What Is Spiritual Care?

What Is Spiritual Care?

Perspectives from Different Professions and Religious Traditions

EDITED BY
PAMELA COOPER-WHITE

Coedited by Claudia Kohli Reichenbach
and Emmanuel Y. Lartey

Epilogue by Ivone Gebara

☙PICKWICK Publications · Eugene, Oregon

WHAT IS SPIRITUAL CARE?
Perspectives from Different Professions and Religious Traditions

Copyright © 2025 Wipf and Stock Publishers. All rights reserved. Except for brief quotations in critical publications or reviews, no part of this book may be reproduced in any manner without prior written permission from the publisher. Write: Permissions, Wipf and Stock Publishers, 199 W. 8th Ave., Suite 3, Eugene, OR 97401.

Pickwick Publications
An Imprint of Wipf and Stock Publishers
199 W. 8th Ave., Suite 3
Eugene, OR 97401

www.wipfandstock.com

PAPERBACK ISBN: 978-1-6667-7497-9
HARDCOVER ISBN: 978-1-6667-7498-6
EBOOK ISBN: 978-1-6667-7499-3

Cataloguing-in-Publication data:

Names: Cooper-White, Pamela, editor. | Kohli Reichenbach, Claudia, editor. | Lartey, Emmanuel Y., editor. | Gebara, Ivone, epilogue.

Title: What is spiritual care? : perspectives from different professions and religious traditions / edited by Pamela Cooper-White ; with Claudia Kohli Reichenbach and Emmanuel Y. Lartey, coeditors ; foreword by Ivone Gebara.

Description: Eugene, OR: Pickwick Publications, 2025. | Includes bibliographical references.

Identifiers: ISBN 978-1-6667-7497-9 (paperback). | ISBN 978-1-6667-7498-6 (HARDCOVER). | ISBN 978-1-6667-7499-3 (ebook).

Subjects: LCSH: Pastoral care. | Pastoral theology. | Pastoral counseling. | Psychology and religion.

Classification: BV4335 W26 2025 (print). | BV4335 (ebook).

05/13/25

Contents

Preface   vii

List of Contributors   xi

PART 1 | PERSPECTIVES FROM DIFFERENT PROFESSIONS

1. Spiritual Care and Medicine   3
   CHRISTINA M. PUCHALSKI

2. Spiritual Care from the Perspective of the Medical Profession   14
   JESSICA ZITTER *INTERVIEWED BY* PAMELA COOPER-WHITE

3. Spiritual Care within Nursing and Midwifery   22
   LINDA ROSS AND WILFRED MCSHERRY

4. Acknowledging the Tragic: Spiritual Care from the Perspective of Public Health   35
   JOHN BLEVINS

5. Spiritual Care from Evolving Psychological Perspectives   45
   KENNETH I. PARGAMENT

6. Towards Wholeness: Caring for the Whole Person Through Listening, Reflecting, and Connecting   54
   PNINIT RUSSO-NETZER

7. Spiritual Care from the Perspective of Hospice and Palliative Care Chaplaincy   69
   KEI OKADA

8	Spiritual Care from the Perspective of Pastoral Theology: Shifting Paradigms Pamela Cooper-White	78
9	Spiritual Care from the Perspective of Pastoral Theology: Postcolonial Views Emmanuel Y. Lartey	91

PART 2 | PERSPECTIVES FROM DIFFERENT RELIGIOUS TRADITIONS

10	What Is Spiritual Care? An Islamic Perspective Mahmoud Abdallah	99
11	The Muslim Counseling Helpline (MuTeS): An Example of Spiritual Care from an Islamic Perspective Mohammad Imran Sagir and Omar Adham Youssef	113
12	Spiritual Care in Light of COVID-19: A Jewish Perspective Mychal B. Springer	122
13	What Is Spiritual Care in Light of Crisis from the Perspective of Orthodox Judaism? Michelle Friedman	131
14	Understanding Spiritual Care: A Christian View Daniel S. Schipani	136
15	Spiritual Care in Light of COVID-19 from an African Christian Perspective Esther Mombo	149
16	What Is Spiritual Care from a Christian Perspective? Pastoral Care for Rage and Joy Angella Son	156
17	Beyond the "Art of Doing Nothing": Reflections on Indigenizing Clinical Pastoral Education to the Buddhadharma Upayadhi S. Luraschi	164

Epilogue: Spirituality: Oh, What Is *This* We Call Spirituality? 183
Ivone Gebara

Preface

What is spiritual care, really? Is there a singular definition or praxis? Who gets to define it and in what contexts? Historically, chaplains, mostly in hospital settings and with fairly uniform training (i.e., Clinical Pastoral Education, or "CPE"), and beginning in the US and Europe, developed the first theological and theoretical foundations, ethics, and normative standards of practice in the mid-1950s to 1980s—usually under the umbrella terms "pastoral care" and "*Seelsorge*." Since its emergence as a religious profession, mostly practiced by ordained clergy and vowed members of religious orders, however, its terminology, ethical and theological underpinnings, normative practices, and range of professional practitioners, have all expanded exponentially—even as the civil rights movement, feminist/Womanist theology and theory, interreligious dialogue, and postmodern and de/postcolonial theology have challenged the white, mostly Protestant status quo throughout theological education and care of both persons and cultures.

There is a vast and growing literature by pastoral theologians and spiritual caregivers over the past half-century, yet fundamental questions of defining "pastoral" and "spiritual" care have largely remained implicit as scholars and practitioners have addressed more granular questions of (mostly Christian) theology, psychology, methodology (theological, theoretical, and practical), social and cultural location, and increasingly, identity of caregivers and care recipients. Especially since professionals in other clinical professions have begun to recognize their own need to recognize and care for the spiritual needs of patients and clients, definitions and practices have expanded and at times remained in the silos of their own disciplines. Approaches to care have also expanded as the hegemony of Christian pastoral theology has given way to a wider diversity of religious traditions with their differing theological foundations, rituals, and indigenous practices of caring. The individualism of American Protestant care and counseling has been challenged and enhanced by other traditions' and cultures' more communal forms of care.

The present volume represents an international, intercultural, interprofessional, and interreligious project to address these questions. This project was the mission of a new international organization—the International Association for Spiritual Care—which was inaugurated in 2015 at the University of Bern, Switzerland, by pastoral theologian the Rev. Dr. Isabelle Noth in collaboration with interdisciplinary colleagues in Bern and five continents around the world. The mission of IASC was stated as:

> IASC's Mission is to enhance the capacities of scholars and practitioners worldwide in acquiring, disseminating, and applying knowledge of theory and practice of spiritual care with an emphasis on interdisciplinary, interreligious, and intercultural scholarly investigation. The Association offers vital continuing education opportunities, encourages networks for professional support and enrichment, and facilitates growth and interdisciplinary innovation engaging medicine, psychology, theology, nursing, and social work.[1]

A series of well-attended annual conferences hosted in Bern (twice),[2] Jerusalem/Beit Jalah,[3] and New York City, respectively, focused on pressing international topics of "pastoral care across religions and cultures"; "pastoral care and migration"; "peace dialogue as pastoral care"; and "religious conflicts, internal and external." The IASC Board (founding members Emmanuel Lartey, Georg Wenz, Claudia Kohli-Reichenbach—secretary/treasurer, and myself as the new President) met in New York in Fall of 2019 to begin a five-year review of IASC's accomplishments in line with its mission. We agreed that we had sponsored excellent conferences, created an engaging website (developed by Emmanuel Schweitzer of Bern) cultivated a participant and email list of hundreds of scholars and practitioners worldwide, and published two (now to be three) scholarly anthologies based on annual

---

1. For more details on IASC, see the IASC website: https://internationalassociationforspiritualcare.org/ and facebook page https://www.facebook.com/profile.php?id=100067558847295.

2. Organized by Dr. habil. Isabelle Noth, Professor of Spiritual Care, Psychology of Religion, and Religious Pedagogy and her colleagues at the University of Bern and the House of Religions, Bern, Switzerland.

3. Organized by Sarah Bernstein, Director of the Rossing Center for Dialogue and Education, Jerusalem, and Ruchama Weiss, Associate Professor of Talmud and Spiritual Care and Director of the Blaustein Center for Pastoral Counseling at Hebrew Union College/Jewish Institute of Religion, Jerusalem.

conferences. (See Noth et al., 2017; Noth & Kohli Reichbenach, 2019; Abdallah et al., 2025.) We felt at that time that we still had not addressed in a systematic or more comprehensive way the definitional challenges of spiritual care, both from the perspectives of different professions and religious traditions. We therefore planned to host two conferences devoted to each of those areas and to publish a volume reflecting what emerged from those presentations and discussions.

The present anthology is a compilation of many of the voices of those scholar-practitioners who participated in those two conferences in 2020 and 2021—which perforce became webinars as the COVID-19 pandemic struck in Spring 2020.[4] Some of the authors here continue to reference the particular challenges and sorrows of spiritual care during those peak years of the epidemic. Their thoughts reflect insights and adjustments to theology and praxis that emerged during those fraught times. These gleanings continue to have relevance to this day, as COVID-19 variants still circulate, with at times deadly consequences—and certainly more generally as spiritual caregivers continue on the front lines of coping with the impacts of racism (including racial disparities in healthcare), personal and familial tragedy, crisis, war, and trauma.

Part 1 includes reflections from the professions of medicine, nursing, public health, spiritual care/hospice chaplaincy, and pastoral theology. Part 2 includes Muslim, Jewish, Christian, and Buddhist perspectives. While each author brings a distinctive perspective and represents a particular context, some red threads run through the entire volume: the importance of deep listening, openness to difference, willingness to recognize the importance of spiritual care as practiced by different professions and religious traditions, refraining from religious proselytizing, respect for the inherent dignity of every person, and support for each individual's unique spiritual journey. At the same time, reading all the chapters taken together, the diversity of voices makes clear—both by juxtaposition and argumentation—that

---

4. Since those two webinars, IASC further hosted a webinar on the topic of "spiritual care and climate crisis," co-sponsored by Union Theological Seminary New York, organized by Pamela Cooper-White, Christopher McFadden, and Ian Rees of Union Theological Seminary, and IASC board colleagues,; and an in-person conference on "Spiritual Care in Times of War and Displacement" in Tübingen, Germany, organized by Georg Wenz and Mahmoud Abdallah in cooperation with the Protestant Academy of Palatinate and the Center for Islamic Theology at the University of Tübingen; a webinar in September, 2024 entitled "Practical Theologies/Wisdom Traditions in Spiritual Care," with presentations from religious traditions including Hinduism Indigenous Wisdom, Judaism, Islam, Buddhism, Humanism, Christianity, and Islam; and in July 2025, a conference in Chicago entitled "Spiritual Care as Resistance." Details about conferences can be found on the website https://internationalassociationforspiritualcare.org/, along with links to recordings of webinars since 2020.

the hegemony of a mid-twentieth-century white American Protestant "tradition" of "pastoral care" is being re-evaluated, contested, expanded, and even decolonized, as voices formerly from the margins are being brought to the center, and the spiritual needs of persons from many different traditions and locations are increasingly being met on their own terms. We are honored to include an Epilogue on "Spirituality" by Brazilian ecofeminist theologian Ivone Gebara, who articulates an overarching assumption of this volume—that spiritual care cannot be divorced from social, political, and economic realities of those for whom we care, and that care is finally inseparable from larger efforts toward justice and peace.

ACKNOWLEDGMENTS

Special thanks are due to all the speakers on our 2020 and 2021 webinars, including all the contributors to this anthology, and also P. Wanjiru Njiru and Mohammed Jalloh (public health), Chanequa Walker-Barnes (psychology and Womanist theology), Maya Zumstein-Shaha (nursing), Hooman Keshavarzi (Islam), Aid Smajic (Islam), Ruchama Weiss (Jerusalem), Geshe Lobsang Tenzin Negi (Buddhism), Chikako Ozawa-de Silva (Buddhism), and Bikshuni Lozang Trinlae (Buddhism). Their presentations and discussions contributed much to this project! We also especially thank Mahmoud Abdallah and Upayadhi Luraschi for adding their voices to this volume.
Pamela Cooper-White, August, 2024

REFERENCES

Abdallah, M., Dreher, T., & Wenz, G., eds. *Spiritual Care in Times of War*, forthcoming 2025.
Noth, I., Wenz, G., & Schweizer, E., eds. *Pastoral and Spiritual Care across Religions and Cultures/Seelsorge und Spiritual Care in interkultureller Perspektive.* (Neukirchener Theologie.) Göttingen: Vandenhoeck & Ruprecht, 2017.
Noth, I. & Kohli Reichenbach, eds., *Pastoral and Spiritual Care across Religions and Cultures II: Spiritual Care and Migration.* Göttingen: Vandenhoeck & Ruprecht, 2019.

Contributors

MAHMOUD ABDALLAH, PhD, is a Senior Researcher at the Zentrum für Islamische Theologie (ZITh—Center for Islamic Theology) at the University of Tübingen and Visiting Lecturer at the Universities of Vienna, Innsbruck, and St Andrews. From 2016 to 2019 he headed at ZITh the project "Academic Education through Social Responsibility" of the Ministry of Science and Research BWB. In 2019–2020, he was Senior Scientists at the Institute for Islamic Theology and Religious Education at the University of Innsbruck—Austria. He studied Arabic Studies, Islamic Theology, and German Studies at al-Azhar University in Cairo, and in 2012 he earned his PhD from the University of Heinrich Heine in Düsseldorf, Germany. His research foci include Islamic Practical theology/ pastoral care in Islam, Theology of coexistence, Muslim religious community Umma in a pluralistic society and the image of man and God in Islam, and state and religion in Islam. He is the author of numerous articles, and two books: "Werbesprache im Deutschen und Arabischen und die kulturelle Problematik ihrer Übersetzung: Eine linguistisch-interkulturelle kontrastive Studie" (Advertising Language in German and Arabic and the Culture Problematic of Its Translation: A Linguistic-intercultural Contrastive Study), and *Islamische Seelsorgelehre. Theologische Fundierung und Perspektiven in der pluralistischen Gesellschaft* (Islamic Pastoral Care Doctrine: Theological Foundations and Perspectives in Pluralistic Society). He is currently working on a project entitled "genealogy of Islamic pastoral care."

JOHN BLEVINS, ThD, is an Associate Research Professor at the Rollins School of Public Health at Emory University (Atlanta USA). Trained in religious and theological studies with an emphasis in pastoral theology, John is the Director of the Interfaith Health Program, an initiative that aims to understand the varied influences of religion on individual and cultural beliefs, perceptions, and practices related to health. John is also affiliate faculty in the Graduate Division of Religion in the Laney Graduate School at Emory. He is actively working on initiatives at the intersection of religion and global health in over a dozen countries around the world. John has authored numerous academic articles on religion and public health and is the author of *To Transfer the Empire of the World: Christianity's Role on United States Global Health and Development Policy*.

PAMELA COOPER-WHITE, PhD, LCPC, is Dean/Vice President for Academic Affairs Emerita and the Christiane Brooks Johnson Professor Emerita of Psychology and Religion at Union Theological Seminary, New York; former Gautier Professor of Pastoral Theology at Columbia Theological Seminary, Decatur, Georgia, and Co-Director of the Atlanta PhD program in Pastoral Counseling. She has published 10 books and over 100 anthology chapters and articles. Book titles include *Old and Dirty Gods: Religion, Antisemitism and the Origins of Psychoanalysis*; *Many Voices: Pastoral Psychotherapy in Relational and Theological Perspective*; *Shared Wisdom: Use of the Self in Pastoral Care and Counseling*; and *The Cry of Tamar: Violence against Women and the Church's Response*. She is Past President of the IASC, and has served as Co-Chair and on the Steering Committee of the Psychology, Culture and Religion unit of the American Academy of Religion, as Editor of the Journal of Pastoral Theology, as well as several editorial review panels. She is an Episcopal priest, licensed and board-certified clinical counselor (LCPC, NBCC), and psychoanalytically trained pastoral psychotherapist, and has lectured frequently in the US and internationally.

MICHELLE FRIEDMAN received her MD from the New York University School of Medicine and has completed advanced training at the Columbia University Psychoanalytic Center for Training and Research. She is the Steven and Marilyn Lieberman Professor of Pastoral Counseling at Yeshivat Chovevei Torah Rabbinical School, a Modern Orthodox yeshiva; Associate Professor of Clinical Psychiatry at the Icahn School of Medicine at Mount Sinai Health System in New York and the co-author *The Art of Jewish Pastoral Counseling: A Guide for All Faiths*.

IVONE GEBARA, PhD, is a Roman Catholic sister in the Augustinian Congregation of the Sisters of Our Lady and recipient of two PhD's—in philosophy and in religious sciences. A Brazilian philosopher and ecofeminist theologian, she has worked for many years in the Northeast of Brazil. She was a professor at the Instituto Teológico do Recife (ITER) which was linked to the liberation theology movement. Since the Instituto was closed by the Vatican in 1989, she has devoted her time to writing and delivering courses and lectures around the world, on the foundations of religious discourse. She has published many books and articles in Brazil and internationally, including the well-known Longing for Running Water: Ecofeminism and Liberation; Out of the Depths: Women's Experience of Evil and Salvation; Mary, Mother of God, Mother of the Poor, and many major works in Portuguese. She continues to work as a writer and public lecturer.

CLAUDIA KOHLI REICHENBACH, ThM (Spirituality), PhD habil., teaches spiritual/pastoral care at the University of Bern and in various formation programs all over Switzerland. She is a board member of the advanced studies program in Palliative Care at the Medical Faculty. From 2014–2019 Claudia was the director of the continuing formation program in Pastoral/Spiritual Care at the University of Bern. She is a founding IASC board member, serving as secretary/treasurer since 2015. Claudia is an ordained minister of the Swiss Reformed Church, working in clinical practice. She promotes spiritual innovation through training programs such as the *école de silence*. Claudia has authored and co-edited books and articles on spiritual care, including *Spiritualität im Diskurs; Palliative und Spiritual Care*, and most recently (with Ralph Kunz) *Verstehen Sie Glauben?*

EMMANUEL Y. LARTEY, PhD, DD, is the Charles Howard Candler Professor of Pastoral Theology and Spiritual Care at Candler School of Theology. He teaches pastoral theology, care, and counseling at Candler, as well as in Emory's Graduate Division of Religion. An internationally acclaimed scholar, Lartey is recognized as a pioneer in the development of an intercultural approach to pastoral care and counseling, which argues for and models respectful engagement across racial, gender, class, cultural and religious boundaries. He is the author of six books including *In Living Color: An Intercultural Approach to Pastoral Care and Counseling; Pastoral Theology in an Intercultural World; Postcolonializing God: An African Practical Theology*; and most recently (with Hellena Moon), *Postcolonial Images of Spiritual Care: Challenges of Care in a Neoliberal Age and Postcolonial Practices of Spiritual Care*. He served as a founding Board member of IASC and has served in leadership for the American Academy of Religion, the Society for Pastoral Theology (US), the International Council for Pastoral Care and Counseling (ICPCC), the Society for Intercultural Pastoral Care and Counseling (SIPCC), the International Academy of Practical Theology (IAPT), and the African Association for Pastoral Studies and Counselling (AAPSC).

UPAYADHI S. LURASCHI, MA, MSc, MDiv, STM, is a doctoral student in Buddhist Studies at the University of Chicago, where she focuses on the Indian Buddhist Revival, transnational Buddhist networks in the modern period, and the relationship between religious narrative and political imagination. Her research has been dedicated to Dr. B. R. Ambedkar's radical Buddhist imagination, which she places in conversation with Womanist and Black liberation theologians. Since 2004, Upayadhi has been practicing with the Triratna Buddhist Community, otherwise known as the Triratna Bauddha Mahāsaṅgha in India, and was ordained in 2018. She undertook Clinical Pastoral Education at NewYork-Presbyterian Hospital and at the Jewish Theological Seminary of New York, in the Religious Leaders' program. A graduate of the Sorbonne University, the ESSEC Business School in Paris, and of Union Theological Seminary, Upayadhi was also part of one of the first cohorts of the Foundations in Contemplative Care offered by the New York Zen Center for Contemplative Care, in collaboration with the Visiting Nurse Service of New York. Integrating her work as a scholar, interfaith chaplain and meditation instructor, she co-founded *Awareness Is Revolutionary*, an international Buddhist collective committed to cultivating Beloved Community and accelerating racial literacy within a Dharmic framework. Born in Paris, Upayadhi moves between France, the US, the United Kingdom, and India.

WILFRED MCSHERRY, PhD, FRCN, is a Professor in Nursing, Department of Nursing and Midwifery, School of Health, Education, Policing and Science, Staffordshire University, England, United Kingdom. He has held joint appointments with the University Hospitals of North Midlands NHS Trust, Staffordshire, United Kingdom and was a part-time Professor at VID University College, Bergen, Norway. He has had a career in nursing spanning over 30 years focusing primarily on acute care advocating dignity, spirituality especially in the care of older people and those receiving end of life care. He has published extensively in the field of spirituality and is one of the most cited nursing authors in this area. As part of his early research, he developed the Spirituality and Spiritual Care Rating Scale (SSCRS) that has been used in many international studies and translated into several languages. In 2010 he led on an important piece of work for the Royal College of Nursing (RCN) exploring members' perceptions of spirituality leading to the development of the following: Spirituality in nursing care: online resource and the Spirituality in care: a pocket guide. He has worked with colleagues in the Australian Nursing and Midwifery Federation (South Australia) Branch replicating the RCN survey. He is a Principal Fellow of the Higher Education Academy (now AdvanceHE). He is a founding and executive member of the International Network for the Study of Spirituality (formerly the British Association for The Study of Spirituality) https://spiritualitystudiesnetwork.org/, and a co-editor in chief of their *Journal for the Study of Spirituality*. In 2012 he was made a Fellow of the Royal College of Nursing for his unique contribution to nursing in the areas of spirituality and dignity. Wilf co-led a European project titled Enhancing Nurses Competence in Providing Spiritual Care through Innovation Education and Compassionate Care (EPICC) website: http://epicc-network.org.

ESTHER MOMBO, PhD, is Lecturer and Director of International Partnerships and Alumni Relations at St. Paul University (formerly St. Paul's United Theological College) in Limuru, Kenya. She teaches and supervises students in the Faculty of Theology in history and theology. She is a member of the Circle of Concerned African Women Theologians and involved in mentorship of young theologians.

KEI OKADA, MDiv, RBCC (Retired Board Certified Chaplain in BCCI, an affiliate of Association of Professional Chaplains), is an associate of Columbia University Seminar on Death, and an ordained minister of American Baptist Churches, USA. A Christian mystic and an artist, born in New York and raised in Kanazawa, Japan, he spent eight years in visual and performing arts before studying at Union Theological Seminary and starting to pursue chaplaincy in 1993 upon graduation. After working at New York-Presbyterian Cornell Medical Center's Pediatric Center for Special Studies, "Program for Children with AIDS" and Housing Works Adult Day Health Care programs for the homeless living with HIV, Kei worked at Visiting Nurse Service of New York (VNS Health) Hospice and Palliative Care as a Spiritual Care Counselor. In the end of 2021, he retired from his position as Program Manager, End-of-Life Spiritual Care. Kei has been a lecturer in US and Japan, focusing on creative integration of inter-sensory & intra/inter-personal end-of-life consciousness and semantics in spiritual care. Kei's first book, *Dialogues in Awe of Life: How Can We Talk with Someone Who Is Facing Death? (Inochi ni Odoroku Taiwa)* was published in September, 2024 by the medical publisher Igaku-Shoin, Tokyo, Japan.

KENNETH I. PARGAMENT, PhD, is a professor emeritus of psychology at Bowling Green State University and adjunct professor in the Department of Psychiatry at Baylor Medical College. He has authored over 300 refereed articles on the relationship between religion and mental health. He has written *The Psychology of Religion and Coping* and *Spiritually Integrated Psychotherapy*. Dr. Pargament is editor in chief of the two-volume *APA Handbook* of *Psychology, Religion, and Spirituality*. With Julie Exline, he has authored the recently released *Working with Spiritual Struggles in Psychotherapy: From Research to Practice*. He was Distinguished Scholar at the Institute for Spirituality and Health at the Texas Medical Center. His awards include the Oskar Pfister Award from the American Psychiatric Association in 2009, the Distinguished Service Award from the Association of Professional Chaplains in 2015, the first Outstanding Contribution to the Applied Psychology of Religion and Spirituality Award from Division 36 of APA in 2017, and an honorary doctor-of-letters from Pepperdine University in 2013.

CHRISTINA M. PUCHALSKI, MD, MS, OCDS, FACP, FAAHPM, is a pioneer and global leader in the movement to integrate spiritual health into clinical settings, education, and policy. Dr. Puchalski is Founder and Executive Director of George Washington University's Institute for Spirituality and Health (GWish) and Professor of Medicine at The George Washington University in Washington, DC. Dr. Puchalski's collaborative work has influenced clinical practice on a global scale, most notably the development of a course for clinicians and chaplains to learn how to create systemic change in their own health settings [Interprofessional Spiritual Care Education Curriculum (ISPEC©)]; and the widely disseminated spiritual history tool (FICA). She currently is leading a global collaborative initiative called The GWish Project: Advancing Interprofessional Spiritual Care. Dr. Puchalski is author of *Time for Listening and Caring: Spirituality*; *Care of the Seriously Ill and Dying*; and co-author of *Making Health Care Whole*; and *The Oxford Textbook of Spirituality and Health*. She has received numerous awards including being named in 2018 as one of "30 Visionaries" in the field by the American Academy of Hospice and Palliative Medicine. In 2022 she received the Debra Sivesind Career Award for Outstanding Contributions to Palliative Care.

LINDA A. ROSS, BA Nursing, PhD, RGN, FHEA, is a Professor of Nursing (specializing in spirituality) at the University of South Wales, UK. Her PhD in 1992 was the first in Europe to explore nurses' perceptions of spirituality and spiritual care which she published as a book in 1997. She has published extensively on the subject of spirituality, contributing to educational resources for the Royal College of Nursing and to spiritual care guidance for Welsh Government. She chairs a group that advises Welsh Government on spiritual matters within health and social care across Wales and she was instrumental in seeing spiritual care education become mandatory across all undergraduate nursing, midwifery and allied health programmes in the country. She is a Director, Trustee, and Founding member of the

International Network for the Study of Spirituality (INSS, formerly BASS) a society set up to foster interdisciplinary debate and study of spirituality (https://spiritualitystudiesnetwork.org/) and she is Co-Editor in Chief for the Society's affiliated 'Journal for the Study of Spirituality'. She co-led (with 5 other partners) an Erasmus funded project (2016–19) to establish best practice in spiritual care nurse/midwifery education across Europe (www.epicc-network.org) which is impacting on spiritual care education, practice and policy internationally, and she Chaired the emerging EPICC Network from 2021–24. Her research on spirituality was independently rated as "internationally excellent" in the UK's 2021 Research Excellence Framework.

PNINIT RUSSO-NETZER, PhD, is a senior lecturer, researcher and the head of the Education Department and the head of the Resilience and Optimal Development Lab at Achva Academic College. Her main research and practice interests focus on meaning in life, positive psychology, existential psychology, spirituality, character strengths, positive change and growth. Dr. Russo-Netzer is the founder and head of the 'Compass' Institute for the Study and Application of Meaning in Life, and the head of the Academic Training Program for Logotherapy (meaning-oriented psychotherapy) at Tel-Aviv University. Dr. Russo-Netzer serves as academic advisor and consultant to both academic and non-academic institutions worldwide. She is the recipient of the International Positive Psychology Association (IPPA) Spirituality and Meaning Researcher Award, and the co-developer and co-instructor of the Mindfulness-Based Meaning Program (MBMP). She has published academic articles and chapters and is the co-author and co-editor of several books on the topics of meaning in life, positive psychology, existential psychology, positive change and growth. Follow her on Facebook, LinkedIn, or visit her website (https://www.pninitrn.com/en).

MOHAMMAD IMRAN SAGIR is a Berlin native with cultural roots in India. He works as a communication and behavioral trainer on the one hand and as an anti-violence and competence trainer on the other. Since December 1, 2008, he is the managing director of the Muslim telephone counseling (*Telefonseelsorge*) in Berlin (https://telefonseelsorge-berlin.de/ueber-uns/aktuelles/).

DANIEL S. SCHIPANI, PsyD, PhD, was born and raised in Argentina. He earned a PsyD from the Universidad Católica in Buenos Aires, Argentina, and a PhD from Princeton Theological Seminary. He is Professor Emeritus of Pastoral Care and Counseling (Anabaptist Mennonite Biblical Seminary), Affiliate Professor of Spiritual Care (McCormick Theological Seminary, and

San Francisco Theological Seminary), Lecturer in Latin America and Europe and author and editor of over twenty-five books on Pastoral and Practical Theology, including *The Way of Wisdom in Pastoral Counseling, Multifaith Views in Spiritual Care,* and *Spiritual Care in Our Multifaith World.*

ANGELLA SON, PhD, is Professor of Psychology and Religion and was awarded The Presidential Award for the Theological School Teacher/Scholar of the Year Award at Drew University. She is past president of the Society for Pastoral Theology and has served on the Executive Committee of the American Association of Pastoral Counselors' Eastern Region and the Status of Racial and Ethnic Minorities in the Profession Committee of the American Academy of Religion. She is a Psychotherapist of the Association of Clinical Pastoral Education and directs the Care and Counseling Program at Blanton-Peace Institute, New York. She has authored numerous academic articles on pastoral care, counseling, and theology. She authored *Spirituality of Joy: Moving Beyond Dread and Duties,* edited and contributed to *Pastoral Care in a Korean American Context,* and translated *Stories That Make History: The Experience and Memories of the Japanese Military Comfort Girls-Women.* She serves on editorial boards for several scholarly juried journals, including *Pastoral Psychology* and the *Journal of Pastoral Care and Counseling.*

RABBI MYCHAL B. SPRINGER, MJS, DD, is the manager of Clinical Pastoral Education at New York-Presbyterian Hospital. She founded the Center for Pastoral Education at the Jewish Theological Seminary (JTS) in Manhattan in 2009. Over a ten-year period, she oversaw an intensive hospice chaplaincy training program in collaboration with Metropolitan Jewish Health System's Hospice. She began her career as a hospital chaplain in New York City, and in the 1990s became the director of the Department of Pastoral Care and Education at Beth Israel Medical Center. Mychal was the first Conservative rabbi to be certified as an Educator by ACPE: The Standard for Spiritual Care & Education. Mychal served as The Rabbinical School at JTS's associate dean and director of Field Education. Her publications include *Sisters in Mourning: Daughters Reflecting on Care, Loss, and Meaning* (2021) with Dr. Su Yon Pak and "Presence in a Time of Distancing: Spiritual Care in an Acute Care Setting," in Friedman, Levin and Raphael, eds., *Jewish End-of-Life Care in a Virtual Age: Our Traditions Reimagined* (2021). Mychal received her BA in Judaic Studies and Religious Studies from Yale College magna cum laude. She was ordained a Conservative rabbi and received her Master's in Judaic Studies and Doctor of Divinity at JTS. Mychal is a certified Jewish chaplain in Neshama: Association of Jewish Chaplains.

OMAR ADHAM YOUSSEF is a Berlin native with cultural roots in Berlin, Egypt and Lebanon. He has a resumé of working as a social worker, teacher, life coach and counselor, with specialization in migration and intercultural work, and is looking forward to pivot into the space of project and event management. He has been an official member of the MuTeS-counseling team since March 2023.

JESSICA ZITTER, MD, MPH, specializes in Critical Care and Palliative Care medicine and practices at a public hospital in Oakland, California. She is the author of *Extreme Measures: Finding a Better Path to the End of Life*. Her work is featured in the Oscar and Emmy-nominated short documentary *Extremis*, and the award-winning short documentary, *Caregiver: A Love Story*. She is at work on her third film, *The Chaplain of Oakland*. Follow her on Twitter, Facebook, Instagram, or visit her website at https://www.jessicazitter.com/.

PART 1

Perspectives from Different Professions

1

Spiritual Care and Medicine

Christina M. Puchalski

Spiritual care is an essential part of whole person care—physical, emotional, social and spiritual. It is the obligation of all clinicians to address the spiritual health of their patients as part of routine clinical care. Identifying spiritual distress is critically important given the rising rates of spiritual distress in the US and globally. Spiritual care is nothing brand new. Within palliative care, Cecily Saunders, the founder of the hospice movement (Richmond, "Dame Cicely Saunders"), spoke about "total pain"—physical, psychosocial, and spiritual pain. She described that pain as a part of how we care for people with serious illness. And in the "whole-person" care model and in narrative medicine, people have talked about addressing all domains. The World Health Organization (WHO) Palliative Care Resolution is probably the first time the word "spiritual" occurred in any WHO document:

> Palliative care is an approach that improves the quality of life of patients . . . through the prevention and relief of suffering employing early identification and correct assessment and treatment of pain and other problems, whether physical, psychosocial, *or spiritual."* (WHO, *Sixty-Seventh World Health Assembly,* emphasis added)

I was involved in the development of that resolution, and there was quite a lot of debate about the spiritual domain. Still, it was recognized that we do have to attend to palliative care that addresses the quality of life, prevention, and early identification by early assessment and treatment of pain and other problems, whether physical, psychosocial, or spiritual.

In the US, spiritual professionals and chaplains have been serving patients since the early 1900s. Yet despite the recognition that spiritual care was needed, there has been a divide between clinical care and professional spiritual care. Our work at the George Washington Institute for Spirituality and Health (GWish) since 2001 has been to bridge that divide by creating clinical models and ways to address spiritual distress and spiritual health. This initially began with palliative care, but palliative care has come primarily to be seen as care for patients with serious and/or chronic illness or dying, so our effort applies to all of care. Increasingly clinicians are recognizing spiritual health across all of healthcare.

The COVID pandemic especially cast light on the need for spiritual care. For everyone, globally, and our friends and neighbors, we didn't exactly know what the future would hold during this pandemic. Such a time of uncertainty triggered reflection. In such a time of isolation, loss, grief, and facing mortality raised many existential questions, and people were recognizing the importance of that element. In my clinical setting, people are seeing that spiritual care is such a critical need! Think about what happens in clinical settings, and the crisis the pandemic caused in California, in New York, and around the world, especially in the early days, seeing overwhelming, increasing numbers of critical care patients, and people who were dying having to face very difficult ethical choices.

So what happens to clinicians in this situation? I work in an outpatient setting, and I also heard from inpatient clinicians, who all said, "There is nothing I can do. We don't have any known treatments" (now is a bit different)—that experience of inadequacy, of not being able to "fix," which is so much a part of our training—but what happened is the that clinicians began to experience the power of presence and compassion in the face of uncertainty. In the experience of COVID, this experience was heightened by the increasing numbers of patients who came in with severe illness or were struck by loss or grief. Clinicians saw even more clearly the need to be able to recognize spiritual distress, and the need to be able to address that.

Many studies have shown a global pandemic of spiritual distress affecting many parts of the world. Rates of spiritual distress were reported as 44% of cancer patients in the US (Hui et al., *Frequency and Correlates*; 65% in Switzerland (Monod et al., "Validation"); 73.1% of patients with HIV-AIDS in Brazil (Pinho et al., "Impaired Religiosity"); and a range of

25–76% of patients in Zimbabwe (Patel et al., "Spiritual Distress"). More studies are ongoing.

A CASE STUDY OF A PATIENT CALLED "MIKE" (PSEUDONYM)

While some of the details are changed for purposes of confidentiality, this was a real patient of mine. He was the first person I saw in Telehealth (virtual patient encounter). So try to picture me trying to figure out how this Telehealth even works, and how nervous I was learning the technique, and then being present to someone who was suffering. Mike had experienced a traumatic relationship in another state, and at the same time was beginning to have difficulty with his memory, shaking, having a lot of workups not knowing what was going on. He moved here at the beginning of the pandemic to be with his daughters and his son, who were in the area. Now I'm seeing him in the middle of the pandemic. He was not able to come in person. He was isolated in his apartment. His daughter joined the call, so we are having a three-way conversation, and he's telling me the story of his pain—of what that meant to him, of how devastated he was. A beautiful man, he had raised his family on his own after his first wife left. She had abandoned the family and had addiction problems. He was very devoted to his children.

He was a highly successful person, but at that moment all of that had been taken away from him. In the first spiritual assessment, he talked about spirituality as more personal, a source of his moral compass. He has found meaning in his family and in his work, in raising his children and continuing to be a good father for his family. He was wondering what he would do now with whatever time he had left in his life. He had a tremendous amount of uncertainty and felt very isolated: "I came here to be with my family and I'm sitting here alone in my apartment." He talked about his faith and how it was very important and did impact how he dealt with stress. As I continued with the spiritual history, he went on to say that he wondered if he was "good enough in God's eyes . . . If I die from all of this, will God see me as a good man?" In that moment of course I wanted to say, "Everything that you are saying to me testifies that you are a good man!" But I didn't. I sat in silence with him as he shared his profound grief and loss, how his sense of who he was was being eroded, and grabbing for any lifeline that was being offered to help him in this moment. That silence went on for quite a while, but I learned so much about the suffering he was going through, and I learned it could not be fixed. Being with him in that suffering was all that I could do at that moment, to learn what was really going on with him. He was willing to see a chaplain if we could find someone who could do that by Zoom, which was a challenge at the beginning of the COVID pandemic but I was able to find a chaplain that could see him virtually.

So, what is spiritual care from the perspective of all of our various professions, and from the particular perspective of clinical care? Spiritual care is at the core of respectful, compassionate care. By understanding what gives a patient meaning, purpose, and hope, providers can play a critical role in relieving suffering for the people and families in their care. By being present and accompanying our patients we can help alleviate suffering. While it is relatively easy and straightforward to write these words, this is not that easy to practice. A colleague wrote a beautiful article in a journal about palliative care. She was struggling with how to attend to a patient who dying from COVID. One of my colleague's struggles was "How can I be present in this moment when I too am terrified of getting the virus, and with all this paraphernalia I must wear? How can I be present?"

It's very difficult to witness extreme suffering, and so much of the training we do is about how can we witness without trying to fix. This is why we need training on compassionate presence. This training is not just communication skills but how we can be open to the sacredness of the encounter and use our heart and intuition to move into a space of deep listening and love.

Therefore, creating models has been important for finding ways to bring spiritual care into the clinical model. By creating clinical models, and working with spiritual care professionals, we can address the spiritual needs of patients, and be present with them in their suffering as a form of accompaniment. Spiritual care, I believe, is the way to operationalize compassionate care. In developing our models, we developed a broad definition of spirituality that is very inclusive. This is a globally based, consensus-based definition that applies to everybody's spirituality, including religion, culture, secular humanism, etc.:

> Spirituality is a dynamic and intrinsic aspect of humanity through which persons seek ultimate meaning, purpose, and transcendence, and experience relationship to self, family, others, community, society, nature, and the significant or sacred. Spirituality is expressed through beliefs, values, traditions, and practices. (Puchalski, Vitillo, Hull, and Reller, "Improving")

The clinical spiritual care model is a generalist model of care, in which every person on the care team is responsible for addressing spiritual issues, but we recognize spiritual care professionals as the experts with whom we need to work closely.

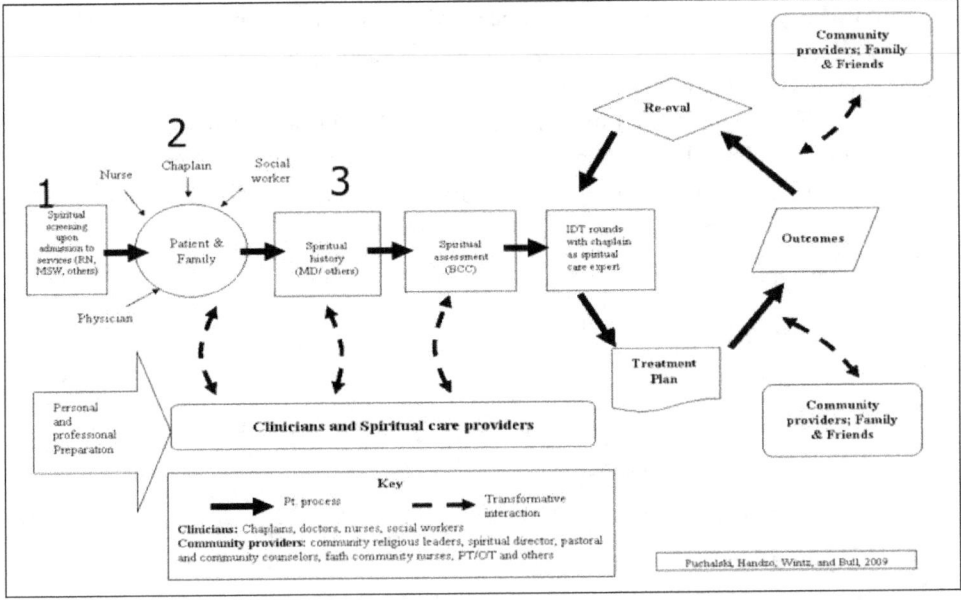

The Consensus Conference Spiritual Care Model (Puchalski, Ferrell, Virani, et al., "Improving") includes:

- Assessment, diagnosis, and treatment of spiritual distress—include spiritual distress in symptom management
- Identification and support of spiritual resources of strength
- Generalist-Specialist Spiritual Care
- Provision of compassionate care
- Training of above commensurate to scope of practice of healthcare workers
- Team-based model

These are our roles as clinicians. Working side-by-side with chaplains is key. And that is a challenge in the US, and probably in other areas, where there are not even trained chaplains or widely available.

In our country and globally, we need more chaplains and spiritual care professionals in both inpatient and outpatient settings. In national consensus projects in the US on palliative care, "Domain 5" is on spiritual care, recognizing it as "an essential component of quality palliative care": "Spiritual care service, including screening, history, and assessment are performed on admission and regularly thereafter. Interventions using professional standards of practice are part of the basic provision of quality care available to all palliative care patients." Spiritual care is provided by all of us, professional spiritual care providers as well as clinicians.

We have published in this space on National Cancer Comprehensive Network spiritual care diagnoses that we are currently working with, in terms of developing ways to understand more what is and how to treat it (Puchalski, Ferrell, Otis-Green, and Handzo, "Overview"):

- Existential
- Abandonment by God/others
- Anger at God/others
- Concerns about relationship with deity/transcendence
- Conflicted belief systems
- Despair/hopeless
- Grief/loss
- Reconciliation
- Isolation
- Religious specific struggle/needs

How Do We Assess Spiritual Distress? Spiritual Screening, History-Taking, and Assessment

- A global survey of 807 palliative care providers from 87 countries ranked spiritual screening tools as the number one priority for spiritual care research. (Selman, 2014)
- Three levels of clinical inquiry for spiritual assessment have been defined:

Type of Clinical Inquiry	Clinical Context	Length	Mode	Clinician
Spiritual Screening	On admission or in the outpatient setting, integrated into other screening instruments	Brief	Open-ended questions or items with scaled response, goal is to identify patients in need of spiritual care referral	Any clinical care provider, nurse, or the person doing general screenings
Spiritual History-taking*	Initial visit, annual visit, acute visit for serious illness or breaking bad news, if patient in distress or experiencing loss or stress, ongoing re-evaluation, and follow-up	Moderate	Open-ended questions using a spiritual history tool; diagnosing spiritual distress and resources of strength and integrating into treatment plan	Clinical medical care provider (e.g., physician, nurse, PA)
Spiritual Assessment	Initial contact, ongoing reassessment	Extensive	Conceptual framework guides interview and development of spiritual care plan	Board-certified chaplain or spiritual care professional with equivalent training

(Balboni et al., 2017)
*Adapted by Christina Puchalski, MD

In terms of assessment, the work that we did with Dr. Tracy Balboni and Dr Karen Steinhauser, who surveyed palliative care providers on how people communicate (Balboni, Fitchett, Handzo, et al., "State of the Science"). The figure above identified three levels of communication about spiritual issues; 1. Screening which is brief, the goal of which is to identify spiritual distress and make a referral to a chaplain. The spiritual history is moderate and is done on intake is done by clinicians as part of their history and assessment. Trained chaplains do a full spiritual assessment which reflects their training as spiritual care experts. So at the bedside, we should do a FICA (Borneman, Ferrell, and Puchalski, "Evaluation") or some other type of assessment measuring spiritual distress and strength, offering compassionate presence is a key part of the spiritual care we should offer. We include values and goals of care and document resources in the chart. And always ensure the dignity of all—the patient and the family. Most importantly we work collaboratively with spiritual care professionals. Below is a figure from a brief we did for global organizations in palliative care for spiritual care and palliative care during COVID (Puchalski, Bauer, Ferrell, et al., "Interprofessional"):

CLINICIANS AT THE BEDSIDE SHOULD:

- **Complete a spiritual history** (FICA—Faith, Importance, Community, Address) to assess patients for spiritual distress and document in note
- **Offer compassionate presence,** listening and connection
- Help patient **identify inner spiritual resources** and access other spiritual resources
- Include **patients' spiritual beliefs and values in goals of care** discussion
- **Document Spiritual Distress and resources of strength** in the patient clinical note including treatment plan, referrals, etc.
- **Ensure dignity** of the patient
- **Refer to spiritual care professionals**

Now what about chaplains and spiritual care professionals? The board-certified chaplains can confirm or change the diagnosis of distress or type of distress. Chaplains are trained in various counseling skills and listening skills, and in identifying spiritual themes. They also have theological training that can help them discern and treat spiritual distress with all patients not just patients who have a faith practice. They can go deeper in their interventions, and also recommend what types of interventions clinicians might do.

CHAPLAIN INTERVENTIONS IN CLINICAL CARE:

- **Confirm/change diagnosis of spiritual distress, and type of distress (Spiritual assessment)**
- Reflective listening, identifying spiritual themes
- **Spiritual interventions (treatment)**
    - Assess for distress/issue and implement appropriate interventions
- **Writing up the assessment and chaplain interventions as well as recommendations for team**

So healing in relationship is core to clinical care. Listening and compassionate presence is just as critical as more reductionistic assessing, diagnosing, and putting it into the chart. One of my favorite quotes is from the spiritual teacher Henri Nouwen: "Listening is a form of spiritual hospitality by which you invite strangers to be friends, to get to know their inner selves more fully, and even to dare to be silent with you" (Nouwen, *Bread for the Journey*). Silence is such a profound intervention, and as I've learned in recent years, it is as possible in Telehealth as it is in person.

Returning to the story of Mike, I did a review of systems just as any other clinician would do, but I've added the spiritual review of systems to my review of systems, and in his case there was grief, loss, profound concern about his relationship with God, existential distress, fear of uncertainty about his health and death, and what would happen especially during that time. Interestingly, in much of our work, our colleagues do the history and the assessment, but charting is the next challenge. It is hard to do that in clinical records, so we are working on ways to do that (see Monod et al., 2012). But the chart is the way that we communicate. If it's not in the chart, it's not seen as an important part of care. Here is an example of charting from Mike's care:

Biopsychosocial-Spiritual Model Assessment and Plan

	Mike, a 68yo male who presents for new visit, has mild cognitive impairment, tremors, gait imbalance, consider parkinsonism, also insomnia, anxiety, grief/loss, existential distress, depression, questions about his relationship with God, fear of uncertainty, self-worth issues.
Physical	Physical therapy, neuro assessment, cont. current medications, sleep hygiene trial of melatonin
Emotional	Anxiety, sadness, maybe mild depression, start Zoloft
Social	Isolated, discussed ways to connect with friends and family during this time. Recommended counselor
Spiritual	Referral to chaplain, continued presence and follow up, meditation apps discussed that help with sleep and also mindfulness approaches

In closing, we have developed an Interprofessional Spiritual Care Education Curriculum (ISPEC) together with my nursing colleague Betty Ferrell at City of Hope (Puchalski, Jafari, et al., "Interprofessional"; Puchalski, Ferrell, Borneman, et al., "Implementing"). We designed this as an online course to train the trainer, and then work with institutions. We have intentionally invited spiritual care professional/chaplain-clinician pairs to these programs. Since 2018, a total of 593 participants in 29 countries and 32 US states have been involved with ISPEC. Adding this number to those who have participated in our other spiritual care education programs, we have trained 2,694 participants.

Below is a quote from one of one of my medical students who took the online course as part of our training:

> I found ISPEC (Gwish training) to be incredibly inspiring. I felt chills and familiarity with the motivations I brought into medical school. What has happened since starting is an excess focus on the technical, and not enough focus on the sacred aspects of medicine. I look forward to putting into practice these principles. I intend to take a "pause" moment before seeing each patient so as to center myself and become prepared for the sacredness of the encounter to come. —Max Ruben, Class of 2020

Spiritual care as part of whole person care is so critical, and it must be practiced by all clinicians who work collaboratively with healthcare chaplains and faith community leaders. Faith community leaders may be important in patients' lives and if so we should integrate them in the "team" that cares for the patient. The essence of the practice of spiritual care is recognizing the sacred in the clinical settings—what is holy or significant for the patient. It enables us to move into silence when we witness suffering of our patients and those we care for and to be fully present to the other. This is for all of care—whether it is at end of life, whether it is a new visit, whether it is at the time of childbirth. Spiritual care enables patients to find hope and healing. Spiritual care enables the clinicians and chaplains to reconnect with each visit to our sense of meaning and purpose and to our call to serve. Integrating spiritual care practiced by all clinicians and chaplains and faith communities in clinical settings results in truly whole person care. It results in the possibility of healing for all—patients, families, clinicians, chaplains, faith community leaders. We are all afforded the opportunity to experience deep sacred moments, healing and joy. That is the path to restoring the heart and humanity to healthcare.

REFERENCES

Balboni, T. A., Fitchett, G., Handzo, G.F., et al. "State of the Science of Spirituality and Palliative Care Research, Part II: Screening, Assessment, and Interventions." *Journal of Pain Symptom Management* 54/3 (2017) 441–53.

Borneman, T., Ferrell, B., Puchalski, C. M. "Evaluation of the FICA Tool for Spiritual Assessment." *Journal of Pain Symptom Management*, 40/2 (2010) 163–73.

Hui, D., de la Cruz, M., Thorney, S., Parsons, H. A., Delgado-Guay, M., and Bruera, E. "The Frequency and Correlates of Spiritual Distress among Patients with Advanced Cancer Admitted to an Acute Palliative Care Unit." *American Journal of Hospice and Palliative Medicine* 28/4 (2011) 264–70. https://doi.org/10.1177/1049909110385917.

Monod S., Martin E., Spencer, B., Rochat E., Büla, C. "Validation of the Spiritual Distress Assessment Tool in Older Hospitalized Patients." *BMC Geriatrics* 12 (2012) 13. https://doi.org/10.1186/1471-2318-12-13; PMID: 22455520; PMCID: PMC3368768.

Patel, V., et al (1995). "Spiritual Distress: An Indigenous Model of Nonpsychotic Mental Illness in Primary Care in Harare, Zimbabwe." *Acta Psychiatria Scandinavica* 92.2 (1995) 103–7. https://doi.org/10.1111/j.1600-0447.1995.tb09551.x

Pinho C. M., Gomes E. T., Trajano, M. F. C., Cavalcanti A. T. A., Andrade, M. S., and Valença, M. P. "Impaired Religiosity and Spiritual Distress in People Living with HIV/AIDS. *Revista Gaucha de Enfermagem* 38/2 (2017) 67712. https://doi.org/10.1590/1983-1447.2017.02.67712.

Puchalski, C. M., Bauer, R., Ferrell, B. R., et al. Briefing Note: "Interprofessional Spiritual Care in the Time of COVID-19." *Global Palliative Care* (2020). http://

globalpalliativecare.org/covid-19/uploads/briefing-notes/briefing-note-interprofessional-spiritual-care-in-the-time-of-covid-19.pdf.

Puchalski, C. M., Ferrell, B. R., Borneman, T., Remein, C. D., Haythorn, T., Jacobs, C. "Implementing Quality Improvement in Spiritual Care: Outcomes from the Interprofessional Care Education Curriculum." *Journal of Health Care Chaplaincy*, 28/3 (2022) 431–42.

Puchalski, C. M., Ferrell, B. R., Otis-Green, S., Handzo, G. "Overview of Spirituality in Palliative Care." In S.D. Block and J. Givens (Ed.), *UpToDate*. Waltham, MA: UpToDate, Inc., 2020.

Puchalski, C. M., Ferrell, B. R., Virani, R., et al. "Improving the Quality of Spiritual Care as a Dimension of Palliative Care: The Report of the Consensus Conference." *Journal of Palliative Medicine* 12/10 (2009) 885–904.

Puchalski, C.M., Jafari, N., Buller, H. Haythorn, T., Jacobs, C., Ferrell, B. R. "Interprofessional Spiritual Care Education Curriculum: A Milestone toward the Provision of Spiritual Care." *Journal of Palliative Medicine* 23/6 (2020) 777–84.

Puchalski, C. M., Vitillo, R., Hull, S. K., Reller, N. "Improving the Spiritual Dimension of Whole Person Care: Reaching National and International Consensus. *Journal of Palliative Medicine* 17/6 (2014) 642–56.

Richmond, C. "Dame Cicely Saunders." *British Medical Journal*, 331/7510 (2005) 238. https://www.ncbi.nlm.nih.gov/pmc/articles/PMC1179787/.

World Health Organization (WHO) *Sixty-Seventh World Health Assembly, Agenda Item 15.5: Strengthening of Palliative Care as a Component of Comprehensive Care throughout the Life Course*, WHA67.19. Geneva: World Health Organization, 2014.

2

Spiritual Care from the Perspective of the Medical Profession

Jessica Zitter
interviewed by Pamela Cooper-White[1]

PCW: I first met Jessica when she was the plenary speaker for an event at the Jewish Theological Seminary that was part of a larger series of events all across New York City and San Francisco the same week around the week of Hallowe'en or All Souls, called "Reimagine Death and Dying." Jessica shared her amazing work in palliative care, and I had the good fortune of being the moderator of that panel. She is a medical doctor who over the years has become engaged in and convicted about the need for compassionate care. Jessica, can you tell us a little bit more about yourself, and what was the pathway that got you from your medical career into palliative and compassionate care?

JZ: Listening to Dr. Puchalski's case example of "Max"[2] gave me chills, because I remember that I came into medicine thinking that I was

---

1. Jan. 5, 2020, as part of IASC Webinar, "What Is Spiritual Care from the Perspective of Different Professions: Medicine." The interview has been edited for clarity.
2. See Chapter 1 in this volume.

coming into a profession where I could actually connect with people. And help them. And before I knew it I was on this *conveyor belt* to becoming a specialist. In my residency program there were 60 people, and 57 of them became specialists. And by the way, of the three who went into primary care, one became a gastroenterologist. So that was the expectation. You go to these programs, and the more interventionist you become, the better doctor you are perceived to be. It's almost subconscious. We call it a hidden curriculum. Being a good soldier, I kept moving forward on that training conveyor belt.

The next thing I knew I was an ICU doctor, and I was all about interventions and machines. And in some ways in those early days it was a relief. Because I was witnessing so much suffering, and I had knobs and tubes and catheters to hide behind. And that's what I did. It numbed me, because I didn't know how to process the suffering I was seeing.

So in those early years of being an ICU doctor, in 2003, my first real job was working in the University Hospital of New Jersey in the ICU. And there was this tiny little pre-palliative care team. They didn't even call themselves the palliative care team. They called themselves the Family Support Team, because who knew what palliative care was!? It was led by a nurse named Pat Murphy who did not suffer fools, and who was very palliative minded. She had trained with Elizabeth Kübler-Ross.[3] She had won an incredible award from the Robert Wood Johnson Foundation to enhance communication in the intensive care unit. And suddenly she was all over the ICU! I didn't know who she was. I didn't know what she was doing. She was talking to my patients, and that wasn't how I was used to it working in the hierarchical world I'd been trained in. There, the ICU doctor was the "boss." And suddenly, there was Pat, and all of her team—walking around the unit, telling me things that I didn't want to hear, like, "Hey, wait a minute, does that patient in Room 7 know what you and I both know, that they're not going to survive? Have you even told them? And that patient in Room 5, who's writhing in pain, have you even thought about starting pain medication?"

At first, I was very defensive. Then suddenly everything changed. I was about to put a Quinton catheter (for dialysis) into a patient's neck.

---

3. Kübler-Ross (1926–2004) was a Swiss psychiatrist whose work focused on the dying and the bereaved. In her 1969 book *On Death and Dying*, she introduced her now classic model of "five stages of grief." For more details, see https://en.wikipedia.org/wiki/Elisabeth_K%C3%BCbler-Ross.

This patient was dying, but I was soldiering on. I would be the one to save her! Suddenly, Pat was standing in front of me, leaning against the doorjamb of the patient's room. She put her hand up to her face like it was a phone and spoke calmly into it, pretending to talk to someone, and she said (for my benefit), "They're torturing a patient in the ICU!" That was my epiphany moment. It broke down my defenses, and my place in that hierarchy, and I felt a rush of shame and guilt, because I knew that what I was doing was wrong. I wasn't going to help this woman. I was just going to hurt her. In her final hours of life. I realized I had gotten off my path and I was lost. Within a few days went to Pat with my tail between my legs. I said "I need you to help me." And that's when I started to learn about palliative medicine. It took me many years to get back to a place where I felt good about my practice of medicine. And it was palliative medicine that led me there.

PCW: Your work in intensive care and palliative care in Oakland was featured in the 2016 documentary "Extremis," which won Best Documentary Short at the Tribeca Film Festival and was also nominated for an Academy Award.[4] Talk a little bit about the making of that film and your relationship with the spiritual care team—the chaplains—as you were involved in making that film.

JZ: That film, the suffering that I described to you, and my opening up to it, after Pat showed me a new way—it's powerful stuff. Dr. Puchalski and I have both spent our careers facing suffering—spiritual distress and physical pain. It's hard to watch—a lot of this is avoidable, even much of this is avoidable. The hospital system is not set up to mitigate it, in fact it exacerbates it. We are completely separated—in fact we think as doctors that we should separate ourselves from people's spiritual condition, their spiritual selves, because we don't think it's scientific. So we are causing more and more distress on top of existential distress in serious illness and death. So I started to write about it.

I've been a writer since I was eleven, with my little journal. But now I really started to write. I felt it was important to share it with my physician colleagues. I think physicians are a big lever for changing healthcare culture because the hierarchical system gives them a lot of power to dictate the environment around them. And, frankly, other health care professions are doing a better job. I spend a lot of time messaging

---

4. Directed and produced by Dan Krauss, 2016. For more detail, see https://en.wikipedia.org/wiki/Extremis_(film).

new approaches that I have learned for my fellow physician colleagues. I felt that this was a way to *justice*, a way to *repair*.

Then one day I saw a film—"The Waiting Room"[5] by filmmaker Pete Nicks—that was made in our hospital's emergency room about issues of access to healthcare. We had a big screening for hospital staff at the Grand Lake Theater. When the lights came up, I went up to the director and said, "You need to come in and do a film about what happens in the intensive care unit—the decision making, the fact that people end up there without any preparation." Even though he was busy, I just kept texting this filmmaker for about a year and a half. Every time I had a conversation that I thought would be important for the public to see. And finally he referred me to another filmmaker named Dan Krauss who came in and made the film, with me in his ear constantly sharing the perspectives that I'd been writing about. A filmmaker wouldn't know about what's really happening in the hospital environment, all the issues that are going on with the physicians and staff, and the barriers between us and our patients. So that's how "Extremis" came to be.

I do want to say something about spiritual care here. My first mentor was the nurse I mentioned, Pat Murphy. My second mentor was Chaplain Betty Clark, with whom I have worked for thirteen years at Highland Hospital in Oakland, and who is featured in the film I am making now, *The Chaplain of Oakland*. Betty has really guided me into this new world of less judgmental, more curious, more humble. She has taught me the importance of obtaining a spiritual history, and thinking about people as full human beings, not just a disease or another variable that doesn't get to the essence of a person. She has taught me everything I know about bringing humanity to the bedside, so I have to commend all of you who are chaplains and spiritual care researchers, doing what I believe is the most important work we do for patients with serious illness. I feel that it is my mission to bring my colleagues, my ICU colleagues, my oncologist colleagues, etc., into an understanding of how critically important it is to have that next team member be a spiritual caregiver—whether it's a hospital chaplain, or a community faith leader. Their work is critically important, and it's time for us to stop diminishing what they do. Not only for our patients, but for ourselves as care team members.

---

5. https://en.wikipedia.org/wiki/The_Waiting_Room_(2012_film).

PCW: In the film, you were working at Highland Hospital in Oakland, California. A very large proportion of patients there are African American and Latinx. In the summer of 2019, you wrote an Op-Ed piece in the *New York Times* on racial disparities in medical care. I wonder if that also entails some particular disparities (I think you called it a polarity) between the faith of the patient and the doctor's typical attitude toward faith, coming from and having been trained in a more scientific approach. Can you talk about that disparity, and how you address this issue, especially for communities of color?

JZ: Ah, that's a huge topic! If you think about it, spirituality is one variable of personhood. There are so many such variables! Race is obviously one. And education. So many things that come into a person's experience in life, and that they bring with them into the hospital. I would say that it's so easy for us, the physicians, who are on this conveyor belt ourselves, trying to manage a lot of suffering and stress, to just categorize people by superficial attributes that don't tell the most important story. We bucket people so we can just push things through the system in order to get through the day. What we do is, again, so damaging. Whether it's about race, whether it's about whether a person is a "spiritual person" or not, whether a person speaks English—we make decisions and assumptions about that person in a millisecond, and it informs how we treat them.

I'm doing some work with an amazing group called the "Alameda County Care Alliance" based in Oakland. The ACCA works within the faith-based African American community, trying to support community members to achieve equal access to good end-of-life care. We're working on a project to educate faith leaders using the film "Extremis." Because the film "Extremis" mostly has African American patients in it, it's a relatable film for the African American community. It's a model for a new way of integrating faith leaders in the community with health care staff, and bringing people together in a more therapeutic way for everybody.

Cynthia Perrilliat, the founder and CEO of the ACCA, is an amazing woman and a friend of mine. She asked me once over coffee, "Can you tell me something? If you hear that somebody is a person of faith, that they believe in God, does it make you think they're less intelligent?" I just thought that question was so telling—that she, whose life's work focuses around supporting communities of faith, is wondering if medical communities somehow look down on that. Obviously my own answer is no, but I hate to admit that I think for some doctors—and I am blaming doctors a lot—feel this way. When people hear that somebody is a person of faith there are some assumptions that are made about what they're going to want, what kind of end-of-life care they're going to want, and yes, some of it has to do with race. Then this disconnection happens. You make this decision in your head: "Oh, this is a person who wants everything, this person believes in miracles, it's not even worth even having a conversation about goals of care." It happens all the time. So just hearing her ask it, that she perceived this herself as a person who works at the intersection of these two worlds all the time, it's heartbreaking. It's true on some level, and it has to be remedied. Because spiritual caregivers all know that it's simplistic and causes tremendous pain and suffering.

PCW: It strikes me that you're addressing different levels of implicit bias that people are not even conscious of, and might consciously disavow, but also the nature of intersectionality. That term gets watered down to just mean "well, we have lots of different aspects to ourselves," but it actually came out of the battered women's movement, and it originally referred to people—Black women—who are experiencing multiple forms of oppression simultaneously. It strikes me that you're pointing how people can get written off if they are "too religious," as yet another added form of implicit bias to pile on top of race and gender and sexuality and all kinds of other ways in which they can be viewed as less-than by doctors who've been educated in a particular system.

JZ: Beautifully said, I couldn't have said it better myself.

PCW: Just last week we had our first graduate from our Doctor of Ministry program for chaplain educators/supervisors-in-training. One of the colleagues, who himself is African American and works in a hospital in West Philadelphia, used a term I'd never heard before: "miracle literacy." Can you say a bit more about doctors' reactions when a patient "believes in miracles"?

JZ: It's shorthand for us. It's "the patient in Room 5 believes in miracles." I've often seen that on a sign-out [notes from another doctor whose shift has just ended]. "Oh, the patient in room 5 believes in miracles." That's shorthand for saying, "Don't even try to talk to this person about the fact that they may actually die. They won't be reasonable. It will be a waste of your time, and theirs." So the word "miracle" somehow—and other words, too—just turn doctors off from engaging. It's a real problem.

I'll tell you one example of how to think differently about patients who believe in miracles. We brought "Extremis" to a group of faith leaders—mostly African American leaders. We watched it, and we talked about the end of life and decisions regarding the use of life-prolonging treatments like ventilators. Discussed how sometimes those treatments don't help, and even cause harm. I could feel the discomfort in the room. We have such a long history in this country of white doctors withholding treatments and technology from Black patients (Zitter, "The Never-ending Mistreatment") you can imagine how it would raise suspicions for me to come to a Black church and suggest that sometimes it can be harmful to use these treatments. But it was a very productive conversation, and one of the pastors came up to me afterwards and said, "Thank you so much, it was incredibly enlightening for me. I appreciate learning more about what those machines are in the ICU and what their limitations are. It reminds me of a time I was with my mother, when she was dying and we prayed for a miracle." I was confused. We had just had a conversation about miracles in the group, and all the faith leaders had talked about challenges with their parishioners who had unrealistic expectations and were praying for miracles. Now, I assumed this man was telling me that prayer can achieve miracles. So I asked for clarification. "I want to make sure I understand. Were you praying for the miracle of her getting cured?" He said "No!" and looked at me like I was nuts. "It was the miracle of reconciliation and spiritual triumph." I realized I had again made the mistake of assuming that the word "miracle" meant continuing to fight on with machinery. And that's not what this pastor was saying at all. We need to be curious and ask more, instead of maintaining fixed thinking and withdrawing from the conversation.

PCW: Yes, and sometimes death *is* the healing and the wholeness that is needed for the family and the individual. You talk about how you used to back out of the room when the chaplain started to pray and you no longer do that. Can you talk briefly about your own shift when it came to praying with patients?

JZ: I'm Jewish, and I just felt that somehow it was inappropriate for me to stay in the room with Chaplain Betty when she would start praying with African American, mostly Christian patients. I felt like I wasn't supposed to be there, and frankly, I was uncomfortable. One day, Betty just put her hand on my arm and said "We're going to pray now, Dr. Zitter." It was probably about three-and-a-half years ago. I remember that moment. I stayed in the room, I put my head down, and she started to pray. It was the most beautiful thing. It was a beautiful moment for me. I never went back. (See also Springer, this volume.)

Since then I always take every opportunity to participate in prayer with patients and their families. It was not only a huge sense of profound connection, and profound healing—healing that I didn't realize would be possible when there was no more life enhancing medical treatment that I could offer. I just wish all of my colleagues could understand what it means, not only to offer to patients to have their physician stay in the room and want to join them in this important sacred moment, but what it means to physicians, how it can provide profound strength and relief from our own suffering and witnessing to sadness, grief. So again one of my life's goals is to raise that awareness among my colleagues.

PCW: Both you and Christina have used the word "witness." I have loved that word for a long time. The Greek New Testament word for that is "*martys*," which also is translated at "martyr." Being present in that way is costly, it takes something out of your whole humanity, you're not just moving machines around or doing charting, but you're bringing your whole self. What is your definition of "spiritual care"?

JZ: It really has to do with what Dr. Puchalski mentioned, which is really being curious, asking questions, wondering about a person, asking them what makes them feel whole and supported, and really respecting it. Really opening up your heart to whatever answer they might give you. Spending time with somebody. There's always time. I will tell you as an ICU Attending in a busy ICU—there's always time. Even if it's only two minutes of silence and holding someone's hand. Even if they're on a ventilator. It's an act of humanity, which is why, like "Max," I went into medicine. It is profoundly powerful and important and humanizing for everybody.

PCW: Thank you for that beautiful answer, and for being with us today.

REFERENCES

Kübler-Ross, E. *On Death and Dying*. New York: Macmillan, 1969.

Zitter, J. N. "The Never-ending Mistreatment of Black Patients." *New York Times*, Opinion, June 29, 2019. https://www.nytimes.com/2019/06/29/opinion/sunday/hospice-end-of-life-racism.html.

3

Spiritual Care within Nursing and Midwifery

Linda Ross and Wilfred McSherry

INTRODUCTION

In this chapter, we focus on the importance of spirituality, particularly in difficult times such as during illness and COVID-19, and the challenges that this presents for professionals such as nurses and midwives who feel unprepared for spiritual care as part of their holistic caring role. We describe how a European project "Enhancing nurses' and midwives' competence in Providing spiritual care through Innovative education and Compassionate Care" (EPICC Project) responded to this challenge by producing outputs that support the preparation of nurses and midwives for spiritual care namely: definitions of "spirituality" and "spiritual care"; competencies for practice; pointers for developing evidence-based education programmes, with a supporting Toolkit; and a network and website for sharing best practice. We conclude by giving examples of how the EPICC outputs are impacting healthcare education, practice and policy internationally to better prepare nurses, midwives, and more recently, other healthcare staff, to include spiritual care within their practice.

IMPORTANCE OF THE SPIRITUAL IN DIFFICULT TIMES

The spiritual part of life can come into sharp focus particularly in times of crisis, whether that be from illness, loss, death, and/or any life changing events, causing our beliefs and faith and our deep-seated sense of meaning, purpose, value and connection to be challenged and may result in spiritual distress. COVID-19 saw both healthcare staff and patients experience spiritual distress over a prolonged period. The global scale of the pandemic meant that large numbers of nurses and patients simultaneously suffered exceptional losses challenging nurses' ability to "journey" with and support patients. The pandemic was unrelenting, staff became exhausted and traumatized by having to make difficult decisions about rationing peoples' care which went against their moral judgment (for some resulting in moral injury). They personally experienced disconnection (some stayed in hospital residences to avoid infecting their families and were unable to continue with their normal self-care activities such as art, music, gardening, and nature) and they certainly witnessed disconnection on a large scale; patients dying in large numbers often alone without family present, trying to facilitate connection with loved ones using iPads and other devices, breaking bad news frequently over the phone rather than in person. On top of this, specialist spiritual support, normally provided by healthcare chaplains to patients and staff, was variable. Some hospitals considered chaplains as "front line" staff providing them with Personal Protective Equipment (PPR whereas others did not, more or less withdrawing them from frontline service (Carey et al., "COVID-19"; Stirling, "COVID-19"). For many staff this meant that valuable specialist spiritual support was unavailable at a time when it was needed most, resulting in patients, staff, and families encountering existential and spiritual distress on an unprecedented scale. Many have still not fully recovered and are struggling with long COVID and/or Post Traumatic Stress Disorder (PTSD) type symptoms consistent with moral injury (Williamson et al., "Moral Injury").

NURSES AND SPIRITUAL CARE

Spiritual care is important to patients and their families, as was highlighted during COVID-19. It is highly valued when provided (de Diego-Cordero et al., "Spiritual Needs") and is associated with greater treatment adherence, clinician trust, and satisfaction with care (Balboni et al., "State of the Science"). Nurses and midwives have an important role to play in general spiritual care alongside the specialist healthcare chaplain. They have a duty to care for the whole person, body, mind and spirit (International Council of Nurses, *The ICN Code*). While they are well prepared to care for the body and the mind, with curricula and exams focusing largely on these aspects and some nurses specializing solely in mental health, they are less well prepared to care for the spirit. Nursing curricular input on spirituality has been variable or non-existent and nurses have been calling for education and guidance for at least two decades (McSherry et al., "Preparing"; Rykkje et al., "Educational"). This call has largely gone unheard and the reasons are complex but include uncertainty about definitions of spirituality and spiritual care, the absence of spiritual care competencies, fears about being suspended by regulatory bodies for inappropriate practice, and absence of evidence-based teaching and learning (Ross et al., "Nursing and Midwifery"). Our research over the past 15 years sought to address these gaps to better prepare nurses for spiritual care.

RESEARCH TO BETTER PREPARE NURSES FOR SPIRITUAL CARE

The EPICC Project has made a significant contribution to the preparation of undergraduate nurses and midwives across Europe and beyond for the delivery of spiritual care. The EPICC Project, funded by the European Commission and led by six partners, brought 31 pre-registration nurse/midwifery educators from 21 European countries and over 60 international stakeholders together from 2016–2019 to co-produce important novel outputs to address the gaps identified above. These outputs are explained below and include:

- Clarification of the terms "spirituality" and "spiritual care" for nursing/midwifery practice (outlined in the preamble of the EPICC Spiritual Care Education Standard, or EPICC Standard)
- Core spiritual care competencies (outlined in the EPICC Standard)

- Synthesis of the factors that help student nurses/midwives to become competent in spiritual care (EPICC Gold Standard Education Matrix or EPICC Matrix)
- A toolkit with teaching and learning activities to help students attain the competencies outlined in the EPICC Standard (EPICC Adoption Toolkit)
- A Network to enable educators, researchers, and other stakeholders to communicate and share ideas about best practice in spiritual care education (EPICC Network)
- A website to house all the above outputs (www.epicc-network.org)

CLARIFICATION OF THE TERMS "SPIRITUALITY" AND "SPIRITUAL CARE" FOR NURSING/MIDWIFERY PRACTICE (EPICC STANDARD, PAGES 1–2)

Among the gaps highlighted earlier was a lack of clarity about how "spirituality" and "spiritual care" are understood for nursing and midwifery practice. Consensus on definitions of these terms was achieved through discussion groups and voting rounds with all groups participating in the EPICC Project, resulting in the following definitions (See Tables 1 and 2 below).

Defining Spirituality

The European Association of Palliative Care (EAPC) definition (EAPC, *Spirituality*), which was itself based on consensus among international stakeholders in key conferences between 2009 and 2014 (Nolan et al., "Spiritual Care"; Puchalski et al., "ImprovingP") was accepted as appropriate for nursing/midwifery practice and can be found on pages 1 and 2 of the EPICC Standard:

Table 1: The EPICC definition of spirituality

Spirituality: "The dynamic dimension of human life that relates to the way persons (individual and community) experience, express and/or seek meaning, purpose and transcendence, and the way they connect to the moment, to self, to others, to nature, to the significant and/or the sacred.

The spiritual field is multidimensional:

1. Existential challenges (e.g., questions concerning identity, meaning, suffering and death, guilt and shame, reconciliation and forgiveness, freedom and responsibility, hope and despair, love and joy).

2. Value-based considerations and attitudes (e.g., what is most important for each person, such as relations to oneself, family, friends, work, aspects of nature, art and culture, ethics and morals, and life itself).

3. Religious considerations and foundations (e.g., faith, beliefs and practices, the relationship with God or the ultimate).

Defining Spiritual Care

The NHS Education for Scotland (*Spiritual Care Matters*, 2010) definition of spiritual care (later replaced by NES, *Spiritual Care Matters*, 2021) was amended to include the wellness perspective, ensuring its relevance to midwives. The changes are highlighted in bold below; the definition is on page 2 of the EPICC Standard:

Table 2: Defining Spiritual Care

Spiritual care: "Care which recognizes and responds to the human spirit when faced with life changing events (such as birth, trauma, ill health, loss) or sadness, and can include the need for meaning, for self-worth, to express oneself, for faith support, perhaps for rites or prayer or sacrament, or simply for a sensitive listener. Spiritual care begins with encouraging human contact in compassionate relationship and moves in whatever direction need requires."

CORE SPIRITUAL CARE COMPETENCIES (EPICC STANDARD PAGE 3)

A further gap was identifying what was reasonable to expect of nurses and midwives as general spiritual care providers to complement the specialist healthcare chaplain. No practical spiritual care competencies yet existed that could be applied to nursing/midwifery practice. One of the EPICC

Partners, Professor Rene van Leeuwen, had developed the Spiritual Care Competency Scale (van Leeuwen et al., "The Validity") and another Partner, Dr. Josephine Attard (Attard et al., "Development" and "Design") built on that work, producing a 54–item spiritual care competency framework from a review of the international literature and Delphi rounds with stakeholders in Malta and international experts. Through a series of voting rounds EPICC participants reduced Attard's 54 spiritual care competencies to four; these four core competencies make up the EPICC Spiritual Care Education Standard and, for the first time, map out the knowledge, skills and attitudes expected of student nurses and midwives at point of registration. Detailed accounts of the development of the EPICC Standard and a self-assessment version of the EPICC Standard can be found in van Leeuwen et al., ("The Development) and Giske et al., ("Developing") respectively.

FACTORS THAT HELP STUDENT NURSES/MIDWIVES BECOME COMPETENT IN SPIRITUAL CARE (EPICC GOLD STANDARD EDUCATION MATRIX OR EPICC MATRIX)

How student nurses/midwives learn to become competent in spiritual care was a further gap in knowledge. Our research over the past 15 years had identified factors important for student learning; this data was synthesized into the EPICC Matrix and its accompanying narrative and is explained in detail in Ross et al. ("Development"). In brief, in the only multinational studies of their kind and size (Ross and McSherry, "The Power"; "Development . . . Matrix"; "Nursing and Midwifery"), we identified factors important for student learning as outlined in Table 3. These key points are supported by examples in the next section where the EPICC Toolkit is discussed.

Table 3: Factors Important for Student Learning
Key point: Spiritual care competency develops over time, even in low scoring students, so a one-off lecture or module is insufficient, rather spirituality should be a key thread running through entire curricula.
Factors important for learning:
The student as a person. Teaching should focus on broadening students' perception of spirituality beyond religion (e.g., "word cloud" activity in EPICC Toolkit (see section below) and should encourage reflection on own beliefs, values and personal life events (e.g., "life tree" and "meaning and purpose" activities in the EPICC Toolkit) and should support self-care (see self-care activities).
The clinical environment, in particular the ethos of the organisation and whether it fosters holistic patient care, and experience in caring for patients i.e. reflecting in and on practice. Students reported that patients are the best teachers.
A teaching/learning environment which encourages reflective practice through personal reflection and group discussion and debate.

TOOLKIT TO HELP STUDENTS BECOME COMPETENT IN SPIRITUAL CARE

(EPICC Adoption Toolkit)

The EPICC Adoption Toolkit contains over 25 activities that can be used by those providing spiritual care education. The activities are designed to help students to become competent in spiritual care. The activities, arranged under the 4 competencies, were provided by EPICC Participants based on their experience of what works in the classroom and for education.

For example, for EPICC Competency 1, which is about intrapersonal spirituality (becoming aware of your own spirituality), one activity invites students to develop a word cloud about "What does spirituality mean to you?" This activity encourages reflection on the wider definition of spirituality. Another activity invites students to draw their life tree, reflecting on the life events and people who have shaped their personal beliefs, values and journey to becoming a nurse or midwife. For self-care, students might reflect on "what gives your life meaning and purpose?" and consider how they might live a more meaningful life. They may also try out a variety of self-care activities such as a gratitude diary, affirmation cards or, breathing exercises to identify what works for them in managing stressful situations.

For EPICC Competency 2 (interpersonal spirituality), which is about recognizing the importance of spirituality for other people, competency 3 (assessment and planning) and competency 4 (intervention and evaluation) we encourage students to try out the 2 Question Spiritual Assessment Model (2Q-SAM, Ross and McSherry, "Nursing and Midwifery") with one patient during one shift and reflect on whether care was more person centred as a result. This activity is useful for encouraging students and healthcare professionals to reflect upon their own understanding of spirituality and how spiritual needs may be expressed by patients in practice. The activity also highlights the usefulness of a systematic approach to assessment, planning, implementation and evaluation when addressing spiritual needs. This approach is fundamental to the achievement of competencies 3 and 4. The 2Q-SAM uses the questions, "What's most important to you right now?" (this is taken from the EPICC definition of spirituality) followed by the question "How can we help?" These two seemingly simple questions can guide nursing care at each care moment. They give permission for people to express things relating to meaning/purpose/transcendence/connection, the deeper spiritual things in life, that might be bothering them but feel unable to voice. By focusing care on the most pressing needs at any care moment, care becomes dynamic, holistic, patient led, and fundamentally person centred. Care is also prudent; only what is needed is addressed at any given moment. In this way spiritual care need not involve extra time or resources, a commonly cited reason for not including it. In fact, some students testing the model reported time saving, because the really important issues for the person were addressed rather than peripheral ones. For example, one student identified that a worry for one patient was that no one was there to look after her cat at home. Arrangement of further tests on an outpatient basis and discharge medication enabled this patient to return home earlier than planned.

A SUPPORTIVE NETWORK AND WEBSITE (EPICC NETWORK)

The EPICC Network is a community of (mainly nursing and midwifery) educators and practitioners who support one another and share best practice in spiritual care research, education and practice. The Network achieves these objectives through biannual webinars, biennial conferences, joint publications and grant applications. It is free to join through the EPICC website which provides an historical record of the EPICC Project and a home for all of the EPICC outputs (www.epicc-network.org).

MOVING FORWARD: IMPACT OF EPICC AND THE RESEARCH ON WHICH IT IS BUILT

The EPICC Project ran from 2016– July 2019. Since then, the impact has been far reaching. Its outputs have had significant impact on nursing and midwifery education, practice and policy internationally. A full account up to October 2020 can be found in the "Use and Value of the EPICC Outputs 2020" report under the "Reach and Impact" tab on the EPICC website (https://epicc-network.org/wp-content/uploads/2021/01/Use-and-Value-of-the-EPICC-Outputs-final.pdf). Some examples from the report are presented in the following sections.

Impact on Education

The education of nurses/midwives changed in 23 universities across 16 countries who adopted the EPICC Standard across their curricula, better preparing practitioners for spiritual care. These were mainly EPICC participants, but usage of the EPICC Standard and Matrix to inform curricula is seeing expansion beyond the original EPICC participants to other parts of Europe and beyond (e.g., Fernández-Pascual et al., "Effectiveness") including countries such as Western Australia, China, Brazil, and Asia and to other disciplines such as medicine and allied health. For example both the original EPICC Standard and the self-assessment version are in the process of being translated into thirteen languages (see EPICC website) by academics suggesting cross-cultural relevance and utility of these tools beyond Europe.

In addition to university education, the EPICC outputs are informing redesign of the UK Royal College of Nursing (RCN) spiritual care educational resources, ensuring that the continuing education of the UK nursing/midwifery workforce is evidence-based. Other, such as South Australia and Ghana have also expressed an interest.

Impact on Policy

The EPICC Project has also influenced government policy. For example, in Wales from 2022 spirituality became a mandatory component of all undergraduate nursing and midwifery programmes (NHS Wales, "Spiritual Care"). The mandatory training is based on the EPICC Standard and students are assessed on the four competencies in clinical practice across all three years of their degree studies (UK Nursing and Midwifery Council,

Future Nurse). Clinical staff assessing students also complete training based on the EPICC Standard which acts as the assessment template.

Additionally, the UK Board of Health Care Chaplaincy adopts the EPICC Standard as what is reasonable to expect of non-specialist spiritual care givers, such as nurses, in providing spiritual care (UK Board of Healthcare Chaplaincy, *Spiritual Care*). This development highlights the relevance and credibility of the EPICC Standard and its application beyond nursing and midwifery.

Impact on Professional Practice

One of the tools in the EPICC Toolkit, the 2Q-SAM referred to earlier, is supporting Specialist Organ Donation Nurses in the UK with difficult end of life conversations (NHS Blood and Transplant, *Advanced*) and it features in the EAPC white paper as a model to support the practice of multidisciplinary palliative care teams (Best et al., "An EAPC White Paper").

Additionally, a long-standing campaign to see spiritual care reinstated within the UK regulatory body's (the Nursing and Midwifery Council, NMC) revised Code for nurses/midwives has resulted in discussions about this possibility, with EPICC's evidence being presented in support of this move (Ross et al., "Spiritual Care"; "Spiritual Shortfall?"; Ross and McSherry, "Spiritual Care"). Recently the NMC launched a campaign about the importance of providing "Holistic Care." We were invited to submit a case study to highlight the importance of spiritual care and how this is a significant dimension of a person-centred and holistic approach (Ross and McSherry, "Holistic Care"). This is an important step for the NMC because it signals a willingness and desire to engage with the spiritual aspects of the person. It is also a positive indicator for reinstating the word "spiritual" within the next revision and iteration of the Code.

CONCLUSION

This chapter has explored the importance of spirituality and spiritual care for nursing and midwifery practice within the context of holistic and person-centred care. The chapter describes the significant contribution that the EPICC Project has made to the preparation of nurses and midwives for spiritual care by defining the terms "spirituality" and "spiritual care," by establishing competencies for education and practice (EPICC Standard) and by identifying factors important for teaching and learning (EPICC Matrix). The EPICC outputs are proving useful vehicles for achieving a more co-ordinated approach to the spiritual care education of nurses, midwives, and more recently allied health professionals internationally. Further work is needed to establish the cross-cultural relevance of these tools beyond European and Western cultures.

REFERENCES

Attard, J., Ross, L., Weeks, K. "Design and Development of a Spiritual Care Competency Framework for Pre-registration Nurses and Midwives: A Modified Delphi Study." *Nurse Education in Practice* 39 (2019) 96–104. https://doi.org/10.1016/j.nepr.2019.08.003.

———. "Developing a Spiritual Care Competency Framework for Pre-registration Nurses and Midwives." *Nurse Education in Practice* 40 (2009) 102604. https://doi.org/10.1016/j.nepr.2019.07.010.

Balboni, T. A., Fitchett, G., Handzo, G. F., Johnson, K. S., Koenig, H.G., Pargament, K. I., Puchalski, C. M., Sinclair, S., Taylor, E. J., and Steinhauser, K. E. "State of the Science of Spirituality and Palliative Care Research, Part II: Screening, Assessment, and Interventions." *Journal of Pain and Symptom Management* 54/3 (2017) 441–53.

Best, M., Leget, C., Goodhead, A., et al. "An EAPC White Paper on Multi-Disciplinary Education for Spiritual Care in Palliative Care." *BMC Palliative Care* 19 (2020) 9. https://doi.org/10.1186/s12904-019-0508-4.

Carey, L., Swift, C., Burton, M. "COVID-19: Multinational Perspectives of Providing Chaplaincy, Spiritual, and Pastoral Care." *Health and Social Care Chaplaincy* 8/2 (2020) 133–142. https://doi.org/10.1558/hscc.41973.

de Diego-Cordero, R., Rey-Reyes, A., Vega-Escaño, J., Lucchetti, G., and Badanta, B. "Spiritual Needs during COVID 19 Pandemic in the Perceptions of Spanish Emergency Critical Care Health Professionals." *Intensive and Critical Care Nursing* 76 (2023) 103373. https://doi.org/10.1016/j.iccn.2022.103373.

European Association of Palliative Care (EAPC). *Spirituality and Spiritual Care Definitions*. Vilvoorde, Belgium: EAPC (2023). https://eapcnet.eu/eapc-groups/reference/spiritual-care/; https://blogs.staffs.ac.uk/epicc/files/2020/08/EPICC-Spiritual-Care-Education-Standard.pdf.

Fernández-Pascual, M., Reig-Ferrer, A., and Santos-Ruiz, A. "Effectiveness of an Educational Intervention to Teach Spiritual Care to Spanish Nursing Students. *Religions* 11 (2020) 596. https://doi.org/10.3390/rel11110596.

Giske, T., Schep, A., Bø, B., Cone, P., Kuven, B., McSherry, W., Owusu, B., Ueland, V., Lassche-Scheffer, J., van Leeuwen, R., and Ross, L. "Developing and Testing the EPICC Spiritual Care Competency Self-Assessment Tool for Student Nurses and Midwives." *Journal of Clinical Nursing* 32/7–8 (2022) 1148–62. https://doi.org/10.1111/jocn.16261.

International Council of Nurses (ICN). *The ICN Code of Ethics for Nurses*, rev. 2021. Geneva, Switzerland: ICN, 2021. https://www.icn.ch/sites/default/files/2023-06/ICN_Code-of-Ethics_EN_Web.pdf.

McSherry, W., and Ross, L. "Spiritual Shortfall?" *Nursing Standard* 29 (2015) 22–23.

McSherry, W., Ross, L., Attard, J., van Leeuwen, R., Giske, T., Kleiven, T., Boughey, A., and the EPICC Network. "Preparing Undergraduate Nurses and Midwives for

Spiritual Care: Some Developments in Education over the Last Decade." *Journal for the Study of Spirituality* 10/1 (2020) 55–71. https://doi.org/10.1080/20440243.2020.1726053.

NHS Blood and Transplant. *Advanced Communication Guide Specialist Nurses in Organ and Tissue Donation.* Bristol: NHS Blood and Transplant, 2020. https://www.nhsbt.nhs.uk/.

NHS Education for Scotland. *Spiritual Care Matters: An Introductory Resource for All NHS Scotland Staff.* Edinburgh: NHS Education for Scotland, 2010.

———. *Spiritual Care Matters: An Introductory Resource for All NHSScotland Staff.* Edinburgh: NHS Education for Scotland, 2021. https://www.nes.scot.nhs.uk/media/xzadagnc/spiritual-care-matters-an-introductory-resource-for-all-nhsscotland-staff.pdf.

NHS Wales/GIG Nymru. "Spiritual Care to Become Part of Welsh Nursing Curriculum." Nantgarw: NHS Wales, [2019]. https://heiw.nhs.wales/news/spiritual-care-to-become-part-of-welsh-nursing-curriculum/.

Nolan, S., Saltmarsh, P., and Leget, C.J.W. "Spiritual Care in Palliative Care: Working towards an EAPC Task Force." *European Journal of Palliative Care* 18/2 (2011) 86–89.

Puchalski, C. M., Vitillo, R., Hull, S. K., and Reller, N. "Improving the Spiritual Dimension of Whole Person Care: Reaching National and International Consensus." *Journal of Palliative Medicine* 17/6 (2014) 642–56.

Ross, L., Giske, T., Boughey, A., van Leeuwen, R., Attard, J., Kleiven, T., McSherry, W. "Development of a Spiritual Care Education Matrix: Factors Facilitating/Hindering Improvement of Spiritual Care Competency in Student Nurses and Midwives." *Nurse Education Today* 114 (2022) 105403. https://doi.org/10.1016/j.nedt.2022.105403.

Ross., L., Giske, T., van Leeuwen, R., Baldacchino, D., McSherry, W., Narayanasamy, A., Jarvis, P., and Schep-Akkerman, A. "Factors Contributing to Student Nurses'/Midwives' Perceived Competency in Spiritual Care." *Nurse Education Today* 36 (2016) 445–51. https://doi.org/10.1016/j.nedt.2015.10.005.

Ross, L., and McSherry, W. "Holistic Care." London: Nursing and Midwifery Council, 2024. https://www.nmc.org.uk/standards/guidance/holistic-care/?utm_source=Nursing%20and%20Midwifery%20Council&utm_medium=email&utm_campaign=14215802_Education%20newsletter%20May%202024&utm_content=holistic%20care&dm_i=129A,8GOZE,39A0YR,YYL9E,1).

Ross, L., and McSherry, W. "The Power of Two Simple Questions." *Nursing Standard.* 33/9 (2017) 78–80.

Ross, L., and McSherry, W. "Spiritual Care Should Be Part of the Code." *Nursing Standard* 31/33 (2017) 29. https://doi.org/10.7748/ns.31.33.29.s25.

Ross, L., McSherry, W., Giske, T., van Leeuwen, R., Schep-Akkerman, A., Koslander, T., Hall, J., Østergaard Steenfeldt, V., and Jarvis, P. "Nursing and Midwifery Students' Perceptions of Spirituality, Spiritual Care, and Spiritual Care Competency: A Prospective, Longitudinal, Correlational European Study." *Nurse Education Today,* 67 (2018) 64–71. https://doi.org/10.1016/j.nedt.2018.05.002.

Ross, L., van Leeuwen, R., Baldacchino, D., Giske, T., McSherry, W., Narayanasamy, A., Downes, C., Jarvis, P, and Schep-Akkerman, A. "Student Nurses['] Perceptions of Spirituality and Competence in Delivering Spiritual Care: A European Pilot

Study." *Nurse Education Today* 34/5 (2014) 697–702. https://doi.org/10.1016/j.nedt.2013.09.014. PMID: 24119953.

Rykkje, L., Søvik, M. B., Ross, L., McSherry, W., Cone, P., and Giske, T. "Educational Interventions and Strategies for Spiritual Care in Nursing and Healthcare Students and Staff: A Scoping Review." *Journal of Clinical Nursing* 31/11–12 (2021) 1440–64. https://doi.org/10.1111/jocn.16067.

Stirling, I. "COVID-19. The Call of Louisa Jordan: The Formation of the Spiritual Care Team at NHS Louisa Jordan, Glasgow, Scotland." *Health and Social Care Chaplaincy* 9/2 (2021) 154–74. https://doi.org/10.1558/hscc.42420.

UK Board of Healthcare Chaplaincy. *Spiritual Care Competencies for Healthcare Chaplains*. Kingston-upon-Hull: UK Board of Healthcare Chaplains, 2020. https://www.ukbhc.org.uk/wp-content/uploads/2024/08/2024_08_01–UKBHC-CCs-182020.pdf.

UK Nursing and Midwifery Council. *Future Nurse: Standards of Proficiency for Registered Nurses: All Wales Practice Assessment Document and Ongoing Record of Achievement*. London: UK Nursing and Midwifery Council, 2018. https://heiw.nhs.wales/education-and-training/nursing-and-midwifery/placement-information/docs/all-wales-practice-assessment-document-nursing/.

Van Leeuwen, R., Tiesinga, L., Middel, B., Post, D., and Jochemsen, H. "The Validity and Reliability of an Instrument to Assess Nursing Competencies in Spiritual Care." *Journal of Clinical Nursing* 18 (2009) 2857–69. https://doi.org/10.1111/j.1365-2702.2008.02594.x.

Van Leeuwen, R., Attard, J., Ross, L., Boughey, A., Giske, T., Kleiven, T., McSherry, W. "The Development of a Consensus-based Spiritual Care Education Standard for Undergraduate Nursing and Midwifery Students: An Educational Mixed Methods Study" *Journal of Advanced Nursing* 77/2 (2021) 973–86. https://doi.org/10.1111/jan.14613.

Williamson, V., Murphy, D., Phelps, A., Forbes, D., and Greenberg, N. "Moral Injury: The Effect on Mental Health and Implications for Treatment." *The Lancet* 8(6) (2021) 453–55. https://doi.org/10.1016/S2215-0366(21)00113-9.

4

Acknowledging the Tragic: Spiritual Care from the Perspective of Public Health

John Blevins

This chapter is a response (too tentative to be an "answer") to the question, "What is spiritual care from the perspective of public health?" As a licensed minister and someone trained in theological studies who now serves on the faculty of a school of public health in the United States, I have spent a number of years working to understand the complex and at times contradictory relationship between religion and the field of public health. Situated within that context, I will offer my perspectives on this question by first defining the field of public health and then identifying two frameworks—positivism and instrumentalism—that, while important to the field, limit its capacity to examine (or even name) spirituality as a topic of research. I will offer two specific examples of such limitations: 1) the inadequacy of the field to understand many complex and contradictory dimensions of our individual and collective spiritual experiences as human beings, especially in relation to health and illness; and 2) the inherent impossibility of the field to achieve its own objectives, an impossibility the field is loath to acknowledge. The critical analysis of public health practice that follows in this chapter raises questions that are spiritual in nature because they represent an encounter with the limitations of our human knowledge and capacity to make sense of the suffering that accompanies illness and death. I close by arguing for an urgent need for those of us in public health to acknowledge such limitations in order to imagine what spiritual care is within our field.

WHAT IS PUBLIC HEALTH? HOW DOES THE FIELD UNDERSTAND RELIGION AND SPIRITUALITY?

The field of public health is interested in improving the health of our communities by decreasing the rates of illness and premature death. To do this, the field focuses on health at the population level. This distinguishes the field from clinical medicine (a field that is still a key partner in public health research and programs), which focuses on the health of patients in the individual clinical encounter. Many in the field rely on the definition of health stated in the constitution of the World Health Organization (WHO): "Health is a state of complete physical, mental and social well-being and not merely the absence of disease or infirmity" (WHO, *Constitution*). The definition obviously lacks any mention of the spiritual dimensions of human existence.

There have been efforts to amend the definition to include this dimension. In 1983, the World Health Assembly of the WHO adopted resolution 37.13 that "invites Member States to consider including in their strategies for health for all a spiritual dimension as defined in this resolution in accordance with their social and cultural patterns"[1] (Peng-Keller, "Ennobling," 55). Building on this resolution, efforts were made to amend the WHO constitution in 1998 to define health as "a dynamic state of physical, mental, spiritual, and social well-being and not merely the absence of disease or infirmity" (Rauch, "Attempts," 165). The effort failed as representatives objected to the implications of the term and criticized it as too vague and imprecise for a field and professional practice that prizes concrete descriptions of observable phenomena and quantifiable, generalizable data.

The reliance on these types of data as the primary type of information to inform public health practice is understandable from the standpoint of public health's overall mission of reducing morbidity and mortality. It is also severely limiting from the standpoint of understanding human experiences (religion and spirituality being two important examples) that are not easily

---

1. Support for the resolution rested in part on a paper authored by Halfdan Mahler, who was then WHO Director-General. Mahler was the son of a Danish Baptist minister; see Blevins *Christianity's Role*, 120–23.

studied through the kinds of methodologies that yield this highly-prized data that guide public health programs. Such a reliance leads to a positivistic and instrumentalist bias in public health research and practice that limits the field's exploration of religion and spirituality.

A positivistic approach prioritizes measurable phenomena and concrete facts as the only sources of knowledge on which one may rely when making truth claims and deciding on a course of action.[2] An instrumentalist approach values pragmatism and prioritizes outcomes and impact. Much of the new-found interest in religion in public health is instrumentalist, focused on religions' contributions to health programs, services, and capacities. For example, religion matters in global health because of the substantial clinical health services provided by faith-based health facilities in low- and middle-income countries, especially in the sub-Saharan African region (Blevins et al., "The Percentage"). Understanding the scale, scope, and quality of such services can be useful in to setting priorities, allocating budgets, developing more effective programs to cover gaps in health services, establishing effective partnerships for community engagement, and building and sustaining capacity (Olivier et. al., "Understanding"). Such priorities reflect a utilitarian approach to ethical deliberation, often summarized as the greatest good for the greatest number.[3] And yet, the negative, unintended consequences of these kinds of programs that take precedence because of instrumentalism are rarely interrogated.[4]

The positivistic bias of the health sciences in relation to religion limits the framing of research questions and studies to the aspects of religion that can be measured and assessed, conceptualizing "religiosity" through clearly defined indicators; these often include measures such as religious

2. For an insightful critique of the problems with positivism for public health education and a call for a deeper engagement with humanities disciplines (including religious and theological studies), see Buchanan, "Beyond Positivism."

3. The field wrestled with the potential and limits of utilitarianism in the 2020 COVID pandemic. For a perspective on the essential role of utilitarianism in response to a health emergency such as COVID, see Savulescu, Persson, and Wilkinson, "Utilitarianism." For a critique of instrumentalism, see **Bispo Júnior and Brito Morais, "Community Participation."**

4. Critiques of instrumentalism in public health usually focus on public health programs that improve health outcomes for the public at-large but may have no positive effects—or even detrimental effects—for communities on the social margins. For example, see Gibson and Porter, "Unpacking." Such studies are often presented as case studies conducted as part of a program review to identify unintended consequences of particular public health initiatives. This chapter offers other examples of such critiques in global health practice and argues that such dynamics are frequent enough to necessitate a proactive critical analysis before a project begins rather than a mere retrospective assessment at a project's termination.

attendance, a content analysis of doctrinal statements or denominational policies, or self-reports of belief in God.[5] Public health researchers prize positivistic approaches because they allow for replicability across a multi-site study or a meta-analysis of different studies that each measure religion according to similar religiosity indicators.

And yet, while positivism and instrumentalism are common approaches for studying religion in public health, both are severely limited in accounting for the complexity of religion. For example, measuring self-reports of the frequency of religious attendance reveal little about the various factors influencing such attendance, the reciprocal influences of belief and practice on each other, and the negotiations between individuals' stated religious beliefs and their daily behaviors outside of religious observance that may be in tension with such belief. Further, such narrow conceptualizations for studying religion limit interdisciplinary scholarship because scholars in religious and theological studies rarely use instrumentalism or positivism to conceive of religion. These vastly different approaches across the disciplines mean that those most interested in religion in the various fields are talking past, not to, one another.

THE LIMITS OF PUBLIC HEALTH ENCOUNTERS WITH RELIGION AND SPIRITUALITY

This section offers two brief examples of the consequences of public health employing positivism and instrumentalism to inform its efforts to work with faith communities and religious leaders. The first example is the 2014–2016 Ebola outbreak and the second is the ongoing global HIV pandemic. When Ebola spread across western Africa in late 2015 in the largest outbreak of the virus ever recorded, a massive public health response ensued. Burial practices were quickly identified as a source of transmission of the virus and the existing 1998 guidance for outbreak response co-developed by the WHO and the US Centers for Disease Control (CDC) contained explicit step-by-step procedures for safely handling the bodies of those who died. That guidance was 209 pages in length; it contained exactly one reference to religion: "Be aware of the family's cultural practices and religious beliefs. Help the family understand why some practices cannot be done because they place the family or others at risk for exposure" (Perry and Lloyd, *Infection Control*). The guidance was dutifully implemented across the West Africa region and still cases skyrocketed. The emergency response was failing

---

5. The staggering varieties of instruments to measure religiosity are seen in Hill and Wood, *Measures*.

miserably and in September 2014, the CDC epidemiologists estimated that as many as 1.4 million could be dead by January 2015 (Meltzer, Atkins, and Santibanez, "Estimating").

The initial response failed as public health officials employed a positivistic framework for assessing causes and determining responses: handling of the bodies during burial rituals was transmitting the virus so suspend such rituals to stop the route of transmission. The logic was sound from the standpoint of public health science. But for millions of people in western Africa such practices were not routes of transmission that must be halted; they were spiritual rituals laden with such significance that suspending them was unimaginable. The observable phenomenon of viral transmission held far less meaning than the spiritual practices associated with burial for most people outside of public health circles. Only when public health officials, working in concert with Christian, Muslim, and traditional spiritual healers, modified the guidance to allow for an adaptation rather than a suspension of burial practice did the rates of new infection drop. In due course, the outbreak was under control, and by June 2016, with over 11,000 deaths recorded, the WHO declared that the outbreak was over (WHO African Region, "WHO Declares"). An over-confident reliance on positivism coupled with a bias that the observable data that matter are the ones that public health scientists prioritize, delayed the public health response to this outbreak for weeks—weeks in which thousands died.[6]

The second example comes from the ongoing global HIV pandemic. I mentioned earlier that increased awareness of the scale of clinical services provided by faith-based health facilities in the sub-Saharan region of Africa has been an influential factor in the rather newfound interest in religion on the part of public health officials. In a report detailing the proceedings from a consultation with religious leaders in 2012, Ambassador Eric Goosby, director of the United States government's HIV response, noted that "In sub-Saharan Africa, it is estimated that 40 percent of health care services are provided by FBOs, many of which serve the most rural areas and the most marginalized people" (US President's Emergency Plan for AIDS Relief, *A Firm Foundation*). Ambassador Goosby was correct in noting the important role of faith-based health facilities. But he failed to acknowledge how the US response to the global pandemic also provided resources to religious institutions in many of the nations that were hardest hit by the pandemic to foment stigma, violence, and severe legal punishment to vulnerable communities such as gay men and sex workers (Evertz, "How Ideology";

---

6. For a more comprehensive analysis of the failure to initially understand religions' influences in the Ebola outbreak, see Blevins, Jalloh, and Robinson, "Faith."

Blevins and Irungu, "Different Ways").[7] A strict instrumentalist approach to strengthening the capacity and funding of faith-based organizations helped ensure that their contributions to HIV health services were leveraged; it also funded religious responses that have fueled stigma and discrimination against some groups most affected by the pandemic and resulted in violence and death for some gay men.

ILLUSIONS AND TRAGEDIES: THE CONSEQUENCES OF PUBLIC HEALTH'S FAILURE TO REFLECT ON THE SPIRITUAL DIMENSIONS OF HUMAN HEALTH . . . AND OF THE SPIRITUAL DIMENSIONS OF OUR FIELD

In this final section, I frame the argument made to this point as a spiritual dilemma for the field of public health—a dilemma that has concrete, measurable consequences for the metrics of morbidity and mortality that public health prioritizes. This dilemma manifests in at least two ways. First, the field's over-reliance on positivism and instrumentalism leaves it ill-equipped to understand and account for its own biases and priorities. We travel all around the world and conduct rigorous research to understand the social-cultural forces that impact health outcomes in those communities but we rarely articulate the assumptions that underwrite our efforts. In short, we treat public health as a value-neutral scientific endeavor when, in fact, it reflects very specific cultural norms and assumptions. Acknowledging those norms is an essential starting point, but we rarely even do that, leaving us ill-equipped even to recognize that millions of people around the world employ frameworks their taken-for-granted lens for understanding health that are far removed from the data that informs our own culturally specific lens. Such a failure leaves us in constant danger of overwriting our framework on top of those of other societies, as we saw in the case of the Ebola outbreak. If this experience were limited to one tragic example, we could express regret and learn from our "unintended consequences" but the experiences are legion and they leave us vulnerable to repeating the worst episodes in the history of our field such as the Tuskegee syphilis experiments.[8]

---

7. These effects continue into the present. Uganda instituted laws criminalizing homosexuality carrying punishments that includes death. The effect on the country's LGBTQ community has been devastating and the law is rolling back hard-won progress against HIV in the country. See Mandavilli, "With Harsh."

8. For background on the Tuskegee study, see Blevins, *Christianity's Role*, 114–17. William Jenkins, one of the foremost researchers on race and health disparities in the

Second, those of us in public health would do well to acknowledge that the field inescapably places us in tragic positions. In describing the field as tragic, I borrow from an analysis that the theological ethicist Stanley Hauerwas first articulated almost fifty years ago when he claimed that medicine is tragic to the extent it places clinicians in the position of deciding among competing goods at play, or deciding if a relative good should be chosen if it also produces a subsequent bad outcome, or deciding what to do when no "good" choice exists but a choice must nonetheless be made. In such conditions, said Hauerwas, the most important thing is "to have the strength to resist false solutions" (Hauerwas, "Medicine," 184). He believed that medicine is inevitably tragic, even if we pretend it is not:

> Our difficulty with such matters is that morally we lack the skills to describe what happens in [medical] dilemmas—especially since the dilemmas result from our own power of intervention. Because we lack a sense of the tragic we are tempted to try to justify what we do in such circumstances by using the language of the good . . . But what we must learn to see is that this is to misdescribe the situation by giving in to our need for moral justification. We must simply learn that often in such situations there is no right or wrong thing to do—whatever we do will involve both. Such situations are tragic and we only pervert ourselves and our medical practice if we try to describe them in terms that deny that they are anything else.
>
> What we must learn to do is accept that medicine, like almost all other aspects of our lives, involves trade-offs that are unhappy. There is no way to avoid that. We will take the goods it offers, and they are great goods, but at the same time, doctors and patients alike must be willing to accept their losses. And they are hard losses, as they may at times involve life itself. Such losses are tragic, but they can be lived with. They only become destructive when we refuse to recognize them for what they are (Hauerwas, "Medicine," 201).

United States, offered the opening plenary address at the 2010 Annual Meeting of the American Public Health Association. In his talk, he referenced a longitudinal public health surveillance initiative with exemplary programs of community engagement according to public health priorities. He stunned the audience when he revealed that he was referring to the Tuskegee study. In doing so, Jenkins obviously was not championing the approach taken in the study but exhorting the audience to acknowledge the dangers of our work—work that intentionally endeavors to intervene in societies around the world—and the essential need for us to critically reflect on the potential for carrying out violence in the name of compassion. See Jenkins, Opening Plenary.

I believe that such tragic conditions are also hard-wired into the fundamental goal of health for all people in all societies. Public health has set this impossible goal that must be carried out across myriad social and political institutions that are by their very definition at odds with one another. Those systems will at times place us in a position where the actions that may achieve health benefits for a large proportion of a population also exact a price for others. In such circumstances, some system of intense moral reflection would be immensely helpful. Of all the benefits that spiritual practices such as reflection and discernment could offer to the field of public health, this may be the most profound and the most needed.

We are ill-equipped to acknowledge the tragic dimensions of our work because this field cannot imagine acknowledging its inescapably tragic dimension—an acknowledgement that is itself a spiritual practice. Paradoxically, such an admission would enliven and provide concrete expressions of spiritual care in our field by placing us on more sound footing when engaging the morally dangerous waters of health interventions carried out at the societal level for the sake of that society's citizens *for their own good* (or so we tell ourselves). And yet, public health cannot tell those chapters in our own history.

Some religious traditions have forged such spiritual narratives—testimonies may be a more accurate term—honest enough to recount their own tragic collusion with power and violence that was rationalized and justified in the name of God. Such narratives offer public health an example of facing uncomfortable truths. Our failure to do this leaves us dangerously prone to minimizing the harm of the prices paid by some through our actions by touting only the health benefits gained. Were we able to fashion such narratives, we could also express more profound gratitude for our efforts to save lives or improve health and double down our commitment to such practices even as we acknowledge that such practices are always, inescapably tragic. That, to me, is what spiritual care is—or could be—from the perspective of public health.

REFERENCES

Bispo Júnior, J. P., and Brito Morais, M. "Community Participation in the Fight against COVID-19: Utilitarianism and Social Justice."*Cadernos de Saúde Pública*, 36/8 (2020) e00151620. https://doi.org/10.1590/0102-311X00151620.

Blevins, J. *Christianity's Role in United States Global Health and Development Policy: To Transfer the Empire of the World.* New York: Routledge, 2019.

Blevins, J., and Irungu, P. "Different Ways of Doing Violence: Sexuality, Religion, and Public Health in the Lives of Same-gender-loving Men in Kenya." *Journal of the American Academy of Religion* 834 (2015) 930–46. https://www.jstor.org/stable/43900144.

Blevins, J, Jalloh, M., and Robinson, D. "Faith in Global Health Practice in Ebola and HIV Emergencies." *American Journal of Public Health* 109/3 (2019) 379–84. https://doi.org/10.2105/AJPH.2018.304870.

Blevins, J., Lemon, E., Kiser, M., and Kone, A. "The Percentage of HIV Treatment and Prevention Services in Kenya Provided by Faith-based Health Providers." *Development in Practice* 27/5 (2017) 646–57. https://doi.org/10.1080/09614524.2017.1327027.

Buchanan, D. R. "Beyond Positivism: Humanistic Perspectives on Theory and Research in Health Education." *Health Education Research* 13/3 (1998) 439–50.

Evertz, S. *How Ideology Trumped Science: Why PEPFAR Failed to Meet Its Potential*. Washington, DC: Center for American Progress/The Council for Global Equity, 2010. https://cdn.americanprogress.org/wp-content/uploads/issues/2010/01/pdf/pepfar.pdf.

Gibson, J., and Porter, F. "Unpacking 'Women's Health' in the Context of PPPs: A Return to Instrumentalism in Development Policy and Practice?" *Global Social Policy* 16/1 (2016) 68–85. https://doi.org/10.1177/1468018115594650.

Hauerwas, S. "Medicine as a Tragic Profession." In *Truthfulness and Tragedy: Further Investigations into Christian Ethics*, edited by S. Hauerwas et al., 184–201. South Bend: University of Notre Dame Press, 1977.

Hill, P. C., and Wood, R. *Measures of Religiosity*. Birmingham: Religious Education, 1999.

Jenkins, W. Opening Plenary of the American Public Health Association 2010 Part 1. [Video]. November 7, 2010. https://www.youtube.com/watch?v=BragfuSDoow.

Mandavilli, A. "With Harsh Anti-LGBTQ Law, Uganda Risks a Health Crisis." *New York Times*, January 19 (2024) A1. https://www.nytimes.com/2024/01/19/health/uganda-lgbtq-hiv.html.

Meltzer, M., Atkins, C., and Santibanez, S. (2014). "Estimating the Future Number of Cases in the Ebola Epidemic—Liberia and Sierra Leone, 2014-2015." *Morbidity and Mortality Weekly Report (MMWR)* 63/3, Supplement 3 (2014) 1–20. https://stacks.cdc.gov/view/cdc/24901.

Olivier, J., Tsimpo, C., Gemignani, R., Shojo, M., Coulombe, H., Dimmock, F., Nguyen, M. C., Hines, H., Mills, E. J., Dieleman, J. L., Haakenstad, A., and Wodon, Q. "Understanding the Roles of Faith-based Health-care Providers in Africa: Review of the Evidence with a Focus on Magnitude, Reach, Cost, and Satisfaction." *The Lancet* 386/10005 (2015) 1765–75. https://doi.org/10.1016/S0140-6736(15)60251-3.

Peng-Keller, S. "Ennobling Ideas: The World Health Assembly Debates the 'Spiritual Dimension.'" In *The Spirit of Global Health: The World Health Organization and the "Spiritual Dimension" of Health, 1946–2021*, edited by S. Peng-Keller, F. Winiger, and R. Rauch, 42–61. Oxford: Oxford University Press, 2022. https://doi.org/10.1093/oso/9780192865502.001.0001.

Perry, H.N., and Lloyd, E. *Infection Control for Viral Hemorrhagic Fevers in the African Healthcare Setting*. Atlanta: US Centers for Disease Control and Prevention, 1998. https://stacks.cdc.gov/view/cdc/21878.

Rauch, R. "Attempts to Reform the WHO Definition of Health (1997–1999)." In *The spirit of Global Health: The World Health Organization and the "Spiritual*

Dimension" of Health, 1946–2021, edited by S. Peng-Keller, F. Winiger, and R. Rauch, 161–81. Oxford: Oxford University Press, 2022. https://doi.org/10.1093/oso/9780192865502.001.0001.

Savulescu, J., Persson, I., and Wilkinson, D. "Utilitarianism and the Pandemic." *Bioethics* 36/6 (2020) 620–32. https://doi.org/10.1111/bioe.12771.

US President's Emergency Plan for AIDS Relief (PEPFAR). *A Firm Foundation on the Role of Faith-based Organizations in Sustaining Community and Country Leadership in the Response to HIV/AIDS*. Atlanta, Emory University and US Centers for Disease Control, Division of Global HIV/AIDS, 2012.

World Health Organization (WHO). *Constitution of the World Health Organization*. Geneva: WHO, 1946. https://www.who.int/about/governance/constitution.

World Health Organization African Region. "WHO Declares the End of the Most Recent Ebola Virus Disease Outbreak in Liberia." *WHO African Region*, June 12, 2016. https://www.afro.who.int/news/who-declares-end-most-recent-ebola-virus-disease-outbreak-liberia-0.

5

Spiritual Care from Evolving Psychological Perspectives

Kenneth I. Pargament

Over the past 100 years, the field of psychology has dramatically changed its approach to the domain of spirituality in both research and clinical practice. This paper takes a "birds-eye" view of this process of evolution. Specifically, it describes three psychological perspectives on spirituality and spiritual care that have and continue to mark this transformation: the insubstantial, the instrumental, and the integral.

THE INSUBSTANTIAL APPROACH TOWARD SPIRITUALITY AND SPIRITUAL CARE

To put this paper into a larger historical perspective, it's important to remember that the founding figures in the field of psychology in the late 19th and early 20th centuries, such as William James, G. Stanley Hall, and James Leuba, were fascinated by religious phenomena, from mystical experience to conversion, and saw them as central aspects of human functioning (Wulff, *Psychology of Religion*). However, in its effort to establish itself as a scientific field, subsequent figures did all they could to distance themselves from anything hinting of religion, superstition, or magic. Several leaders of the field were quite outspoken about their anti-religious views. Freud (*Future of an Illusion*), for example, was clear in his belief that religion was delusional, developed to defend the individual against the terrors of living in the world. Freud instead argued for the head-on confrontation with reality. Similarly, B. F. Skinner, the founder of behaviorism, saw God as an "explanatory fiction" (Skinner, *Beyond Freedom and Dignity*, 201) and in his fictional vision of a utopian community, *Walden Two*, wrote that "[r]eligious faith becomes irrelevant when the fears which nourish it are allayed and hopes fulfilled—here on earth" (Skinner, *Walden Two*, 165). Albert Ellis, creator of rational-emotive therapy, was perhaps even harsher. Religion, he said, "is on almost every conceivable count, directly opposed to the goals of mental health" (Ellis, *Case against Religion*, 12). He went on to say that to help patient's live with their religions is "equivalent to trying to help them live successfully with their emotional illness" (*Case against Religion*, 15). (Ellis did later shift to a more nuanced and sensitive view of religion.)

Not all psychologists have adopted antagonistic views toward religion. Many, however, have distanced themselves from religious life. In one study, psychologists reported a tenfold shift from holding a religious affiliation as children to describing themselves currently as "nones" (Shafranske and Cummings, "Religious and Spiritual Beliefs"). This movement toward religious disaffiliation has led to a "religiosity gap" between psychologists and the general population. For example, while over 90% of the US population reportedly believes in a personal God, only 26% of clinical and counseling psychologists do so, and while 75% of the US population prays regularly, only 54% of psychologists do the same (Shafranske and Cummings, "Religious and Spiritual Beliefs"). As a result of this gap, psychologists have likely underestimated the prevalence and power of religious beliefs, practices, and experiences among those they serve. True, many people adhere to religious beliefs and practices, but the religion they devote themselves to is said to lack substance. From this "insubstantial perspective," religious or spiritual issues are simply irrelevant to human functioning.

According to this point of view, religion and spirituality are expressions of more fundamental biological, social, or psychological forces. A number of major theorists have maintained that religion at its core serves non-religious functions, including the needs for connectedness and community (Durkheim, *Elementary Forms*), emotional comfort and self-control (Freud, *Future of an Illusion*), and meaning in life (Geertz, *Religion*). These are radical reductionist perspectives that encourage a focus on the presumably more basic functions of religion rather than religion itself. In this sense, religion is "explained away," and the distinctive role that religion and spirituality may play in peoples' lives as well as the need to attend to it in healthcare is discounted (Pargament, "Is Religion Nothing but . . . ?").

It follows that spiritual care is unnecessary from an insubstantial perspective because religion and spirituality do not contribute directly to the problems people bring to healthcare or to their solutions. The prevalence of this perspective may help to explain why only a minority of psychologists receive any training in religion and spirituality in their graduate education (Shafranske and Cummings, "Religious and Spiritual Beliefs"). Lacking training in this area, healthcare providers may feel uncertain how to respond when their patients raise religious issues in treatment and instead shift the subject to what is seen as more relevant territory or, even worse, interpret the client's religious involvement critically.

This perspective is problematic for many reasons. For one, it overlooks the results of literally hundreds of studies that demonstrate significant links between religion/spirituality and health (Oman, *Why Religion*), as well as the challenges people experience in their lives. In addition, it overlooks the facts that people dealing with significant problems often turn early to their faith as a way of coping, and that many find religion to be a valuable resource or, in some instances, a source of struggle. And the insubstantial perspective overlooks the reality that a number of people who seek out healthcare would like to be able to discuss religious and spiritual issues in treatment (Rose, Westefeld, and Ansley, "Spiritual Issues in Counseling").

THE INSTRUMENTAL PERSPECTIVE TOWARD SPIRITUALITY AND SPIRITUAL CARE

A second psychological perspective on spiritual care emerged in the late 1960s and 1970s when the rise of psychopharmacological treatments and the mass deinstitutionalization of mental health patients triggered a community mental health movement. This movement marked a shift away from purely individual approaches to mental health care to a view of problems and their solutions as rooted in social systems. Thus, we saw the rise of community-based mental health centers, marital and family therapies, and preventive programming. Paraprofessional programs became popular in which non-mental health professionals—from bartenders to police to funeral directors—were taught basic mental health skills. Other mental health programs were located in school systems to help children develop good problem solving and social skills.

In this context, psychologists began to take a serious look at religion as a mental health resource, with good reason. Statistics told the tale, with vastly more religious congregations in the US than mental health centers, many more clergy than mental health professionals, and studies showing that people turn to their clergy in times of stress more often than they do mental health professionals (Chalfant et al., "The Clergy"). Moreover, it became apparent that the community mental health system was not reaching underserved groups, such as African Americans, people with serious psychological problems, and those unable to access or fully trust the healthcare system. And gradually, practitioners in the community came to recognize that, apart from the focus of religious institutions on theological matters, religious and healthcare systems shared a concern with the health of the whole person. Both had an interest in fostering community and connectedness, meaning in life, emotional comfort, good impulse control, healing, and a healthy lifestyle.

Building on this realization, psychologists reached out to religious institutions and clergy as potentially useful vehicles or platforms for expanding the scope of programs to foster better physical and mental health. For example, programs were developed to train clergy and congregation members with skills in crisis intervention and disaster response (e.g., McCabe et all, "Psychological First-aid Training"), promote screening and early intervention for physical illnesses within religious congregations (e.g., Maxwell et al., "Promoting Cancer Screening"), and teach clergy how to provide therapy to people with mental disorders (e.g., Iheanacho et al., "Utilizing").

Many of these programs proved successful in expanding the reach of healthcare services and continue today. However, these activities were also limited in an important respect. They reflected an instrumental approach to religion, one in which religion was understood and approached merely as a useful tool or method for enhancing the physical and mental health of people underserved by the healthcare system. The programs themselves were standard healthcare activities that made no mention of religious beliefs, practices, or resources; they were secular activities that were simply transplanted into religious contexts. Overlooked in this process was the fact that religious institutions are designed first and foremost to help members cultivate their sense of connectedness with the divine, and that no other institution has spirituality as its primary goal. By neglecting the distinctive spiritual function and resources of religious institutions, these instrumental programs may have compromised their effectiveness.

THE INTEGRATIVE PERSPECTIVE TOWARD SPIRITUALITY AND SPIRITUAL CARE

A third psychological perspective on spiritual care is now evolving. It grows out of the emergence of the concept of spirituality. Writings and research on spirituality dramatically increased in number from 1965 to 2000 (Weaver et al., "Trends"). Why was that? Perhaps, because of the empirical literature noted earlier demonstrating ties between religion and health. But, more basically, the upsurge of interest in spirituality likely grew out of an evolution in the meaning of the terms "religion" and "spirituality" themselves. It is worth taking a brief tangent here to talk about that shift (see Zinnbauer and Pargament, "Emerging Meanings"; Pargament et al., "Envisioning" for more complete discussion).

Traditionally, scholars in the field focused largely on the term religion or religiousness. Religiousness was used to refer to a variety of beliefs, practices, and experiences that had some connection to the superhuman or divine and religious institutions. Until the latter part of the twentieth century, spirituality was not often discussed in the field. Instead, phenomena that were spiritual in nature, such as mysticism, were seen as a part of the broader concept of religion. And 50 years ago, spirituality had a very different connotation than it does today. It referred to spiritualism, séances, the occult, and something a bit off center.

However, some people in the field felt that religion, as traditionally understood and practiced (e.g., congregational attendance, prayer, ritual practice, doctrinal beliefs), was not capturing the heart and soul of what religion is about—the virtues, the *mysterium tremendum*, feelings of uplift, and awe, and the yearning for something sacred, transcendent, or greater than ourselves. Not only that, but what about the alternate ways religion was expressing itself: Eastern and other non-Western, indigenous, feminist, earth-based, ecological, nontraditional practices (e.g., meditation, yoga, astrology, 12-step programs), and broader understandings of what people hold sacred, such as the environment, work, loving relationships, the arts, and our ultimate purposes in living? These new expressions seemed to call for an injection of new spirit into our understanding of religious life.

At the same time, phenomena that were once seen as religious in nature began to be removed from their religious moorings. As early as the 1960s, Abraham Maslow argued that many so-called religious phenomena were not the exclusive property of religious institutions (Maslow, *Religion*). He said that there is nothing inherently religious about: "the holy; humility; gratitude and oblation; thanksgiving; awe before the *mysterium tremendum*; the sense of the divine; the ineffable; the sense of littleness before mystery

... a sense of fusion with the whole of the universe; and even the experience of heaven and hell" (Maslow, *Religion*).

In one sense, the introduction of spirituality into the psychology of religion (now the psychology of religion and spirituality) broadened the field, opening it up to new groups, new practices, and new beliefs. In another sense, it deepened the field by zeroing in on the heart and soul of spirituality, and what it means to be human. Spirituality itself was defined in ways that even atheists might endorse. One illustrative definition that came out of an International Consensus Conference on Spirituality in 2014: "Spirituality is the aspect of humanity that refers to the way individuals seek and express meaning and purpose and the way they experience their connectedness to the moment, to self, to others, to nature, and to the significant or sacred" (Puchalski et al., "Improving," 643). Other definitions of spirituality placed even more prominence on the sacred: "Spirituality is a search for the sacred"; it refers to what people do to discover, hold on to, and at times, transform whatever they may hold sacred in their lives (Pargament et al., "Envisioning," 14).

The evolution in the meaning of spirituality has led to a third psychological perspective on spiritual care—the integrative perspective. This perspective rests on several premises: that we are spiritual as well as psychological, social, and physical beings; that the spiritual dimension cannot be reduced or explained away by the psychological, social, or physical dimensions; and that we cannot understand or help people live lives of greater wholeness without attending to their spirituality. What is called for is an integrative perspective—a biopsychosocialspiritual—that approaches people with an eye toward greater wholeness.

An integrative perspective underscores the importance of helping people who are hurting identify what they hold sacred and then fan the flames of these divine sparks to add light and warmth to their lives. Several texts have been written that describe how practitioners can integrate spirituality into psychotherapy (e.g., Jones, *Spirituality in Session*; Pargament, *Spiritually Integrated Psychotherapy*; Rosmarin, *Spirituality, Religion, and Cognitive-behavioral Therapy*) as well as into outreach programs such as disaster training and marital communication training (e.g., Aten and Boan, *Disaster Ministry*; Stanley, Trathen, McCain, and Bryan, *A Lasting Promise*). And research studies have shown that by attending to spirituality, healthcare providers can enhance their effectiveness (e.g., Margolin et al., *Preliminary Study*; Richards et al., "Comparative Efficacy"; Wachholtz and Pargament, Is Spirituality a Critical Ingredient").

The integrative perspective honors the clients' spirituality as a core part of who they are. It weaves the spiritual dimension along with psychological, social, and physical dimensions into a holistic process of caregiving. If an integrative approach is to become more commonplace among healthcare providers, training in the process of integration will need to become a regular part of graduate and postgraduate education. Is this possible? Advances are being made in this direction. For example, Pearce et al. developed a novel program to train mental health professionals in spiritual competencies (Pearce et al., "Novel Training Program"). The online program consists of eight modules that focus on topics, such as how to assess spirituality in psychotherapy and how to address spiritual resources and struggles in treatment. In an evaluation of the program, participants demonstrated significant improvements in spiritual skills, attitudes, and knowledge (Pearce et al., "Novel Online Training"). A revised version of the program is currently being integrated into graduate education across mental health disciplines. Hopefully, an integrative perspective will become increasingly widespread within healthcare.

REFERENCES

Aten, J., D., and Boan, M. *Disaster Ministry Handbook*. Downers Grove, IL: InterVarsity, 2016.

Chalfant, H. P., Heller, P. L., Roberts, A., Briones, D., Aquirre-Hochbaum, S., and Farr, W. (1990). "The Clergy as a Resource for Those Encountering Psychological Distress." *Review of Religious Research* 31 (1990) 306–13.

Durkheim, E. *The Elementary Forms of the Religious Life*. New York: Free Press, 1915.

Ellis, A. *The Case against Religion: A Psychotherapist's View and the Case against Religiosity*. Austin: American Atheist Press, 1986.

Freud, S. "The Future of an Illusion." In *The Standard Edition of the Complete Works of Sigmund Freud*, edited by J. Strachey, 21:5–56. 1927. Reprint, London: Hogarth, 1961.

Geertz, C. "Religion as a Cultural System." In *Anthropological Approaches to the Study of Religion*, edited by M. Banton, 1–46. London: Tavistock, 1966.

Iheanacho, T., Nduanya, U. C., Slinkard, S., Ogidi, A G., Patel, D., Itanyi, I, Naeem, F. Spiegelman, D., and Ezeanolue, E. E. "Utilizing a Church-based Platform for Mental Health Interventions: Exploring the Role of Clergy and the Treatment Preference of Women with Depression." *Global Mental Health* 8/35 (2021) 1–8. https://www.ncbi.nlm.nih.gov/pmc/articles/PMC8127631/.

Jones, R. S. *Spirituality in Session: Working with Your Clients' Spirituality (and Your Own) in Psychotherapy*. Rutgers: Templeton, 2019.

Margolin, A., Schuman-Olivier, Z., Beitel, M., Arnold, R. M., Fulwiler, C. E., and Avants, S. K. "A Preliminary Study of Spiritual Self-schema (3-S+) Therapy for Reducing Impulsivity in Drug Users." *Journal of Clinical Psychology* 63/10 (2007) 979–99.

Maslow, A. H. *Religion, Values, and Peak Experiences*. Columbus: Ohio State University Press, 1964.

Maxwell, A. E., Lucas-Wright, A., Santifer, R. E., Vargas, C., Gatson, J., and Chang, C. "Promoting Cancer Screening in Partnership with Health Ministries in 9 African American Churches in South Los Angeles: An Implementation Pilot Study." *Implementation Evaluation* 16 (2019) 1–13.

McCabe, O. L., Perry, C., Azur, M., Taylor, H. G., Bailey, M., and Links, J. M. "Psychological First-aid Training for Paraprofessionals: A Systems-based Model for Enhancing Capacity of Rural Emergency Responses." *Prehospital and Disaster Medicine* 26/4 (2011) 251–58.

Oman, D., ed. *Why Religion and Spirituality Matter for Public Health: Evidence, Implications, and Resources.* Cham, Switzerland: Springer, 2018.

Pargament, K. I. *The Psychology of Religion and Coping: Theory, Research, and Practice.* New York: Guilford, 1997.

———. *Spiritually Integrated Psychotherapy: Understanding and Addressing the Sacred.* New York: Guilford, 2007.

———. "Is Religion Nothing but . . . ? Explaining Religion versus Explaining Religion Away." *Psychological Inquiry* 13 (2002) 239–44.

Pargament, K. I., Mahoney, A., Exline, J. J., Jones, J., and Shafranske, E. "Envisioning an Integrative Paradigm for the Psychology of Religion and Spirituality." In *APA Handbooks in Psychology: APA Handbook of Psychology, Religion, and Spirituality, Vol. 1: Context, Theory, and Research,* edited by K. I. Pargament (ed.-in-chief), J. Exline and J. Jones (assoc. eds.), 3–20. Washington, DC: American Psychological Association, 2013.

Pearce, M. J., Pargament, K. I., Oxhandler, H., Vieten, C., and Wong, S. "A Novel Training Program for Mental Health Providers in Religious and Spiritual Competencies." *Spirituality in Clinical Practice* 6/2 (2019) 73–82.

Pearce, M. J., Pargament, K. I., Oxhandler, H., Vieten, C., Wong, S., and Hung, J. "Novel Online Training Program Improves Spiritual Competencies in Mental Health Care." *Spirituality in Clinical Practice* 7/3 (2020) 145–61.

Puchalski, C. M., Vitillo R., Hull, S. K., and Reller N. "Improving the Spiritual Dimension of Whole Person Care: Reaching National and International Consensus." *Journal of Palliative Medicine* 17/6 (2014) 642–56.

Richards, P. S., Berrett, M. E., Hardman, R. K., and Eggett, D. L. "Comparative Efficacy of Spirituality, Cognitive, and Emotional Support Groups for Treating Eating Disorder Inpatients." *Eating Disorders: Journal of Treatment and Prevention* 41 (2006) 401–15.

Rose, E. M., Westefeld, J. S., and Ansley, T. N. "Spiritual Issues in Counseling: Clients' Beliefs and Preferences." *Journal of Counseling Psychology* 48 (2001) 61–71.

Rosmarin, D. H. *Spirituality, Religion, and Cognitive-behavioral Therapy: A Guide for Clinicians.* New York: Guilford, 2018.

Shafranske, E. P., and Cummings, J. P. "Religious and Spiritual Beliefs, Affiliations, and Practices." In *APA Handbooks in Psychology: APA Handbook of Psychology, Religion, and Spirituality. Vol. 2: An Applied Psychology of Religion and Spirituality,* edited by K. I. Pargament, A. Mahoney, and E. Shafranske, 23–41. Washington, DC: American Psychological Association, 2013.

Skinner, B. F. *Walden Two.* New York: Macmillan, 1948.

———. *Beyond Freedom and Dignity.* New York: Knopf, 1971.

Stanley, S., Trathen, D., McCain, S., and Bryan, M. *A Lasting Promise: A Christian Guide to Fighting for Your Marriage.* San Francisco: Jossey-Bass, 1998.

Wachholtz, A. B., and Pargament, K. I. "Is Spirituality a Critical Ingredient of Meditation?: Comparing the Effects of Spiritual Meditation, Secular Meditation, and Relaxation on Spiritual, Psychological, Cardiac, and Pain Outcomes." *Journal of Behavioral Medicine* 28 (2005) 369–84.

Weaver, A., Pargament, K. I., Flannelly, K., and Oppenheimer, J. "Trends in the Scientific Study of Religion, Spirituality, and Health: 1965–2000." *Journal of Religion and Health* 45 (2006) 208–14.

Wulff, D. H. *The Psychology of Religion: Classic and Contemporary*. 2nd ed. Hoboken: Wiley, 1996.

Zinnbauer, B. J., Pargament, K. I., and Scott, A. B. "Emerging Meanings of Religiousness and Spirituality: Problems and Prospects." *Journal of Personality* 67 (1999) 889–919.

6

Towards Wholeness

Caring for the Whole Person Through Listening, Reflecting, and Connecting

Pninit Russo-Netzer

INTRODUCTION

> The individual presented himself in the therapy room of the nineteenth century, and during the twentieth, the patient suffering breakdown is the world itself . . . The new symptoms are fragmentation, specialization, expertise, depression, inflation, loss of energy, jargonese, and violence. Our buildings are anorectic, our business paranoid, our technology manic.
>
> —Sardello, *Acts of the Heart*

Our contemporary world is characterized by unprecedented levels of fragmentation, polarization, and alienation. A widening gap is emerging between our swiftly evolving society, characterized by rapid changes, economic affluence, and technological advancements, and the ongoing quest for connection, meaning, and purpose in life (see, for example, Cacioppo et al., "Alone in the Crowd"; Kesebir and Kesebir, "Cultural Salience"; Twenge et al., "Worldwide Increases"). In line with this, Otto Scharmer (in *Theory U*) identifies three distinct divides confronting modern societies: the ecological divide (a disconnection between individuals and nature), the social divide (a disconnection between individuals), and the spiritual divide (a disconnection of the self from the soul or higher self).

These divides align with some of the most pressing challenges of our era, including elevated levels of loneliness, intolerance, and detachment. Processes of cultural and traditional deconstruction and fragmentation have played a role in fostering a feeling of community and tradition loss, contributing to a rising sense of isolation and disconnection (see, for example, Cacioppo et al., "Alone in the Crowd"; Kesebir and Kesebir, "Cultural Salience"). Data indicates a global increase in loneliness rates, with roughly 42 million American adults aged 45 and above estimated to grapple with chronic loneliness—a number projected to escalate as the population ages (Holt-Lunstad, "So Lonely"). These challenges are compounded by various global crises, including, but not confined to, racial and ethnic discrimination, waves of political and social changes, natural and technological disasters, the climate crisis, and the enduring repercussions of the recent COVID-19 pandemic. This presents new challenges—social, therapeutic, societal, organizational, educational, and most of all—human.

Spirituality has played a key role in the human experience as an integral part of an individual's life, throughout history and across cultures (Benson, Roehlkepartain and Rude, "Spiritual Development"; Vaughan, "What Is Spiritual Intelligence?"). The definitions of spirituality have evolved with the ebb and flow of historical and cultural contexts (Berdyaev, *Spirit and Reality*), as well as across religions and traditions. However, unlike other domains of human development such as the cognitive, motor, or emotional, relatively little attention has been paid to spiritual development within canonical lifespan theories and models, recognizing it as integral to human normative development (e.g., Benson and Roehlkepartain, "Spiritual Development"; Oser, Scarlett, and Bucher, "Religious and Spiritual"). Some scholars associate this gap in the literature with the tendency of social scientists to reduce or explain spirituality in terms of other human motivations or forces (Pargament, "Spirituality as an Irreducible Human Motivation and Process").

The Cartesian mind-body dualism of the seventeenth century led to an ideological split between empirical science and theology (Haynes, "Holistic"), and the scientific awakening of the modern era contributed to a positivistic scientism which posited the scientific method as the only legitimate path to knowledge (Mehta, "Mind-body Dualism"), echoing the challenging relationship between the psychological and spiritual characterized in many cases by tension and misunderstandings (Pargament and Mahoney, *Sacred Matters*). The emergence of postmodernism in the late twentieth and early twenty-first centuries paved the way to a resurgence of spirituality as part of a larger cultural and intellectual movement away from mechanistic conceptions of reality and toward more non-dualistic and holistic views (Haynes, "Holistic"). In addition, the pluralist and complex postmodern world challenged the existing processes of continuity and socialization, as well as the transmission of traditional patterns (Buxant, Saroglou and Tesser, "Freelance"). The void left by the collapse of stable structures and binding values instigated an individual search for meaning, including the search for a spiritual meaning, which could provide answers to individuals' ultimate concerns and respond to their "passion for the infinite" (Tillich, *Dynamics of Faith*, 8).

Another reason for the revival of the scientific interest in spirituality has to do with its perception as a potential resource for optimal development (Seligman and Csikszentmihalyi, "Positive Psychology") and its observed association with health and well-being (e.g., Van Dierendonck and Mohan, 2006). The growing number of theories and models that have discussed issues of spirituality in fields such as education, psychology, social work, nursing, sociology, and counseling, reflect the current broad acknowledgment of the meaningful significance of spirituality in human experience (e.g., Furman, Benson, Grimwood and Canda, "Religion and Spirituality"; Mohan and Uys, "Towards Living"; Rose, Westefeld and Ansley, "Spiritual Issues in Counseling"; Tanyi, "Towards Clarification"). An increasing number of people view the spiritual as central to their lives, demonstrate active involvement in its cultivation, and experience spiritual development (e.g., Heelas, *New Age Movement*; Fuller, *Spiritual, but not Religious*; Russo-Netzer, "Healing the Divide"; Wuthnow, *After Heaven*).

Although the potential for spiritual concerns and experiences is considered inherent to human nature (Grof and Grof, *Stormy Search*), the manner in which such potential is manifested in depth, development, and expression may vary between individuals (Vaughan, "What Is Spiritual Intelligence?"). Furthermore, the specific contents of the practices, beliefs, and experiences may be manifested differently across spiritual traditions and can be both individually or institutionally oriented (Gorsuch and Miller, "Assessing Spirituality"). In this sense, spirituality embodies a dynamic and evolving process rather than a static and fixed one (Pargament and Mahoney, "Spirituality"). Similarly, human wholeness is an ongoing and vibrant process, not a static state (Russo-Netzer, "Clinical Perspectives on Meaning"). When we examine the origins of the word 'health', we find that the Latin source of the word is *hal*, which means whole—to heal is to make whole. Similarly, the Hebrew word *shalem* (being whole) corresponds with the word *shalom* (peace). Wholeness therefore encompasses the peace and healing of the divided and fragmented aspects within an individual, a system, or society at large. Consequently, our goal should focus on cultivating the holistic well-being of the client and communities, rather than merely their well-being alone (cf. Russo-Netzer, Schulenberg and Batthyány, "Clinical Perspectives on Meaning").

This chapter advocates for broadening our ways of understanding by embracing diverse dimensions and perspectives, thereby comprehensively addressing the whole person when navigating existential questions in a turbulent world. In our attempts to develop healthy and optimal environments to support mental health, spiritual care is not a luxury, but a necessity.

EXPANDING WAYS OF KNOWING

In former days, people frustrated in their will to meaning would probably have turned to a pastor, priest, or rabbi. Today, they crowd clinics and offices. The psychiatrist, then, frequently finds himself in an embarrassing situation, for he now is confronted with human problems rather than with specific clinical symptoms. Man's search for a meaning is not pathological, but rather the surest sign of being truly human. Even if this search is frustrated, it cannot be considered a sign of disease . . . It is not a sickness to be cured but rather a spiritual challenge to be met.

—FRANKL, *WILL TO MEANING*, 93

This quote by Viktor Frankl, a neurologist, psychiatrist, Holocaust survivor, and the founder of *logotherapy* (meaning-oriented psychotherapy), reflects the importance of a paradigm shift—from a reductionist perspective of the patient to a whole-person perspective that addresses and honors the various aspects that make us uniquely human. As this quote conveys, therapists, clinicians, and scholars today are confronted with existential questions, questions about which existing textbooks and diagnostic manuals carry little, if any, information (Hage, "A Closer Look").

Frankl conceptualizes a person as comprised of mind (*psyche*), body (*soma*), and spirit (*noos*—in Greek: νοῦς). He built his logotherapy, a meaning-oriented psychotherapy, on the concept of non-reductionism, treating it as a guiding heuristic principle. This principle signifies that every facet or dimension of a human—be it physiological, psychological, or noetic (spiritual)—comprises layers of properties and functions that interconnect yet maintain a certain ontological and, to some extent, causal independence (Frankl, "Spiritual Dimension"). Despite these aspects operating independently to a degree, they collectively define what it means to be human, consequently none of these facets can be dismissed or overlooked (Russo-Netzer, Schulenberg and Batthyany, "Clinical Perspectives on Meaning"). According to logotherapy, spirituality is not a mere projection of human desires but rather a fundamental source of meaning. The suppression of human spirituality gives rise to what Frankl termed 'spiritual unconsciousness'. Frankl's concept of the spiritual unconscious and its connection to existential meaning holds significant importance for advancing our understanding of the intricate relationship between spirituality and mental health, especially in addressing the complex question of how spiritual factors may influence mental well-being (de Carvalho and Moreira-Almeida, "Existential Meaning").

In a rather parallel, yet similar vein, spiritual care is grounded in the understanding that human distress often stems from spiritual issues as well as psychological and biological ones (Vieten et al., "Spiritual and Religious Competencies"). As such, spiritual care goes beyond religious affiliation to nurture sources of meaning, purpose, hope, love, peace, comfort, strength, and connection (Sulmasy, "Biopsychosocial-Spiritual Model"). Accumulating recent research demonstrates the psychological benefits of addressing spirituality in mental healthcare, emphasizing that caring for the whole person requires attention to spiritual needs alongside other aspects of care. Indeed, spiritually integrated therapies have shown positive outcomes for disorders including depression, anxiety, PTSD, and addiction (e.g., Aten and Worthington, "Psychotherapy with Religious and Spiritual Clients"; Pargament, *Spiritually Integrated Psychotherapy*), and spiritual practices may reduce stress, enhance coping, foster inner peace, and give meaning to suffering (Desai and Pargament, "Predictors"). By providing a supportive space for spiritual exploration, clinicians allow clients to access inner resources to enhance resilience and well-being (Vieten et al., "Spiritual and Religious Competencies"). Hence, much can be gained from expanding our ways of knowing, as will be highlighted in three main directions for a potential mutually enriching dialogue: listening, reflecting, and connecting, each of which plays a crucial role in facilitating a journey towards wholeness.

Listening: The Whole Is Greater than the Sum of the Parts

A crucial aspect of establishing a successful therapeutic alliance may center around the spiritual dynamics within the connection between the provider and the client. While spirituality is commonly perceived as an individual dimension, it can also manifest, be expressed, and be encountered in a relational context (Mahoney, "Spirituality of Us"). Numerous theorists and practitioners have delineated diverse elements contributing to a deeply spiritual and therapeutic relationship. These elements encompass the therapist's ability to be interpersonally attuned to, or mindful of, the client (e.g., Bruce, Manber, Shapiro, and Constantino, "Psychotherapist Mindfulness"). More specifically, active and empathetic listening lie at the heart of both spiritual care and mental health practices (Aadam, Poon and Fernandez, "Listening"; Puchalski et al., "Improving"). This involves creating a safe and non-judgmental space where individuals can express their deepest thoughts, fears, and anxieties without fear of criticism or dismissal (e.g., Mowat et al., "Listening"; VandeCreek and Burton, "Professional Chaplaincy"). Such attentiveness allows for the co-creation of meaning—a process by which the professional facilitates the individual's exploration of their experience, helping them discover personal significance and value within their challenges (Frankl, *Will to Meaning*). Creating a space for vulnerability and shared meaning necessitates mindful listening to the client's own words, beliefs, and experiences. It also serves as a fertile ground for expanding the spectrum of human experience beyond psychological symptoms and spiritual struggles to also include attention to:

Sacred Moments:

brief intervals during which individuals encounter spiritual qualities such as transcendence, ultimacy, boundlessness, interconnectedness, and spiritual emotions (Lomax, Kripal, and Pargament, "Perspectives"; Pargament and Mahoney, "Spirituality of Us"). It has been found that the occurrence of such sacred moments in the interactions between therapists and their clients contributes to enhanced well-being for both parties, underscoring the significance of carefully acknowledging the spiritual dimension within the provider-patient relationship. This suggests that sacred moments could play a crucial role in therapeutic change, fostering the health and overall well-being of clients and strengthening the therapeutic alliance, as well as offering support and sustaining mental health providers amidst the challenges inherent in mental health care (Pargament et al., "Sacred Moments").

Synchronicity and Meaningful Coincidence:

defined as psychologically meaningful connection between an inner event (e.g., thought, image or dream) and one or more external events occurring simultaneously (Jung, "Synchronicity"), synchronicity pertains to noteworthy and meaningful coincidences that establish a connection between an individual's internal and external realms. Clinical case studies have shown that acknowledging synchronicity experiences is beneficial within therapeutic contexts (Connolly, "Bridging"; Roxburgh et al., "Exploring the Meaning"), involving an identification of an emotional resonance and attributing significance to the coincidence within the context of one's current life narrative. Findings from a phenomenological study suggest three major building blocks of such experiences: receptiveness (R) or increased attention and openness to feelings and cognitions and to the external environment; viewed as a precondition for an exceptional encounter (E), a sudden unexpected event that echoes an inner feeling or thought, commonly evoking memorable and distinctive emotions; and meaning detecting (M), a conscious process of connecting the event to oneself while revalidating a sense of coherence, purpose and control in life (Russo-Netzer and Icekson, "Engaging with Life"). A follow-up study suggests that awareness of synchronicity experiences is rather widespread and that individuals who search for meaning and are open to synchronicity events and manage to make sense of them may experience more meaning and optimism, which eventually may contribute to greater life satisfaction (Russo-Netzer and Icekson, "Unexplored Pathway").

Transformative Life Experiences (TLEs):

TLEs are profound, unintentional changes triggered by a wide range of events, from trauma and adversity to peak and transcendent experiences. An in-depth exploration of such experiences (Russo-Netzer and Davidov, "Transformative Life Experience") identified some common elements in the change process: a distinctive experience, acute awareness of sensations/surroundings, surrendering to the experience, dissolution of contextuality, glimpse into potentiality, and shift in intentionality. TLEs seem to challenge people's core beliefs and worldviews, creating an awareness of new possibilities for living. These factors, in sequence, facilitate the dissolution of contextual constraints, leading individuals to recognize their previously taken-for-granted reality. This realization opens the door to exploring potentialities, offering alternative ways of living, thereby setting the stage for a potential shift in intentionality. These findings carry practical implications for therapy. By closely listening to the client's narratives about their experiences through the lifeworld existentials (i.e., temporality, spatiality, corporality, and relationality), therapists can extract valuable insights into how the client constructs their reality. This, in turn, may empower practitioners to develop heightened sensitivity and attunement to the various nuances and expressions of the client's experiential organization. Deeply listening to clients' holistic experiences, including transformative events, can provide understanding about their meaning-making, core beliefs, and processes of change. This phenomenological lens may help therapists better grasp clients' subjective realities and support desired transformations. Exploring TLEs could reveal pivotal moments when clients became aware of new possibilities and freedoms in life.

Overall, the examples discussed above underscore the importance of paying attention to critical moments in the client's life and experience. By inviting them into the therapeutic encounter, these moments and experiences may facilitate powerful change and transformation for the client, therapist, and the therapeutic relationship. Consequently, the encounter between therapist and client can be understood at a deeper, more profound spiritual level—broadening perspectives, allowing for a deeper reflection to uncover new possibilities, and fostering self-discovery.

Reflecting

Through a phenomenological approach that focuses on the lived experience (van Manen, "Beyond Assumptions"), an individual listens critically to the meanings that intuitively arise in their flow of experiences. For example, perceiving what is meaningful via experiential explorations and meaningful coincidences, such as synchronicity awareness (Russo-Netzer and Icekson, "Engaging with Life") or mindfulness (e.g., Russo-Netzer "Finding Meaning"), while reflecting to differentiate the more meaningful from the less meaningful. Such reflection processes may enable individuals to gain new insights into themselves and their place in the world, along with an opportunity for the emergence of "inner wisdom" and "meaning clues" such as strengths, values, spiritual resources, uniqueness, and priorities. This may address the client's need for comprehension and making sense, preserving a sense of mattering and significance, and providing broader purpose and direction in life as essential ingredients of their overall sense of meaning in life (George and Park, "Meaning in Life"; Martela and Steger, "Three Meanings"). Such reflection may also involve nonverbal exploration such as visual methods of photographs or images that represent their sense of meaning, purpose, or values.

The process of choosing an image and discussing its significance seems to facilitate self-reflection and expression (Russo-Netzer, "Preliminary Exploration . . . Ikigai"). These processes may involve using metaphor elicitation by having clients come up with a metaphor or symbol for their life purpose and discuss its implications. This approach may also provide access to nonverbal knowledge. Additionally, exploring client stories for moments when they felt aligned with their inner values: What activities, thoughts, and feelings characterized those peak experiences? Such creative techniques allow for more holistic processing than verbal discussion alone. They also complement approaches integrating spirituality and psychology by revealing clients' subjective experiences and meaning-making. Creative reflections could reveal how clients' values connect to spiritual perspectives or experiences. These methods help therapists access clients' wholeness beyond diagnoses.

Connection to Life Through Self-transcendence

When we are being heard and can reflect on what is meaningful and valuable to us, we are more able to reconnect with life, through self-transcendence, to reach beyond ourselves. Frankl asserted that "Meaning is to be discovered in the world rather than within man or his own psyche, as though it were a closed system" (Frankl, *Man's Search for Meaning,* 110–11) and suggested three many pathways through which individuals can discover meaning in life, known as the categorical values: creative values, experiential values, and attitudinal values (Frankl, *Man's Search for Meaning*). The creative pathway consists of what we give to the world, in terms of our unique footprints, through creation, taking action, volunteering, acts of kindness, and contribution. The experiential pathway refers to what we get from the world in terms of experiences of life's gifts, experiences of truth, beauty, and love toward another human being. These can include rituals, prayers, and sources of inspiration such as nature, art, and music. The attitudinal pathway involves the stand we take toward an unchangeable situation or unavoidable suffering, and our ability to rise up and imbue spiritual meaning to challenges, adversity, and wounds (Frankl, *Man's Search for Meaning*).

An illustrative instance of this concept can be found in the practice of *kintsugi*. Kintsugi, which translates to "golden rejoining" in Japanese, involves revealing the concealed beauty and resilience within shattered objects. In this process, fractured ceramic pottery undergoes a transformative journey, evolving into a splendidly restored masterpiece. Instead of concealing the imperfections, the cracks are accentuated with the addition of gold. Similarly, the triumph of the human spirit arises not from discarding our wounded aspects but from embracing our imperfections and reintegrating them into a magnificent masterpiece—a more comprehensive and unified whole (Russo-Netzer, "Healing the Divide"). Overall, these directions may allow spiritual development and growth in three dimensions—deep within, up and beyond (the transcendent), and sideways and interconnected (Mayseless and Russo-Netzer, "Vision"). Similarly, spiritual care aims to foster a sense of connection—both within oneself and with others. This includes connecting with one's inner resources, such as resilience, wisdom, and compassion.

Another potential point of integration between the spiritual and psychological perspectives may refer to the integral relationship between character strengths/virtues and spirituality, as they both aim to promote human flourishing, through two main pathways: *The grounding path*, where character strengths offer tangibility and depth to spiritual practices and experiences (for example, using curiosity and judgment in exploring the sacred), and *the sanctification path*, where spiritual perspectives elevate character strengths, imbuing them with sacred meaning. For example, seeing kindness as a "fruit of the spirit" (Niemiec, Russo-Netzer and Pargament, "Decoding"). Such an integrated perspective could help make both spirituality and character frameworks more rounded, meaningful, and impactful. Considering specific spiritual practices, such as cultivating sacred moments or finding one's calling, these could be enhanced by integrating relevant character strengths.

Similarly, character strength practices like strengths spotting could be amplified by adding a spiritual lens. For spiritual care providers, this integration gives concrete ways to utilize clients' character strengths to deepen their spiritual growth, and to draw out the sacred/virtuous qualities in various practices. For psychology practitioners, it may highlight the importance of tapping into clients' spirituality to amplify strengths practices and development, as spiritual perspectives align closely with virtues/character goals. Overall, an integrative approach could benefit both fields and enhance practitioners' ability to foster wholeness and meaning in those they serve.

WITH AN EYE TO THE FUTURE

Collaboration between spiritual care providers and other healthcare professionals is crucial to ensure a holistic approach to patient care. By working together, they can address the multifaceted needs of individuals facing difficult situations, promoting not just physical and mental health, but also inner strength, meaning, and a sense of connection. More specifically, spiritual care, when conceptualized and practiced through the lens of listening, reflecting, and connecting, has the potential to significantly enhance the well-being and resilience of individuals navigating difficult life experiences. By attending to the whole person, we may identify "docking stations" where opportunities and pathways can be cultivated for spiritual growth, deep within, sideways, and interconnected. Continued research and training is needed to advance competent, ethical spiritual care provision in psychology. Attending to spirituality allows clinicians to meet humanity's universal search for meaning at the very heart of our inner lives.

REFERENCES

Aadam, B., Poon, A. W. C., and Fernández, E. "Listening in Mental Health Clinical Practice." *British Journal of Social Work* 54/1 (2024) 246–66. https://doi.org/10.1093/bjsw/bcad193.

Benson, P., Roehlkepartain, E. C., and Rude, S. P. "Spiritual Development in Childhood and Adolescence: Toward a Field of Inquiry." *Applied Developmental Science* 7/3 (2003) 205–13. https://doi.org/10.1207/S1532480xads0703_12.

Benson, P., and Roehlkepartain, E. C. "Spiritual Development: A Missing Priority Youth Development." *New Directions for Youth Development* 118 (2008) 13–28. https://doi.org/10.1002/yd.253.

Berdyaev, N. *Spirit and Reality*. Translated by George Reavey. London: Centenary, 1939.

Bruce, N., Manber, R., Shapiro, S. L., and Constantino, M. J. "Psychotherapist Mindfulness and the Psychotherapy Process." *Psychotherapy* 47/1 (2010) 83–97. https://doi.org/10.1037/a0018842.

Buxant, C., Saroglou, V., and Tesser, M. "Free-lance Spiritual Seekers: Self-growth or Compensatory Motives?" *Mental Health, Religion and Culture* 13/2 (2010) 209–22. https://doi.org/10.1080/13674670903334660.

Cacioppo, J. T., Fowler, J. H., and Christakis, N. A. "Alone in the Crowd: The Structure and Spread of Loneliness in a Large Social Network." *Journal of Personality and Social Psychology* 97/6 (2009) 977–91. https://doi.org/10.1037/a0016076.

Connolly, A. "Bridging the Reductive and the Synthetic: Some Reflections on the Clinical Implications of Synchronicity." *Journal of Analytical Psychology* 60/2 (2015) 159–78. https://doi.org/10.1111/1468-5922.12142.

De Carvalho, J. M., and Moreira-Almeida, A. "Existential Meaning, Spiritual Unconscious and Spirituality in Viktor Frankl." *Journal of Religion and Health* 63/1 (2023) 1–15. https://doi.org/10.1007/s10943-023-01902-8.

Desai, K. M., and Pargament, K. I. "Predictors of Growth and Decline Following Spiritual Struggles." *International Journal for the Psychology of Religion* 25/1 (2015) 42–56. https://doi.org/10.1080/10508619.2013.847697.

Frankl, V.E. "Psychiatry and Man's Quest for Meaning." *Journal of Religion and Health* 1 (1962) 93–103.

———. *Man's Search for Meaning*. 1946. Reprint, New York: Simon & Schuster, 1985.
———. "The Spiritual Dimension in Existential Analysis and Logotherapy." *Journal of Individual Psychology* 15/2 (1959) 157–65.
———. *The Will to Meaning: Foundations and Applications of Logotherapy*. New York: New American Library, 1969.
Fuller, R. C. *Spiritual, but not Religious: Understanding Unchurched America*. Oxford: Oxford University Press, 2001.
Furman, L. D., Benson, P. W., Grimwood, C., and Canda, E. R. "Religion and Spirituality in Social Work Education and Direct Practice at the Millennium: A Survey of UK Social Workers." *British Journal of Social Work* 34/6 (2004) 767–92. https://doi.org/10.1093/bjsw/bch101.
George, L. S., and Park, C. L. "Meaning in Life as Comprehension, Purpose, and Mattering: Toward Integration and New Research Questions." *Review of General Psychology* 20/3 (2016) 205–20. https://doi.org/10.1037/gpr0000077.
Gorsuch, R. L., and Miller, W. R. "Assessing Spirituality." *American Psychological Association eBooks* (1999) 47–64. https://doi.org/10.1037/10327003.
Grof, C., and Grof, S. *Stormy Search for the Self*. London: Taylor & Francis, 1992.
Hage, S. M. "A Closer Look at the Role of Spirituality in Psychology Training Programs." *Professional Psychology: Research and Practice* 37/3 (2006) 303.
Haynes, C. J. "Holistic Human Development." *Journal of Adult Development* 16/1 (2009) 53–60.
Heelas, P. *The New Age Movement: The Celebration of the Self and the Sacralization of Modernity*. Oxford: Blackwell, 1996.
Holt-Lunstad, J. "So Lonely I Could Die." American Psychological Association 125th Annual Convention, Washington, DC, 2017. Summary: https://www.apa.org/news/press/releases/2017/08/lonely-die.
Jung, C. G. "Synchronicity: An Acausal Connecting Principle." In *Collected Works of C. G. Jung*, Bollingen Series 8. 1931. Reprint, Princeton: Princeton University Press, 1968.
Kesebir, P., and Kesebir, S. "The Cultural Salience of Moral Character and Virtue Declined in Twentieth Century America." *Journal of Positive Psychology* 7/6 (2012) 471–80. https://doi.org/10.1080/17439760.2012.715182.
Lomax, J. W., Kripal, J. J., and Pargäment, K. I. "Perspectives on 'Sacred Moments' in Psychotherapy." *American Journal of Psychiatry* 168/1 (2011) 12–18. https://doi.org/10.1176/appi.ajp.2010.10050739.
Mahoney, A. "The Spirituality of Us: Relational Spirituality in the Context of Family Relationships." In *APA Handbook of Psychology, Religion, and Spirituality*, Vol. 1: *Context, Theory, and Research*, edited by pp. K. I. Pargament, J. J. Exline, and J. W. Jones, 365–89. Washington, DC: American Psychological Association, 2013. https://doi.org/10.1037/14045-020.
Martela, F., and Steger, M. F. "The Three Meanings of Meaning in Life: Distinguishing Coherence, Purpose, and Significance." *Journal of Positive Psychology* 11/5 (2016) 531–45. https://doi.org/10.1080/17439760.2015.1137623.
Mayseless, O., and Russo-Netzer, P. "A Vision for the Farther Reaches of Spirituality: A Phenomenologically Based Model of Spiritual Development and Growth." *Spirituality in Clinical Practice* 4/3 (2017) 176–92. https://doi.org/10.1037/scp0000147.

Mehta, N. "Mind-body Dualism: A Critique from a Health Perspective." *Mens Sana Monographs* 9/1 (2011) 202–9. https://doi.org/10.4103/0973-1229.77436.

Mohan, D. L., and Uys, K. "Towards Living with Meaning and Purpose: Spiritual Perspectives of People at Work." *SA Journal of Industrial Psychology* 32/1 (2006). https://doi.org/10.4102/sajip.v32i1.228.

Mowat, H., Bunniss, S., Snowden, A., and Wright, L. "Listening as Health Care." *Scottish Journal of Health Care Chaplaincy* 16/1 (2013) 35–41. http://researchrepository.napier.ac.uk/id/eprint/8987.

Niemiec, R. M., Russo-Netzer, P., and Pargament, K. I. "The Decoding of Human Spirit: A Synergy of Spirituality and Character Strengths toward Wholeness." *Frontiers in Psychology* 11 (2002) 1–24. https://doi.org/10.3389/fpsyg.2020.02040.

Oser, F. K., Scarlett, W. G., and Bucher, A. "Religious and Spiritual Development throughout the Life Span." In *Handbook of Child Psychology: Theoretical Models of Human Development*, 6th ed., edited by R. M. Lerner and W. Damon, 942–98. Hoboken, NJ: Wiley, 2006.

Pargament, K. I. "Spirituality as an Irreducible Human Motivation and Process." *International Journal for the Psychology of Religion* 23/4 (2013) 271–81. https://doi.org/10.1080/10508619.2013.795815.

Pargament, K. I., and Mahoney, A. "Sacred Matters: Sanctification as a Vital Topic for the Psychology of Religion." *International Journal for the Psychology of Religion* 15/3 (2005) 179–98. https://doi.org/10.1207/s15327582ijpr1503_1.

Pargament, K.I., and Mahoney, A. "Spirituality: The Search for the Sacred." In *Oxford Handbook of Positive Psychology*, edited by S. J. Lopez and C. R. Snyder, 611–19. Oxford: Oxford University Press, 2009.

Pargament, K.I., Lomax, J. W., McGee, J., and Fang, Q. "Sacred Moments in Psychotherapy, from the Perspectives of Mental Health Providers and Clients: Prevalence, Predictors, and Consequences." *Spirituality in Clinical Practice* 1/4 (2014) 248–62. https://doi.org/10.1037/scp0000043.

Puchalski, C. M., Vitillo, R. J., Hull, S. K., and Reller, N. "Improving the Spiritual Dimension of Whole Person Care: Reaching National and International Consensus." *Journal of Palliative Medicine* 17/6 (2014) 642–56. https://doi.org/10.1089/jpm.2014.9427.

Rose, E., Westefeld, J. S., and Ansely, T. N. "Spiritual Issues in Counseling: Clients' Beliefs and Preferences." *Journal of Counseling Psychology* 48/1 (2001) 61–71. https://doi.org/10.1037/0022-0167.48.1.61.

Roxburgh, E. C., Ridgway, S., and Roe, C. A. "Exploring the Meaning in Meaningful Coincidences: An Interpretative Phenomenological Analysis of Synchronicity in Therapy. *European Journal of Psychotherapy and Counselling* 17/2 (2015) 144–61. https://doi.org/10.4324/9780429464249-4.

Russo-Netzer, P. "Building Bridges, Forging New Frontiers: Meaning Making in Action." *Social Sciences* 12 (2012) 574. https://doi.org/10.3390/socsci12100574.

———. "Finding Meaning in the Unexpected: Underexplored Pathways to Discovering and Cultivating Meaning in Life." In *Cultivating, Promoting, and Enhancing Meaning in Life Across Cultures and Life Span*, edited by A. Chan, 57–68. Amsterdam: Atlantis (Springer Nature), 2022.

———. "Healing the Divide through Wholeness: Holding on to What Makes Us Human." *International Journal of Existential Psychology and Psychotherapy* 7 (2018) 1–17.

———. "Preliminary Exploration of Creative Expressions of Ikigai." In *Ikigai: Towards a Psychological Understanding of Life Worth Living*, edited by Y. Kotera and D. Fido, 49–71. Woodbridge: Concurrent Disorders Society Publishing, 2021.

Russo-Netzer, P., and Davidov, J. "Transformative Life Experience as a Glimpse into Potentiality." *Journal of Humanistic Psychology*. Online First (2020). https://doi.org/10.1177/0022167820937487.

Russo-Netzer, P., and Icekson, T. "Engaging with Life: Synchronicity Experiences as a Pathway to Meaning and Personal Growth." *Current Psychology* 41/2 (2020) 597–610. https://doi.org/10.1007/s12144-019-00595-1.

Russo-Netzer, P., and Icekson, T. "An Underexplored Pathway to Well-being: The Development and Validation of the Synchronicity Awareness and Meaning-Detecting (SAMD) Scale." *Frontiers in Psychology* 13/22 (2023) 1–17. https://doi.org/10.3389/fpsyg.2022.1053296.

Russo-Netzer, P., Schulenberg, S. E., and Batthyány, A. "Clinical Perspectives on Meaning: Understanding, Coping and Thriving through Science and Practice." In *Clinical Perspectives on Meaning: Positive and Existential Psychotherapy*, edited by P. Russo-Netzer, S. E. Schulenberg, and A. Batthyany, 1–13. New York: Springer, 2016. https://doi.org/10.1007/978-3-319-41397-6_1.

Sardello, R.J. *Acts of the Heart: Culture-building, Soul-researching, Introductions, Forewords, and Prefaces*. Barrington: Lindisfarne/Steiner.

Scharmer, C. O. *Theory U: Learning from the Future as It Emerges: The Social Technology of Presencing*. Oakland: Berrett-Koehler, 2009.

Seligman, M. E. P., and Csíkszentmihályi, M. "Positive Psychology: An Introduction." *American Psychologist* 55/1 (2000) 5–14. https://doi.org/10.1037/0003-066x.55.1.5.

Sulmasy, D. P. A "Biopsychosocial-Spiritual Model for the Care of Patients at the End of Life." *The Gerontologist*, 42/Supplement 3 (2002) 24–33. https://doi.org/10.1093/geront/42.suppl_3.24.

Tanyi, R. A. "Towards Clarification of the Meaning of Spirituality." *Journal of Advanced Nursing* 39/5 (2002) 500–509. https://doi.org/10.1046/j.1365-2648.2002.02315.x.

Tillich, P. *Dynamics of Faith*. New York: Harper & Row, 1957.

Twenge, J. M., Haidt, J., Blake, A. B., McAllister, C., Lemon, H., and Roy, A. L. "Worldwide Increases in Adolescent Loneliness." *Journal of Adolescence*, 93/1 (2021) 257–69. https://doi.org/10.1016/j.adolescence.2021.06.006.

Van Dierendonck, D., and Mohan, K. "Some Thoughts on Spirituality and Eudaimonic Well-being." *Mental Health, Religion and Culture* 9/3 (2006) 227–38. https://doi.org/10.1080/13694670600615383.

van Manen, M. "Beyond Assumptions: Shifting the Limits of Action Research." *Theory into Practice* 29/3 (1990) 152–57. https://doi.org/10.1080/00405849009543448.

VandeCreek, L., and Burton, L. A. "Professional Chaplaincy: Its Role and Importance in Healthcare." *Journal of Pastoral Care* 55/1 (2001) 81–97. https://doi.org/10.1177/002234090105500109.

Vaughan, F. "What Is Spiritual Intelligence?" *Journal of Humanistic Psychology* 42/2 (2002) 16–33. https://doi.org/10.1177/0022167802422003.

Vieten, C., Scammell, S., Pilato, R., Ammondson, I., Pargäment, K. I., and Lukoff, D. "Spiritual and Religious Competencies for Psychologists." *Psychology of Religion and Spirituality* 5/3 (2013) 129–44. https://doi.org/10.1037/a0032699.

Worthington, E. L., and Aten, J. D. "Psychotherapy with Religious and Spiritual Clients: An Introduction." *Journal of Clinical Psychology* 65/2 (2008) 123–30. https://doi.org/10.1002/jclp.20561.

Wuthnow, R. *After Heaven: Spirituality in America since the 1950s*. Berkeley: University of California Press, 1998.

7

Spiritual Care from the Perspective of Hospice and Palliative Care Chaplaincy

Expanding Life

Kei Okada

Spiritual Care has been continually evolving and expanding the scope of its understanding of our human needs and its service to humanity, in the field of clinical chaplaincy. In this paper, I would like to present how spiritual care can be understood, in attending to the spiritual, existential, and/or religious needs of those who are called "patients" (from the Latin: those who suffer) or "clients," based on my clinical experiences from the times of CPE (Clinical Pastoral Education) training to the present time, with the emphasis upon how spiritual care is significant, especially in hospice and palliative care to address the end-of-life care needs.

In recent years I have been seeing more frequent articles and books addressing end-of-life issues and support needs, making "death" less a taboo, showing how people are taking the courage to contemplate our shared mortality and death as part of life. Public awareness has been increasing regarding the need for meaningful end-of-life preparation and effective support systems. Questions emerge at the core of this awareness about the spiritual aspect of suffering and healing.

Various cultures have their spiritual and religious customs and traditions. The meaning, purpose, and well-being of our human life have been the subject of our humanity's everlasting quest. Our sense of life's dignity and fulfillment, wholeness and healing, peace, sacredness, and transcendence are some of the keywords we use to express our spirituality. In this spiritual quest, we face and review how we interpret and evaluate what we perceive, based on what we trust and believe as valuable and meaningful to us.

When I first served children living with HIV/AIDS at a pediatric clinic as their Chaplain, and years later adult homeless clients living with HIV/AIDS at a daycare program as their Pastoral Counselor, I assumed the role of their spiritual caregiver, to nurture and care for them. Hearing the most diverse expressions and serving the most diverse needs (in every sense) of New Yorkers, I was further presented with profoundly inspiring challenges and invitations to keep redefining spiritual care, in order to meet each person where they were. Many were not affiliated with a faith community or religious practice, and I had to explore how to meet the needs of those who called themselves "spiritual but not religious," "being open to the unknowns and mystery of life," or "keeping my faith in God private without religion," and so forth. For many of them, religious implications associated with "pastoral care" evoked painful memories of alienation, or became a chance to revisit their need for reconciliation or forgiveness with the higher power, or affirmation and assurance of divine compassionate presence.

Then years later, as I served those hospice patients and their families as their Spiritual Care Counselor, it also became clearer through their lens of seeing life in the face of death, that their living process in their spiritual quest for how life can be meaningful or fulfilled, became an inspiring, pastoral moment to witness and follow. It was as if the questions that emerged through their dire experiences had pastorally invited my deeper listening and spiritual presence, in order to attend our shared Life. After they died, they left with me a sense of having to live with their heritage, with the lasting gifts of what they had shared with me. Such a heritage of the deceased is also felt as a pastoral presence.

We find inspiring words that expand our view of faith and belief: "Faith is not the clinging to a shrine, but an endless pilgrimage of the heart" (Heschel, *Man Is Not Alone*, 174); "Faith is the state of being ultimately concerned" (Tillich, *Dynamics of Faith*, 1); "There are three sources of belief: reason, custom, inspiration" (Pascal, *Pensées*, 72). We have another beautiful articulation of spiritual care and spirituality by the popular *New York Times* personal health columnist Jane Brody:

> Spirituality is about a person's relationship with the transcendent questions that confront one as a human being and how a person relates to these questions. Spirituality can be about a relationship with a higher power, but it can also be about nature, art, music, family, or community—the beliefs and values that give a person's life meaning and purpose. Spirituality involves such matters as a person's relationships with family members or friends; the meaning of the person's illness, suffering, and death; the value of the person's life and what of value might persist after the person dies. Spiritual care, then, helps people who are dying feel whole, fulfilled, and in harmony with their world and the people in it. (Brody, *Guide to the Great Beyond*, 132)

The medical field of palliative care includes a spiritual aspect of care in this definition by the World Health Organization (WHO Fact Sheets): "Palliative care improves the quality of life of patients and that of their families who are facing challenges associated with life-threatening illness, whether physical, psychological, social or spiritual. The quality of life of caregivers improves as well."

The founder of the hospice movement, Dame Cicely Saunders said, "You matter because you are you. You matter to the last moment of life, and we will do all we can to help you not only to die peacefully, but also to live until you die" (Cicely Saunders Institute, "Dame Cicely Saunders"). Spiritual care first affirms and empowers the sacred significance and intrinsic dignity of each person's life, in times of pain and distress, grief over the loss of their attributed dignity. To assist and empower each person to live as fully as possible, she understood we must attend to each person's suffering as "total pain," including physical, social, psychological, and spiritual pain. Spiritual pain happens when one's values, beliefs, or faiths are challenged by or disconnected from what the person is experiencing, according to how the person is interpreting it to compose and experience his/her integrity of life.

Spiritual pain may have a diminishing force on one's perspective of life's "reality" with its sinking sand kind of "gravity," as one suffers grief, a sense of guilt, hopelessness, or despair over what is perceived as an unresolved or irreconcilable loss. As it is in touch with this dimension, spiritual care is intended to empower a person's sense of intrinsic dignity—"*You matter because you are.*" Spiritual care encourages each person to transcend the pain-induced perspective to expand the scope of spiritual trust and quest, and to experience owning the process of exploration as meaningful.

The definition of spirituality according to the National Consensus Project for Quality Palliative Care (NCP) reads:

> Spirituality is a fundamental aspect of compassionate, patient and family-centered palliative care. It is a dynamic and intrinsic aspect of humanity through which individuals seek meaning, purpose, and transcendence, and experience relationship to self, family, others, community, society, and to the significant or sacred. Spirituality is expressed through beliefs, values, traditions, and practices. (NCP, *Clinical Practice Guidelines*, 32)

For the initial screening and assessment of each patient and their family's spiritual needs, it is important first to offer a safe, non-judgmental, empathic, encouraging, and compassionate space to "hold" whatever they express. Spiritual care begins with the spiritual care provider's intentional awareness of how the interpersonal space is affected by his or her own state of mind, and by their patients and their families, and exploration of therapeutic use of presence, words, body language, and nonverbal palliative approach for their benefit.

Then the spiritual assessment focuses on the patient's/family's sense/interpretation of their reality; expectation/hope regarding: their life and the support they are receiving; and their current support system, both external (family, friends, caregivers, and communities) and internal (awareness, openness, resilience, coping skills, "lived wisdom," self-empathy, and the source of their strength, peace, and hope).

Spiritual pain of moral, ethical, or existential disconnection includes relational disconnection; moral, ethical dilemma related to one's role and identity; disconnections between one's expectation/value/belief and the reality the way one sees, loss/need of life's meaning and purpose, and/or disconnection from one's sense of potential and fulfillment.

Spiritual care can focus on these questions as entry points:

BELIEF (Trust, Faith, Mindset, Ethical perspective/meaning-making): *How do you see what is happening to you? What are and can be trustworthy, reliable, and certain? What is your ultimate concern? How do you want our service to reflect your belief/faith?*

FREEDOM: *What kind of freedom are you fighting for? What would you be free from?*

PAIN: *In between alleviating pain and retaining lucidity, how would you purpose your comfort and consciousness? Which aspects of your life can be affecting/causing the pain; and is affected/impaired by the pain? What is the need and message your pain may be expressing?*

LIFE (in the contexts of relationships, dignity, time, and space): *What makes your life meaningful? What is most important or fulfilling now, for yourself/whom? Which aspects or moments of your life make you say, "My life has/had a good purpose and I am at peace"?*

LOVE (with self, loved ones, society, life, and the sacred): *Whom would you spend your life with and for? What relationships would you want to resolve, to reconcile? What would be your life's lasting impact/legacy/gift beyond physical death you'd leave with your loved ones?*

BEAUTY: *What kind of beauty can fulfill your life? How can you find with your loved ones the "seeds" of stories to grow beauty in their lives?*

Spiritual care is at the heart of our human act of caring when we look into the original meanings of "care" as "to grieve with." Another keyword associated with spiritual care is *compassion*, whose original meaning in Latin is "to suffer together with." We may find a source of healing and empowerment in the caring and compassionate presence of someone who accompanies, witnesses, suffers, and grieves with those who suffer or mourn. Furthermore, in biblical Hebrew, the word for womb, when made plural (*Rachamim*) comes to mean "compassion," in which we may find an inspiring connection between pain and birth. A spiritual care provider may find his/her role as a "midwife" to serve and guide someone's "birthing labor process" to envision what may be born out of each "labor pain."

The transformative, even transcendental nature of our life manifests both suffering and healing. Providing spiritual care requires one to trust and anticipate, thereby empower and facilitate the innate potential of what/how life reveals its healing nature and spiritual mystery. That is when we experience transcending our customary mindset/perspective of suffering and compulsory sense of having to fix problems:

> "Healing is the personal experience of the transcendence of suffering." (Egnew, "Meaning of Healing," 258)

> "A new way of seeing, combined with a new way of acting—that is what we need." (de Chardin, *Activation of Energy*, 295)

> "Out beyond ideas of wrongdoing and rightdoing, there is a field. I'll meet you there. When the soul lies down on that grass, the world is too full to talk about. Let the beauty we love be what we do." (*Essential Rumi*, 36)

Inspired by these perspectives above, we may see spiritual care as an intentional, "musical tuning" of versatile ways of seeing and acting to generate healing interactions with those who suffer, empowering and participating in their exploration of new ways to see beyond their old dichotomy of rights and wrongs, to experience transcending their suffering. To do so, we first need to nurture the vast field of spiritual silence within us, in order to be fully present with those we serve.

In the book of Job in the Hebrew Bible, Job's friends were led to live their spiritual care with a silent presence for Job, when they "saw that his grief was very great" (Job 2:13). When they could not remain silent to listen to how Job expressed his suffering, it became a "miscarriage" of their spiritual care as "grieving and suffering with." Job called to them, "You are all worthless physicians. Oh, that you would be silent, and it would be your wisdom! Now hear my reasoning, and heed the pleadings of my lips" (Job 13:4–6, NKJV). There is the sacred, healing dimension of our caring, compassionate presence for one another.

The spiritual care provider, thus needs to be well-connected with self in empathy, in order not to have his/her caring focus on the patient diverted to one's own pain and needs triggered by what he/she hears and witnesses in the suffering of those he/she serves, so as to avoid triggered self-defense reaction. Formational clinical training required of spiritual care providers, such as Clinical Pastoral Education (CPE), is designed to cultivate their in-depth empathic self-knowledge/integration to remain grounded and non-anxious in their presence, and to become intentional in focusing on the patients' needs, by maintaining objective awareness of one's triggered moments and utilizing what may emerge in one's consciousness therapeutically for the benefit of the patients.

The ancient Greeks believed, "We are the medicine (*pharmacon*)" with the word *pharmacon* having two opposing meanings of "cure" and "poison," thus expressing their awareness of the interpersonal dynamics' potential impact. Henri Nouwen expressed his insights into our human woundedness and healing potential with the phrase "wounded healers," and asked this valuable question of spiritual care, "How can we put our woundedness in the service of others? When our wounds cease to be a source of shame, and become a source of healing, we have become wounded healers" (Nouwen, *Wounded Healer*, 79).

To put our woundedness as well as our potential for healing in the service of others, spiritual care operates in the awareness of our interdependency as both sufferers and healers to one another. It also means spiritual care explores how to bring integrity to a sufferer's spiritual pain of disintegration torn in the dichotomy of "either-or," such as living or dying, health or illness, healing or suffering, right or wrong, doing or being, success or failure, joy or sorrow, dying self or dying to self, and so forth.

Spiritual care thus seeks to affirm and empower the person's intrinsic dignity and humanity by exploring the semantic layers in both ends of dichotomy, to empower the healing process of becoming whole. The spiritual care assessment can offer a transformative process of self-discovery. When one's mind is acutely awakened by pain, suffering, and the shared human condition of mortality, to be urged to explore living life to the fullest, the hidden healing potential of human presence can be most vividly experienced and trusted. This shows a mysterious paradox of our human nature: "Healthy" people are often "asleep" as to their spiritual nature, whereas those who have faced mortality are awakened to the healthy dimension of spiritual integrity and wholeness, where our life and our mortality can reconcile and unite.

When the COVID pandemic threatened our lives and communities, it became like our collective hospice experience, and spiritual care practice was also challenged on the field. During the lockdown here in New York, home visits were limited to the most necessary nursing visits to minimize the chance of infection, and telehealth spiritual care began. The challenge revealed to many an exceptionally fertile ground of profound spiritual quest for the meaning of life in the face of limitations or even the absence of what should otherwise fulfill life. The most fundamental questions such as "Who am I?" in their drastically changed or lost "stage" and context of meaningful and fulfilling life; "Who are we?" in light of "Whose keeper am I?" or "Who is my keeper?" in our shared wilderness experience, surfaced from the depth of our yearning for real connection as a passage of transformation or a kind of initiation to a new stage of our human consciousness.

When long-hidden and closeted emotions were triggered by the fearsome circumstances to overflow, spiritual care counselors were to focus on holding a safe space to affirm what was being expressed, and empowering them to take courage to come out onto the wider field, when felt assaulted or traumatized by the threats upon their normalcy and well-being. The human solidarity normalized all reactions, and spiritual care at best offered a compassionate, caring presence to affirm all of life's aspects and trust life's potential for healing and growth.

Through this extreme challenge, the spiritual dimension of care was explored, expanded, and experienced: when transcendental shifts in semantics and perspectives happen, the human bodies can be sensed and experienced as temples, houses, musical instruments, or communities; emotional feelings and their movements as ocean tides; words and stories as confessions; inter-personal space of shared hearts and remembered spirits of the deceased as a sacred gathering; family or caregiver's loving care as anointing (with the spirit of love); and so on. Spiritual care is called to channel and embody spiritual love, whose compassionate (suffering together) "wombs" may willingly share the pilgrimage of labor pangs leading towards new birth.

Spiritual care trusts and seeks our daily spiritual opportunity of writing and rewriting our stories to share, encouraging the "audience" of the musical performance of those they care for to cherish and grow the resonance of the music remaining within them beyond the termination of the performance. Spiritual care affirms our human life as an ever-growing hub of encounters and communes with those whose impact we have chosen to receive and keep.

And when we are on the land of the living, we seem to have a responsibility of honoring our late loved ones by looking deeper into what they have left behind for us as their growing gifts entrusted to us, as long as we seem assigned to live the "afterlife," following the "death" of our living together with their physical presence. Courageous patients and their families have boldly invited me to hold their personal creeds as I experienced their responses to my spiritual care service, born out of the sacred encounters with their living and dying, expressing and exploring.

Certain essences of what our patients have left with us seem to remain alive with us to this day, raising spiritual questions on the mystery of our life: whether "death" may not be an end, but a mere dimensional shift of life's manifestation; how our relationships seasonally shift with it; how we may choose to tune into what has impacted us—to unbox these as seeds to sow; and how we have already impacted others. These and many more questions may grow from the multitude of stories we are invited to hear. Until we finally reach the ocean of human spirit in one body, after all the individual journeys flow like the rivers and "converse" with one another in community, we continue to explore how to nurture our best gifts to be remembered and spread, until we may reach "the ocean." Spiritual care may seek to celebrate our human life in such an expanded dimension of life's questions and quests.

REFERENCES

Brody, J. *Jane Brody's Guide to the Great Beyond*. New York: Random House, 2009

Cicely Saunders Institute of Palliative Care, Policy and Rehabilitation, "Dame Cicely Saunders: A Palliative Care Pioneer." London: King's College [n.d.]. https://www.kcl.ac.uk/cicelysaunders/about-us/cicely-saunders.

de Chardin, T. *Activation of Energy*. London: Collins, 1970.

Egnew, T. "The Meaning of Healing: Transcending Suffering." *Annals of Family Medicine* 3/3 (2005) 255–62.

Heschel, A.J. *Man Is Not Alone: A Philosophy of Religion*. New York: Macmillan, 1976.

National Consensus Project for Quality Palliative Care. *Clinical Practice Guidelines for Quality Palliative Care*. 4th ed. Richmond, VA: National Coalition for Hospice and Palliative Care; 2018. https://www.nationalcoalitionhpc.org/wp-content/uploads/2020/07/NCHPC-NCPGuidelines_4thED_web_FINAL.pdf.

Nouwen, H. *The Wounded Healer*. New York: Penguin Random House, 1979.
Pascal, B. *Pascal's Pensées*. Translated by W. F. Trotter. New York: Dutton, 1958.
Rūmī, Maulana Jalāl al-Dīn. *The Essential Rumi: New Expanded Edition*. Translated by J. Moynes and C. Barks. New York: HarperCollins, 2004.
Tillich, P. *Dynamics of Faith*. New York: Harper, 1957.
World Health Organization (2020). WHO Fact-sheets. https://www.who.int/news-room/fact-sheets/detail/palliative-care.

8

Spiritual Care from the Perspective of Pastoral Theology

Shifting Paradigms[1]

Pamela Cooper-White

A longstanding metaphor for the Christian pastoral caregiver had been the *shepherd* (the literal meaning of the word *pastor*.) One of the great articulators of pastoral theology of the mid-twentieth century, Seward Hiltner first described the three primary functions of the shepherd-pastor as healing, sustaining, and guiding (Hiltner, *Preface*). This helped to differentiate pastoral care and counseling in the 1950s from the hegemony of psychiatry and to restore a biblical, theological, and historically grounded paradigm to the work of pastoral caregivers, who were struggling to find their own distinctive identity as professionals. But it also participated in a paternalistic paradigm that was then common. The shepherd tends the flock, feeds and guides the sheep, protects them from wolves and marauders, and generally steers them in the direction they are to go. And, drawing on Christ's own words, the shepherd "lays down his life for the sheep" (John 10:11).

This model was taken seriously by generations of clergy who felt a call to sacrificial love of their flock and the task of moral and spiritual guidance. But herein lies a serious pitfall, that is, the tendency to see self-sacrifice as a

---

1. Expanded and updated from Cooper-White, *Shared Wisdom* (2004), 122–28. (NB: This section does not appear in the 2nd ed., Cooper-White, *Shared Wisdom*, 2024.)

defining image of ministry. While some sacrifice is probably always necessary in ministry, or, for that matter, in any devoted Christian life, the dominance of a sacrificial image has caused numerous problems. In particular, it can lead to taking ourselves so seriously that we might view our pastoral ministry as so uniquely indispensable that our own needs as caregivers can be neglected indefinitely. If we or our family should suffer for this, it is all within the framework of the self-sacrificial love of the shepherd.

By the 1990s, this paradigm began to shift, especially in mainline Protestantism. In large part, this was due to the influence of two very important and interrelated strands of theological thinking and pastoral praxis: (1) the growing presence of women in both lay and ordained leadership, and (2) the emergence, in part through liberation theology, of voices of the developing world in theology and some growth in diversity of racial, ethnic, and class leadership in these churches. These leaders brought critiques from their social locations and theological perspectives to the shepherd paradigm. There came to be an increasing awareness of the limitations of this individualistic, heroic model and a concomitant opening of a wider horizon for pastoral care and pastoral theology. This opening or widening process may be seen in three dimensions: *just listening, contextualization,* and *diversification.*

JUST LISTENING

The phrase "just listening" carries two connotations. First, as the Clinical Pastoral Education (CPE) movement has been teaching for many years now, it is important to trust that silence is truly facilitative. "Just listening" means being able to be still and invite the spiritual dimensions of a patient's or client's reflections to emerge, without undue influence or intervention from us, e.g., by probing, giving advice (which may simply be an artifact of our countertransference), or making leading assumptions. As I have written elsewhere, "just listening..."

> entails more than what we do with our ears. Listening is attending. It involves using all of one's self—mind and heart, body and soul, conscious and unconscious. It involves attending not only to the patient's communications (verbal and nonverbal), but to what happens inside ourselves as we spend time deeply immersed in the patient's reality. Relational analyst Donnel Stern uses the term *witness* to describe this form of deeply engaged attention, in which he says "we are called into being by acts of recognition by the other" (Stern, *Partners in Thought*, 110).

As infants, our minds are first brought into being by recognition from parental figures. As adults, we continue to need witnesses—"partners in thought" in Stern's words—in order for events of our lives to fall into narrative awareness.

> This practice of witnessing is sacred. By serving as witness to another's story, we create space where new images, symbols, words, narratives, and meanings can emerge. . .By listening, witnessing, deeply attending, we are perhaps most able to approximate the way God knows and loves us. For most of us, God may seem to be silent much of the time. Maybe this is because God is attending to us to intently and deeply! God is listening! (Cooper-White, "On Taming the Fox," 41)

There was a turn beginning in the 1960s, through the 1980s when I was in training, toward a more clinical model. The social status and professional authority of the clergy was waning in America, while the medical profession, including psychiatry, was still high. The movement toward training as pastoral counselors and psychotherapists arose, in part, from this desire to go deeper and to have proper clinical training and credentialing. "Theological reflection," however, did not always maintain the same scholarly rigor as the clinical case formulation, and was often done somewhat pro forma. In the 1990s, pastoral theologians began to reclaim a more distinctive spiritual and theological character for the discipline of pastoral care and counseling.

I believe that professional spiritual care providers—understood now both ecumenically and interreligiously—should be understood under the umbrella of ministry, and not merely as an adjunct clinical or medical profession. Board certification in the US by the Association of Professional Chaplains (APC), while broadened from its former requirement of a Master of Divinity degree in order to accommodate candidates from multiple religious and spiritual traditions, still requires a minimum two-year graduate degree in theology, philosophy, or psychology, with required coursework in three of four areas: "Spiritual Practices/Practical Ministry, History of a Religious or Philosophical Tradition, Sacred or Foundational Texts, and World Religions," and endorsement from one's religious body (BCCI, *FAQs*).[2] Such

---

2. The Master of Divinity degree or equivalent 72 hours' theological education is no longer required. "A candidate needs to hold a conferred qualifying graduate degree from a CHEA-accredited institution of at least 30 graduate semester hours in one of the following disciplines: theology, or philosophy, or psychology. All applicants must have completed two years of graduate level study, demonstrated by submitting a minimum of 48 graduate semester hours recorded in official transcripts. All applicants must demonstrate graduate coursework in three of four subject areas essential to the practice of professional chaplaincy: Spiritual Practices/Practical Ministry, History of a Religious or

in-depth knowledge of one's own—and others'—spiritual and theological tradition grounds our provision of care. We then bring this specialized knowledge in partnering with professionals trained in medicine, nursing, psychology, and social work. In this volume, Christina Puchalski and Jessica Zitter provide excellent examples of how medical and clergy professionals can collaborate. A sound theological foundation in one's own religious tradition does not preclude the ability to provide spiritual care *across* religious and spiritual boundaries—but, rather, sensitizes pastoral and spiritual caregivers to the importance of noticing and validating differences, and being attentive to others' spiritual needs as a practice of justice-making.

CONTEXTUALIZATION

A second important trend has been the turn toward social, economic, political and cultural context. Traditional one-on-one models of pastoral care, based on the medical model, tended to operate in the arena of the individual psyche, and by extension, the family system. However, the individual and nuclear family model, while still helpful to many in our care, nevertheless ignored larger dimensions of human experience, including the social, political, economic, racial, ethnic, and cultural surround in which any individual's or family's life is embedded, bringing its own additional pressures, stresses, and traumas, both acute and ongoing (Watkins Ali, *Survival and Liberation*).

The increasing awareness of these contextual realities led pastoral theology into a greater social systems perspective, expanding the scope of pastoral care to encompass the work for *justice*, as Larry Kent Graham advocated: a shift from "relational humanness," to "relational justice." (Graham, "From Relational"; see also, e.g., Couture and Hunter, *Pastoral Care and Social Conflict*). Emmanuel Lartey then made further important contributions in this area with his writings on the resources of non-Western modes of care, which are often much more communal (as he also writes in this volume) and how we need to bring a postcolonial/decolonial lens to the way we conceptualize our field (Lartey, *In Living Color*; *Pastoral Theology in an Intercultural World*; and *Postcolonializing God*; see also Byun, *Where Is the* Bachata *in Spiritual Care?*"; Kwok and Burns, *Postcolonial Practice of Ministry*; Lartey and Moon, *Postcolonial Images*; McGarrah Sharp, *Misunderstanding Stories* and *Creating Resistances*; Moon, *Liberalism and Colonial*

Philosophical Tradition, Sacred or Foundational Texts, and World Religions. Applicants must have completed at least one graduate course in three of the core subjects and must show a minimum of 24 graduate hours earned among the four subjects." (BCCI, *FAQs*)

Violence; Moon and Lartey, *Postcolonial Practices of Care*; see also Lartey, this volume).

This turn toward social context has further meant that the arena of care has broadened, toward doing "public theology," that is, getting out into the public arena as activists as well as personal caregivers, to address the underlying societal causes of suffering, and to join in coalition with other advocates for social change. The shift from "relational humanness to relational justice" means that pastoral care can no longer focus on the individual in isolation. This takes pastoral care and counseling out into the arena of advocacy as well as individual care.

To use an example from my years in specialized ministry with survivors of intimate partner violence, it would mean the difference between individual counseling only and counseling plus advocacy in the wider community. This broader approach would seek to empower each woman to identify her own strengths and options, while also preaching, teaching, working collaboratively with shelters for survivors of violence and agencies for batterers, and advocating with others in the community for the eradication of gender-based violence and the social structures that reinforce it (see, e.g., Cooper-White, *Cry of Tamar* and *Gender, Violence and Justice*).

DIVERSIFICATION

This commitment to relational justice, leads to a third aspect of change in pastoral care: diversification.

Diversification of Caregivers, Recipients, and Resources

This refers to diversification of caregivers, care recipients, and the resources made available to those seeking pastoral help. It also calls for an expanded awareness, in which our own openness as caregivers to the reality and the wisdom of those for whom we care can model the kind of mutuality and correct for the kind of top-down, power-over expert role that once held sway. We are also called to hold in our awareness the wider contextual realities in which individuals struggle to live, and to refrain from "diagnosing" as individual psychological or spiritual problems what are, in fact, outcomes of societal rather than individual illness and spiritual malaise.

Pastoral or spiritual care has never been dispensed exclusively in the one-on-one setting of a professional office with a fixed appointment, nor has all pastoral care ever been dispensed solely by the clergy. (This, too, is predominantly a Western model, and an artifact of the medicalization of care.) The one-on-one model has all too often perpetuated a one-up expert role that tends subtly to "fix" rather than empower the one coming for help. However, there is now a growing respect for the wide variety of resources available for pastoral care and for the clergyperson as one resource—albeit an important one with particular gifts—among many. Many pastoral theologians, now understand clergy and religious leaders—to use a phrase from Bonnie Miller-McLemore—as "facilitators of networks of care" rather than lone caregivers (Miller-McLemore, "Living Human Web"). Margaret Kornfeld similarly framed pastoral care as a paradigm of "cultivating wholeness," in which a variety of counselors with a variety of expertise collaborate in the facilitation of spiritual growth and healing of both individuals and communities (Kornfeld, *Cultivating Wholeness*).

Miller-McLemore revised another paradigm that was widely circulated from the mid-twentieth century: Anton Boisen's idea of the "living human document" (Boisen, *Exploration*). In his time, Boisen was concerned that pastoral caregivers turn from an overreliance on theory and texts to a more existential respect for the life of individuals in all their uniqueness. He called for "the study of living human documents rather than books." This phrase—"living human documents"—struck a resonant chord in pastoral caregivers who sought, legitimately, to get closer to the lived inner experience of their helpees (Gerkin, *Living Human Document*). However, this paradigm, too, was limited by its individualistic bent. Miller-McLemore proposed replacing the "living human document" with the "living human web" as the "appropriate subject for investigation, interpretation, and transformation." Miller-McLemore advocated "a shift toward context, collaboration, and diversity," in which the work of caregiving includes both individual and communal care, respecting the complexity and multiple contextual realities of people's lives (Miller-McLemore, "Living Human Web," 16).

In a congregational context, for example, this means that the notion of "care" expands from that lone pastor in the study with a lone congregation member or couple or even family to a web of resources gathered collaboratively to address the complex, layered needs and struggles of the helpee. It means having a well-developed contacts list, in which there are entries representing a wide variety of *personally known and trusted* helpers in the community with various expertise, including spiritual directors, therapists, social workers, school officials and educators, medical professionals, attorneys, public agency workers, and community organizers. It means sharing the responsibility and authority for pastoral care with trained and empowered lay caregivers, such as Lay Eucharistic Ministers, small-group ministry leaders, Stephen Ministers (Stephen Ministries, "Equipping God's People"), Faith Community Nurses/Parish Nurses (FCNI, "Welcome to FCNI"), and lay pastoral care teams. It means hitting the pavement to identify and join with others who are working in the community to change the conditions that perpetuate suffering and bringing those individuals back into our congregations as witnesses to the wider needs of the community. In other settings of spiritual care, such as chaplaincy, an analogous commitment to consultation and interdisciplinary collaboration within one's institution or organization, and beyond it as appropriate, is equally essential.

Consultation and Collaboration

It also means seeking consultation and inter-professional collaboration. The metaphor of the shepherd, as noted above, was central to the self-understanding of Christian clergy in the postwar era, and had long historical precedent. Feminist pastoral theologian Jeanne Stevenson Moessner critiques the shepherd paradigm as overly heroic and self-sacrificing in emulation of Christ himself (Moessner, "From Samaritan to Samaritan"). She counterposes the biblical narrative of the Good Samaritan who enlisted resources from others and kept his boundaries as he went on his own journey after ensuring that the man lying injured on the road was being properly cared for (see also Katherine, *Boundaries*).

Even in one-on-one caregiving, one need not rely solely on one's own wisdom and experience, but can be supported by the accumulated wisdom and experience of many peers and senior colleagues, both in pastoral and spiritual care and secular psychotherapy, and in other allied disciplines represented throughout the wider community.

There is a hidden benefit to this community-based approach. Although this may sound initially like a lot of extra work, it is actually less taxing over time than bearing the burden of ministry entirely on one's own shoulders. The pastor no longer needs to be seen as having sole responsibility for the welfare of the "flock." While providing spiritual leadership is still important in congregations and other institutions, especially in the in times of crisis or conflict when a group looks to their clergy for guidance, pastoral leadership is ultimately meant to focus on equipping and empowering others to do the shared work of ministry. To use a Christian image, ministry is a collaboration of the whole body of Christ by virtue of the baptismal covenant, and also to be shared with the wider community.

Religious Pluralism: "Pastoral" and "Spiritual" Care

Diversification also means a significant widening of the scope of care beyond a predominantly Christian model grounded in Christian scripture and tradition. Increasing interreligious engagement, especially in non-parochial settings, has called for a critique of the term "pastoral care" itself.

The shepherd image was drawn from the Gospel of John (Ch. 10), and although there are many other shepherds in the Hebrew Bible, the shepherd as a model for pastoral caregivers has carried a distinctively Christian history and character. In a modern, globalized, and religiously plural world, however, Christian-based pastoral care is not enough. The spiritual needs of persons of other faiths—on their own terms and not merely through some kind of analogizing and translation by Christian caregivers—has come to the attention of practitioners working in pluralistic settings. Many hospital, prison, and military chaplains led a shift in recent decades to the more nonsectarian term "spiritual care.

This shift has resulted in many organizations replacing the term "pastoral care" with "spiritual care," and widening the circle of care providers to incorporate chaplains from multiple religious and humanist traditions. "Pastoral care," as noted above, then becomes a subset (referring largely to Christian and some Jewish chaplaincies) of "spiritual care," which is the umbrella term for care for persons of (potentially) all traditions, and also those who identify as "spiritual but not religious," the unaffiliated (in America, sometimes called the "nones"—see Pew, "Nones in America"), agnostics, and atheists.[3] Where representatives of all faith traditions are not available, all chaplains should now be trained to provide at least essential spiritual care to persons of other faiths and none (Schipani, *Multifaith Views in Spiritual Care;* "Navigating Religious Difference"; *Spiritual Care in our Multifaith World*; Schmidt, "Interfaith Chaplaincy"; Snodgrass, ed., *Navigating Religious Difference*; Weiss et al., *Healing*). "Spiritual care" might well be served by theologian Paul Tillich's definition from the founding days of pastoral care—with which he was directly involved (Cooper-White, "Paul Tillich's Legacy," 212; see also Cooper, *Paul Tillich and Psychology*)—a "helping encounter in the dimension of ultimate concern" (Tillich, "Theology of Pastoral Care," 22).

What is the appropriate role of a chaplain trained in one particular faith tradition to respond to those of another faith? At the very first conference of the IASC in Bern, Switzerland, we probed this question from an

---

3. For a moving case discussion of an atheist spiritual caregiver's experience with praying, see Schipani, *Spiritual Care in our Multifaith World*, 2–7.

interreligious perspective, and came to an understanding that "pastoral care" is probably best understood as a sub-specialty within "spiritual care." The important skills of listening, compassionate presence, and advocacy for those in our care, can fluently move between religious boundaries, whereas sacramental and tradition-specific rituals, and questions of theology, doctrine, and tradition, require caregivers of the same tradition as the patient or client. Chaplains should refrain from performing liturgies or giving dogmatic instruction to a person of another faith—and it should go without saying, never, ever to proselytize for their own tradition.

This has further heightened awareness in our field of the wider social and economic context, and political realities in which we and our patients and clients live (in particular the captivity of all our institutions and practices to the sweeping realities of neo-liberalism, Western imperialism, and racism), how Western models of care have been captive to the capitalist commodification of care; how have the spiritualities of black, brown and indigenous peoples, and LGBTQ persons have been disregarded or devalued historically in our fields of pastoral theology, care and counseling. We must continue to examine the ways in which our field has done harm in the past.

Diversity as Multiplicity within, between, and among Persons

As a psychoanalytically trained pastoral psychotherapist and theologian, I have also continued to encourage our field not to lose the rich insights of our earlier attention to the ways in which *the unconscious* influences us *as individuals and in groups*. The school of relational psychoanalysis, in particular, over against the rigid, authoritarian mode of so-called "classical psychoanalysis" of the 1950s and '60s[4] offers us a new richness in its understanding of intersubjectivity and unconscious relationship (e.g., Mitchell and Aron, *Relational Psychoanalysis*; Aron and Harris, *Relational Psychoanalysis*, vol. 2; Suchet and Aron, *Relational Psychoanalysis*, vol. 3; Mitchell and Aron, *Relational Psychoanalysis*, vol. 4). Pastoral theologians and clinicians rejected the old ego psychology mode of rigid psychoanalytic theory and practice—rightly so, I think—in favor of family systems and Rogerian person-centered models of counseling. But psychoanalysis as a field, often led by relational analysts, is now addressing systemic racism and gender

---

4. For some of the reasons behind the rigidity of "classical psychoanalysis" having to do with the trauma of the Holocaust and the medicalization of psychoanalysis in the US, see Kuriloff, *Psychoanalysis and the Third Reich* and Jacoby, *Repression of Psychoanalysis*. Psychoanalysis in Europe before WWII had a distinctly social and political orientation, which was lost in the postwar US.

inequality within its own training institutes and practices. Psychoanalysts are also now probing within our own psyches—our countertransference—to examine our own deeply ingrained racial and gender biases. In conclusion, psychoanalysis, too, is a partner with whom we should re-establish ties and continue to collaborate—without abandoning any of the ethical and moral strides our field has taken and is taking, both in the US and internationally, in providing spiritual care today.

A number of relational psychoanalysts have proposed—prompted by an extension of object relations theory, postmodern philosophy, and clinical work around dissociative disorders—that we ourselves, as individuals, *all* contain considerable *internal* diversity—non-pathologically. Our psyches are constituted as multiple subjects, not intrinsically singular, monolithic selves from birth. Our internal world is characterized by a kaleidoscopic, ever-changing, swirl of affect-laden experiences and introjects of other people, especially from early childhood, which are stimulated and come to the fore at different times, depending on different contexts (Davies, "Multiple Perspectives on Multiplicity," 195). Our capacity to experience our self as one continuous being is a developmental achievement (Bromberg, "Speak!," 521; see also Bromberg, *Standing in the Spaces*). Self-fragmentation, often caused by trauma, is not healthy multiplicity, but healthy multiplicity is characterized by a capacity to move fluently from one affect state to another (as an internal "we") without losing a healthy sense of "I." Inviting ourselves to be flexible and complex, and a rejecting rigid, monolithic notions of selfhood and identity, can even be understood as another liberative practice, and a source of creativity (Flax, "Multiples"). Spiritual caregivers, by attending to our own multiplicity, can find in ourselves a greater empathy toward the complexity and changeability of those "others" for whom we care—and find echoes of this multiplicity even in many traditions' conceptions of the divine or the sacred (Cooper-White, *Shared Wisdom*, 181–93; *Many Voices*; and *Braided Selves*).

CONCLUSION

In conclusion, psychoanalytic, systems, person-centered, existential, and intersubjective multiple-self theories, alongside *and accountable to* our multiple theological traditions, and to postcolonial and other liberative social theories, all have a place in grounding our work. And the diversification of caregivers likewise demands that we must do this work (even when we are sitting one-on-one with a patient or client) in collaboration and consultation with other professionals, and with others in the community.

Our theories, theologies, and our collegial relationships are all important resources, not only for understanding our patients and clients, but also for nurturing our own growth, healing, and empathic sensitivity—both in our consulting rooms, and in our activism and advocacy for the *tikkun 'olam*—the mending of the world.

To end with a word from my own Christian theological perspective, Jesus sent the disciples out two by two (Luke 10:1). He did not send individuals, but partners. And when those partners went forth, he foretold that they would be empowered to do great healing works in his name—not to be the messiah themselves, but to be his emissaries. This is the metaphor that for me replaces the paradigm of the shepherd: the image of the disciples, going out as partners, without excess provisions, but with the confidence of the Gospel and the reliance on the hospitality of strangers that would make their mission complete. In this paradigm, we become companions to one another on the journey, and as we go, we may find, as did the disciples on the Emmaus road, that we even end up, without realizing it, walking side by side with Christ himself (Luke 24:13–35).

REFERENCES

Aron, L. and Harris, A., eds. *Relational Psychoanalysis*, Vol. 2: *Innovation and Expansion*. Hillsdale, NJ: Analytic, 2005.

———, eds. *Relational Psychoanalysis*, Vol. 4: *Expansion of Theory*. London: Routledge, 2012.

Boisen, A. *The Exploration of the Inner World*. New York: Harper, 1952.

Board of Certified Chaplaincy, Inc. (BCCI) *FAQs Regarding Certification*. Hoffman Estates: BCCI, 2024. https://www.apchaplains.org/bcci-site/becoming-certified/certification-frequently-asked-questions/.

Bromberg, P. M. "'Speak! That I May See You': Reflections on Dissociation, Reality, and Psychoanalytic Listening." *Psychoanalytic Dialogues* 4/4 (1994) 517–47.

———. *Standing in the Spaces: Essays on Clinical Process, Trauma, and Dissociation*. New York: Psychology/Taylor & Francis, 1998.

Byun, C. "Where Is the *Bachata in Spiritual Care?*: Decolonial Spiritual Care after Religion. Lanham, MD: Lexington, under contract for 2025; PhD dissertation, Union Theological Seminary New York, 2023, Proquest #30637831.

Cooper, T. D. *Paul Tillich and Psychology: Historic and Contemporary Explorations in Theology, Psychology, and Ethics*. Macon: Mercer University Press, 2005.

Cooper-White, P. *Braided Selves: Collected Essays on Multiplicity, God, and Persons*. Eugene, OR: Cascade Books, 2011.

———. *The Cry of Tamar: Violence against Women and the Church's Response*. Minneapolis: Fortress, 1995.

———. *The Cry of Tamar: Violence against Women and the Church's Response*. 2nd ed. Minneapolis: Fortress, 2012.

———. *Gender, Violence, and Justice: Collected Essays on Violence against Women*. Eugene, OR: Cascade Books, 2019.

———. *Many Voices: Pastoral Psychotherapy in Relational and Theological Perspective*. Minneapolis: Fortress, 2007.

———. "On Listening: Taming the Fox." In *Transforming Wisdom: Pastoral Psychotherapy in Theological Perspective*, edited by F. Kelcourse and K. B. Lyon, 28–43. Eugene, OR: Cascade Books, 2015.

———. "Paul Tillich's Legacy in Psychology and Pastoral Psychotherapy." In *Why Tillich? Why Now?*, edited by T. G. Bandy, 207–219. Macon, GA: Mercer University Press, 2021.

———. *Shared Wisdom: Use of the Self in Pastoral Care and Counseling*. Minneapolis: Fortress, 2004.

———. *Shared Wisdom: Use of the Self in Pastoral Care and Counseling*. Rev. and exp. 20th anniversary ed. Minneapolis: Fortress, 2024.

Couture, P. and Hunter, R., eds. *Pastoral Care and Social Conflict*. Nashville: Abingdon, 1999.

Davies, J. M. "Multiple Perspectives on Multiplicity." *Psychoanalytic Dialogues* 8/2 (1998) 195–206.

Faith Community Nurses International (FCNI). "Welcome to FCNI." FCNI [2024]. https://www.fcninternational.org/.

Flax, J. "Multiples: On the Contemporary Politics of Subjectivity." In Flax, J., *Disputed Subjects: Essays on Psychoanalysis, Politics and Philosophy*, 92–110. New York: Routledge, 1993.

Gerkin, C. *The Living Human Document: Revisioning Pastoral Counseling in a Hermeneutical Mode*. Nashville: Abingdon, 1984.

Graham, L. K. "From Relational Humanness to Relational Justice: Reconceiving Pastoral Care and Counseling." In *Pastoral Care and Social Conflict*, edited by P. Couture and R. Hunter, 220–234. Nashville: Abingdon, 1995.

Hiltner, S. *Preface to Pastoral Theology: The Ministry and Theory of Shepherding*. New York: Abingdon, 1948.

Jacoby, R. *The Repression of Psychoanalysis: Otto Fenichel and the Political Freudians*. New York: Basic, 1983.

Katherine, A. *Boundaries: Where You End and I Begin*. Center City: Hazelden, 2010.

Kornfeld, M. *Cultivating Wholeness: A Guide to Care and Counseling in Faith Communities*. New York: Continuum, 1998.

Kuriloff, E. *Psychoanalysis and the Third Reich: History, Memory, Tradition*. New York: Routledge, 2014.

Kwok, P. L. and Burns, S. eds. *Postcolonial Practice of Ministry: Leadership, Liturgy, and Interfaith Engagement*. Lanham: Lexington, 2016.

Lartey, E. Y. *In Living Color: An Intercultural Approach to Pastoral Care and Counseling*. 2nd ed. London: Kingsley, 2003. (Orig. publ. 1997.)

———. *Pastoral Theology in an Intercultural World*. Cleveland: Pilgrim, 2007. Reprint, Eugene, OR: Wipf & Stock, 2013.

———. *Postcolonializing God: An African Practical Theology*. London: SCM 2013.

Lartey, E. Y. and Moon, H. eds. *Postcolonial Images of Spiritual Care: Challenges of Care in a Neoliberal Age*. Eugene, OR: Pickwick Publications, 2020.

McGarrah Sharp, M. *Creating Resistances: Pastoral Care in a Postcolonial World*. Theology in Practice 7. Leiden: Brill, 2019.

———. *Misunderstanding Stories: Toward a Postcolonial Pastoral Theology*. Eugene, OR: Pickwick Publications, 2013.

Miller-McLemore, B. "The Living Human Web: Pastoral Theology at the Turn of the Century." In *Through the Eyes of Women: Insights for Pastoral Care*, edited by J. S. Moessner, 9–26. Minneapolis: Fortress, 1996.

Mitchell, S. A. and Aron, L., eds. *Relational Psychoanalysis: The Emergence of a Tradition*. Hillsdale: Analytic, 1999.

Moessner, J. S. "From Samaritan to Samaritan: Journey Mercies," in *Through the Eyes of Women: Insights for Pastoral Care*, edited by J. S. Moessner, 322–334. Minneapolis: Fortress.

Moon, H. *Liberalism and Colonial Violence: Charting a New Genealogy of Spiritual Care*. Eugene, OR: Pickwick Publications, 2023.

Moon, H. and Lartey, E. Y., eds. *Postcolonial Practices of Care: A Project of Togetherness during COVID-19 and Racial Violence*. Eugene, OR: Pickwick Publications, 2022.

Pew Research Center. "Religious 'Nones' in America: Who They Are and What They Believe." Washington, DC: Pew, 2024. https://www.pewresearch.org/religion/2024/01/24/religious-nones-in-america-who-they-are-and-what-they-believe/.

Schipani, D. S. "Navigating Religious Difference in Spiritual Care." *Religions* 15 (2024) 41–53. https://doi.org/10.3390/rel15010041.

———. *Spiritual Care in Our Multifaith World*. Eugene, OR: Wipf & Stock, 2024.

———, ed. *Multifaith Views in Spiritual Care*. Kitchener: Pandora, 2013.

Schmidt, H. "Interfaith Chaplaincy in a Post-secular Context." *Studies in Interreligious Dialogue* 30/2 (2020) 163–85.

Snodgrass, J., ed. *Navigating Religious Difference in Spiritual Care and Counseling*. Claremont: Claremont University Press, 2019.

Stern, D. B. *Partners in Thought: Working with Unformulated Experience*. Hillsdale: Analytic, 2010.

Stephen Ministries. "Equipping God's people for Ministry since 1975." St. Louis: Stephen Ministries, 2024. https://www.stephenministries.org/.

Suchet, M. and Aron, L., eds. *Relational Psychoanalysis*. Vol. 3: *New Voices*. Mahwah, NJ: Analytic, 2007.

Tillich, P. "The Theology of Pastoral Care." *Pastoral Psychology* 10/7 (1959) 21–26.

Watkins Ali, C. *Survival and Liberation: Pastoral Theology in African American Context*. St. Louis: Chalice, 1999.

Weiss, H., Federschmidt, K., Louw, D., and Bredvik, L. S. *Healing and Human Wellbeing within Iinterreligious Discourse*. Stellenbosch: African Sun Media, 2021.

9

Spiritual Care from the Perspective of Pastoral Theology: Postcolonial Views

Emmanuel Y. Lartey

In this chapter, I engage in a discussion of the meaning and practice of spiritual care from a pastoral theological perspective in the ecra of COVID-19 and the context of ongoing racialized violence. My pastoral theological stance is decidedly postcolonial in the sense that it is critical of colonial perspectives and practices that have characterized Western Christian discourse. It is critical, in particular, of Hegelian conceptions that overly privilege the Caucasian race as paradigmatic of freedom and rationality while consigning Asians and Africans to the realm of the "inferior, ignorant and superstitious."[1] The postcolonial perspective that is the main point of this chapter instead raises African and Asian thought and demonstrates how approaching Christian thought through those lenses serves to redeem Christianity from an oppressive and dehumanizing ethos.

---

1. For references to Hegel's writings, see Lartey and Moon, "Introduction," in *Postcolonial Images*, 4.

EVERY HUMAN PERSON IS SPIRITUAL

A foundational view of humanity that emerges from a postcolonial pastoral theological perspective on spiritual care is that of humanity as created in and bearing the image and likeness of God. This view of humanity taken as a given that is seminal to all practices of spiritual care is derived from Gen 1:27 "So God created *adam* (humans) in his own image, in the image of God he created them, male and female he created them." God is Spirit and all humans, being created in God's image, are spiritual. There is no human being who is not spiritual, and every human being is by nature a spiritual being.

WHAT IS "SPIRITUAL" ABOUT HUMANS?

In contrast to G. W. F. Hegel, whose philosophy almost completely underpins modern Western thought, and for whom *spirit* meant rationality, mind, consciousness, and selfhood, and of which the European individual modeled its fullest and highest development, *spirit* in postcolonial African thought lies at the core of human's capacity to relate. Here, the essential meaning of "spirit" is the God-given energy, driving force and ability of relationship. What is spiritual about us is not so much our ability to think but much more our capacity to relate. As such, to speak of spirituality is to refer to characteristic ways in which we relate. It follows therefore that spirituality is not the preserve of a particular group, class, or type of human being. Instead, spirituality is a human attribute and capacity which is present in all humans and has reference to the ability and characteristic manner in which we relate.

Spiritual care from a postcolonial pastoral theological perspective is more of an exercise in exploration of the manner and health of our human relationships than it is a cognitive science. Of course, exploring 'relationality' requires and does utilize cognitive and rational abilities. However, what is under scrutiny in spiritual care is not cognition itself but rather how relationality functions.

I have defined spirituality as "the human capacity for relationship with self, others, world, God, and/or that which transcends sensory experience, which is often expressed in specific activities and forms of action in historical, spatial, and social contexts in the world" (Lartey, *In Living Color*, 140–41).

SPIRITUAL CARE ADDRESSES FIVE DIMENSIONS OF RELATIONALITY

Spiritual care explores five dimensions of relationship that characterize our humanity. From a pastoral theological standpoint, spiritual care seeks to help us maintain a balance between and among all these dimensions of our relational life. Spiritual care practices help us develop a healthy balance between all aspects of our lives. Reductionism and an exclusive focus on any one dimension skew our humanity and result in toxicity.

Sin and illness are and result from an imbalance, a reductionist disharmony in our relational life, a distortion and displacement of the relational balance within the network of relationships in which we are embedded as humans.

The spiritual care provider enters into relationships with care seekers, and with them explores each of these relational dynamics.

Relationship with Transcendence

First, relationship with transcendence: Transcendence is understood, experienced, and spoken of in many different ways. Explicit "God" language is one way in which people express and explore this dimension of their lives. However religious language is by no means the only form of language available to articulate this experience of life. Spiritual caregivers privilege the forms of expression of the care seekers and help them explore the nuances of this relationship and how it promotes wellbeing or else disease.

Relationship with Self

Second, relationship with self: Spiritual care includes exploring "relationship with self.ġ Such exploration includes looking closely at issues of self-awareness and self-esteem, namely the degree of recognition that a person has of themselves—their thoughts, feelings, and behavior—and just how they regard themselves, either with a sense of appreciation and gratitude or with disdain and loathing. To what extent can one be said to be wrapped up in their own minds and narcissistically absorbed by themselves or else able to make use of their knowledge of self in a self-differentiated recognition and extension of self towards others? Such explorations are often the preserve and operation of psychologists. In this regard, postcolonial spiritual care providers operate in a manner captured well by spiritual director Wilkie Au and Jungian analyst Noreen Cannon, who argue that "neither a spirituality that ignores the dynamics of psychological growth nor a psychology that denies the spiritual nature of the human person can serve as an adequate guide today for people who seek to live with greater harmony and integration" (Au and Cannon, *Urgings of the Heart*).

Relationship with (An)other

Third, relationship with (an)other: Spiritual care accounts for, reviews, and explores the dyadic relational dynamics that are typical for us, examining how they can promote or hinder health and wholeness. In the teaching of Jesus love of neighbor is ranked equal to, or at least a close second to, love of God. In the First Letter of John (1 John 4:20) anyone who claims to love God while hating his or her neighbor is nothing but a liar.

Relationships among People

Fourth, relationships among people: One-on-one relationships, though crucial, are not to be equated in quality or value to group relationships. There is something qualitatively different between them. Group relationships are not simply an extension or elongation of dyadic ones. Cultivating a communitarian ethos requires something quite different. In this regard, Gestalt psychology makes an important contribution when it argues that the whole is greater than the sum of its parts. To capture this communal quality, I have coined the term *communiopathy*. By communiopathy, I refer to the sense and feeling of being a part of a group that transcends oneself and one's individual relationships even with people within the group. It has to do with a sense of belonging and participation, loyalty, and commitment that goes beyond the individuals to that corporate entity that the group is and represents.

Communiopathy then, is a form of group empathy shared within groups as well as felt 'for groups' by those both within them and outside of them. This calls for a systemic and structural approach to spiritual care, able to gauge the health-promoting and death- or disease-dealing ways in which groups may operate.

Relationships with Place, Space, and Things

Fifth, relationships with place, space, and things: Many people bear testimony to the fact that for them spirituality is deeply connected with material culture, space, nature, and place. Going up a mountain, walking beside a river, strolling on the shore of the ocean, swimming in the sea, walking in the forest or jungle—these and many other experiences in nature are often reported to be not only health-promoting but spiritual experiences in which one feels drawn closer to the divine. This is true of the land, rivers, mountains, and trees, as well as with works of creative arts, and the built environment.

POSTCOLONIAL IMPULSES OF SPIRITUAL CARE

Hellena Moon and I, in an anthology that is illustrative of postcolonial practices of spiritual care, have gathered "stories of care—care of self, care of others, and supportive communal practices that have sustained people—during the year 2020–21, so marked by the dual pandemics of COVID-19 and the unsettling racial violence against communities and individuals of color. The contributors to this volume are lawyers, parents, students, chaplains, educators, as well as other professionals. Stories here speak of relationality, nature, pilgrimages, cooking, etc. that are practices grounded in our humanity" (Moon and Lartey, Introduction, *Postcolonial Practices*, 15). Postcolonial spiritual care calls into question dominance and hegemony in human relations, seriously disrupting top-down, hierarchical, patriarchal, and paternalistic forms of "pastoral" or even "spiritual" care."

I would like, finally, to name three features of postcolonial spiritual care that characterize a pastoral theological contribution to the theory and practice of spiritual care. First, postcolonial spiritual care *celebrates plurality*. It affirms and celebrates the fact that, as in the words of Jesus in John 3: 8 "The wind blows where it wishes, and you hear its sound, but you do not know where it comes from or where it goes," so does spiritual care come from unknown places and in many and varied forms. In pastoral theological terms, it truly is a work of the Spirit of God, which impacts human spirits in profound ways.

Second, postcolonial spiritual care is necessarily *polyvocal*. It recognizes and encourages many voices to speak, practice, and be heard on both theory and practice of spiritual care. No one voice assumes a privileged position and exclusive right to speech with all others relegated to the place of hearers or consumers. All are both producers and consumers.

Third, postcolonial spiritual care advocates *courageous activity* unafraid of upsetting settled apple carts and confronting sacred cows. Such activity aims at healing, liberating, and empowering all, especially the many who have been silenced, marginalized, oppressed, or beaten down. At the end of the day, postcolonial spiritual care works for human flourishing everywhere humanity is to be found.

CONCLUSION

Postcolonial spiritual care operates for all human beings throughout the entire world, under the assumption that all are created in the image and likeness of God, the creator. No one is outside the scope or purview of the care on offer. It understands that as a direct result of being created in the image of God all humans are spiritual beings. In this reckoning what is spiritual about human beings is a capacity to relate, and this relational capacity constitutes the core and lies at the heart of every human person.

Based on an African anthropological presupposition of relational wholism as being characteristic of humanity—in other words, that "persons are relational beings in every respect—each component of their beings is relational," spiritual care seeks to nurture and enhance health in all dimensions of the relational network in which humans are embedded. The practice of spiritual care whether for individuals or communities, seeks and works to promote harmony and balance throughout the entire cosmos.[2]

REFERENCES

Au, W. and Cannon, N. *Urgings of the Heart: A Spirituality of Integration*. Mahwah, NJ: Paulist, 1996.

Lartey, E. Y. "Be-ing in Relation: The Goal of African Spiritual Practice." In *Postcolonial Images of Spiritual Care: Challenges of Care in a Neoliberal Age*, edited by E. Y. Lartey and H. Moon, 17–28. Eugene, OR: Pickwick Publications, 2020.

———. *In Living Color: An Intercultural Approach to Pastoral Care and Counseling*, 2nd ed. London: Kingsley, 2003.

Lartey, E. Y. and Moon, H., eds. *Postcolonial Images of Spiritual Care: Challenges of Care in a Neoliberal Age*. Eugene, OR: Pickwick Publications, 2020.

Moon, H. and Lartey, E. Y., eds. *Postcolonial Practices of Care: A Project of Togetherness during COVID-19 and Racial Violence*. Eugene, OR: Pickwick Publications, 2022.

---

2. For a fuller exposition of "relational wholism" see Lartey, "Be-ing in Relation," 20–21.

PART 2

Perspectives from Different Religious Traditions

10

What Is Spiritual Care? An Islamic Perspective

Mahmoud Abdallah

BASIC KNOWLEDGE AND INTRODUCTION

Spiritual care as inter-professional care in the hospital context is gaining increasing attention and is challenging the traditional forms of Islamic pastoral care ("IPC"). However, ambivalence concerning the concept of care within Islam becomes evident through a multitude of publications. There is a fundamental difference of opinion in Islamic discourse regarding the terminology of Islamic pastoral care and its positioning within the scientific community. Definitions often either stand side by side or are in conflict with one another. Some definitions place IPC close to dogmatics and the normative doctrine and make the "self-edification" and "maintenance" of the Muslim community its object (cf., Abdallah, *Islamische Seelsorgelehre*, 90–114). The impression arises that this is not so much a matter of "knowledge" but of "ability." The reference to *aṭ-Ṭibb ar-Rūḥānī*—Abū Bakr Zakarīya ar-Rāzī (d. 313/925), and Ibn Qayyim al-Ǧawziyya (d. 751/1350)—in order to locate the new discipline in the lineage of the Prophet, Islamic pastoral care is often directly linked to religious topics such as prayer and zikr (remembrance of God) and attributes the authority of interpretation to a particular religious current. In doing so, it is often not asked how the diversity of the Islamic tradition presents itself and how it can be incorporated into a comprehensive understanding of Islamic pastoral care. Theological approaches can be divided into four categories: 1. systematic-theological approaches, 2. virtue-ethically oriented approaches, 3. ritual-based approaches and 4. pragmatic-historical approaches (cf., Abdallah, *Islamische Seelsorgelehre*, 122–24; and Dziri, "Muslimische Seelsorge im Aufbruch," 13). The attention that Islamic pastoral care attracts raises the question of the professionalization and quality assurance of this new research and career field. On the one hand, the aim is for Islamic pastoral care to emancipate itself from the professional structures of the Christian churches (Schmid, 2020); on the other hand, one might argue that it has a lot to learn from them. With its centuries-old traditions and firmly established structures, already-existing Christian pastoral care services can serve as inspirations and resources for Muslims who (want to) work as spiritual caregivers in secular public institutions. Secondly, the question arises about possible concepts in regard to cooperation with people of other faiths and perspectives on life. And thirdly, the interrelationship between Islamic pastoral care and other disciplines of Islamic theology has not yet been clarified.

This situation is echoed—at times even subconsciously—in the discussion about spiritual care in Islam. In this context, translations pose a particular challenge for international publications from German-speaking regions and possibly for this chapter as well. How can we convey the Christian-influenced concept of (Islamic) chaplaincy that is so common within German-speaking countries into English? Do we speak of (Islamic) chaplaincy, (Islamic) pastoral care, or (Islamic) spiritual care? Despite its importance, this discussion is not taken into account in my article. To me, it appears to be a context-specific question that receives little attention beyond the German-speaking world. In England and the Netherlands, for example, colleagues speak of Muslim chaplaincy (Gilliat-Ray, Ali, and Paterson, *Understanding Muslim Chaplaincy*; Ajouaou and Bernts, "Imams and Inmates"); in the Canadian context, the literature speaks of spiritual care or of counseling Muslims in the US (cf. Meier et al., 2005; and Ahmed and Amer, *Counseling Muslims*). In this article, I speak of spiritual care in a phenomenological sense, i.e. it is about a relatively new development, which claims to consider the spiritual dimension of the person as part of medical care and thus does not only want to leave it to professional pastors.

WHAT IS SPIRITUALITY?

"Spirituality" is a widespread term according to both emic and etic concepts to describe the (individual) search for meaning in today's society, and attracts increasing attention as well as much criticism and praise. "The use of the term is thus openly formulated and immanently oriented." (Mezger, *Religion, Spiritualität, Medizin*, 25) However, according to Roser, this openness is precisely one of the term's strengths. It lies in its ability to connect with the most diverse forms of searching for and giving meaning in a religiously and ideologically pluralistic society (Roser, "Seelsorge," 246). The European Association for Palliative Care (EAPC) supports the opinion that "spirituality is universal, deeply personal, and individual" (Best et al., "EAPC White Paper," 3).

In Arabic, spirituality has an etymological reference to soul or spirit. The term immediately evokes the hidden and transcendent and conveys a sense of inner peace and blessing. In the Arabic language, "spirituality" literally means—depending on the context—*rūḥānīya*, *rūḥīya* or *ma'nawīya*. But all these lexical meanings, which in English can mean either spirituality or counseling, but cannot describe Islamic spirituality in its conceptually comprehensive meaning. Polat defines spirituality as follows: "Spirituality is first and foremost a spiritual longing and search for the eternal truth (al-Ḥaqq) and as an experience of this truth" (Polat, "Spiritualität als pädagogischer Ansatz," 107). According to Isgandarova, Islamic spirituality is based on three key concepts, namely Iman (the belief to be safe), Islam (to be integral and not to disperse), and taqwa (piety or God-consciousness), the source of Islamic spirituality (Naser, *Islamic Spirituality*). According to him, the Qur'an is the origin and source of all that is Islamic, including, of course, the spirituality and grace of Muhammad and the entire spiritual path that starts from the substance of the Prophet (Naser, 53). According to Naser, the concept of spirituality in Islam is associated with a journey to the proximity of God, to the inner, imperishable and immaterial—a connection to the mystical that can also be found in the sources of spiritual medicine (*Islamic Spirituality: Foundations*, xvii).

In this sense, spirituality in Islam has to do with character building (cf., Isgandarova "Islamic Spiritual Care"; Polat, "Spiritualität als pädagogischer Ansatz"). It is based on an anthropological concept, namely the expression of moral aspiration (Chilian et al., "Zur moralischen Dimension"). Spirituality is not merely a search for meaning but is also and very importantly considered to be the realization of consciousness in thought, feeling and action. "Spiritual/mental development is at the same time to be understood as development in moral judgment and behaviour" (Polat,

"Spiritualität als pädagogischer Ansatz," 113). We can determine from these statements that spirituality simultaneously encompasses both spiritual and intellectual activity. In this case, we can speak of a mutual relationship between spirituality, values, feelings, and actions. From an Islamic point of view, the realities of a person's life include not only his material and social needs, but also his inner world of feelings and experiences, namely his spirituality (Polat, "Spiritualität als pädagogischer Ansatz," 112). Thus, spirituality is considered a form of re-education of the soul, a spiritual localization of the self within the universe, an ontological and functional search for identification, and ultimately a process of finding identity in the face of and through dialog with all that exists. From this meaning-seeking and meaning-giving interpretation, a morally and religiously qualified way of life should develop (Q 22:46).

This led some researchers to use the term *tasawuf* as the Arabic equivalent of spirituality. Islamic Sufism, however, strives for an interpretation that does not exclusively concern itself with transcendence. Instead, it is also an interpretation of life and the world, an imaginary and active description of the relationship of the self with God, fellow human beings, and nature (e.g., Polat, "Spiritualität als pädagogischer Ansatz"; Tittus-Düzcan, "Spiritualität"). Sufism aims at enriching faith with love, mercy, and compassion and strives to contribute to people shaping their achievements as acts worthy of both God and humanity. Spirituality would then not be understood as a state of areligious or agnostic spirituality, but as a religious ability that facilitates the convergence and interrelation between religious expectations and profane realities of life (Polat, "Spiritualität als pädagogischer Ansatz," 112).

Spirituality keeps alive the idea that faith is actually an inner process, and that religiosity should be its outward expression, because otherwise, it would be compulsion. Together with faith-based spirituality as an affective guide, people's inherent mind can lead to self-orientation, self-knowledge and self-commitment. This—inner—mature guidance is very valuable in terms of pastoral care. Polat regards spirituality as an educational process in the sense that it entails the following of religious rules. If this inner guidance is accompanied by trust in God, empathy, compassion towards people, and vigilance (sensitivity) towards ego and one's own tendencies, it can contribute to the development of a morally demanding religiosity. In his work "The Elixir of Happiness," al-Ġregard repeatedly emphasizes that absolute happiness can only lead to true knowledge of God through self-knowledge, i.e. the understanding of the relationship between heart and body. This, in turn, brings about absolute happiness; a state in which a person has completely surrendered to God, no longer attaches any importance to the world, and is no longer plagued by suffering (cf. al-Ġandi, 2017).

In contrast to piety and religious spirituality, a different kind of spirituality can be observed in today's secularized world. The term generally stands for radical individuality in an environment that is designed for generalizations and comparisons in diagnostics, therapy, and care. This understanding focused on the religiosity of spirituality is challenged in the context of spiritual care with a use of the term spirituality that points to an unconventional and individually defined religion or religiosity (see Glicksman and Glicksman, "Apples and Oranges").

Spirituality is understood as an inner state and attitude without a theologically defined binding content of faith and may be seen as a spiritual alternative to religion. Empirical studies show that palliative patients also associate spiritual care with interpersonal encounters, i.e. locate it as a relational dimension in care (see Edwards et al., "Understanding"). It focuses on the individual and his or her recovery and not so much on the cultivation of character or the re-education of moral values. Ignoring the development may work for a short time. In the long term, however, it will prove to be a disruption to Islamic pastoral care practice. Last but not least, the consideration of spiritual beliefs in the recovery of patients or in their ability to cope with illnesses has proven its effectiveness, so much so that spirituality is increasingly regarded as an essential dimension of holistic care (see Frick, "Spiritual Care").

In an Islamic-anthropological sense, spirituality specifically describes the dynamic connection between the immanent and the transcendent, between body and the soul, the physical and the sacred: thus, the spiritual does not stand in contrast to the physical; rather, the consideration of body and soul as a unity is an essential part of Islamic anthropology. It is therefore important to note at this point that Islam also ascribes spirituality to other creatures. The Qur'an sees itself as a source of meaning and spirituality. At the same time, however, it recognizes that spirituality is not limited to this. Meaning and interpretation can also be initiated and accompanied by other creatures and phenomena. Understanding human existence as God's grace and understanding human reason and maturity as reasons for responsibility go hand in hand with the task of understanding the universe and recognizing the signs of God in it. Both holy scriptures and material resources such as water, food etc. are sources of spirituality.

Accordingly, Sura 25 describes material resources such as rainwater as a purification of the soul and a sign of God's mercy in addition to divine revelation (cf., Q 25:1 and 25:48). This is accompanied by a reorganization of instances of a spiritual nature: the self, others, religious practice and their relationships with each other, as well as the universe. In this sense, spirituality can not only be of a religious nature but can also encompass aspects of a natural nature, so that the whole universe is seen as the source of spirituality. In this sense, one speaks of the written book, *al-kitāb al-masṭūr*, and the seen book, *al-kitāb al-manẓūr*. An Islamic understanding of spirituality can at least protect spirituality from being marketed as a product, commodity, or service due to the vagueness of the term. It is just as important to ensure that the discourse does not degenerate and lead to demarcation by attempting to popularize the spirituality of the East against the materializing civilization of the West (cf., Nehring, "Spiritualität im religiösen Pluralismus," 60).

SPIRITUAL CARE

In pre-Islamic times, a primitive concept of medicine and healing prevailed, which was partly influenced by popular beliefs and ideas about sorcery. The calling of Muhammad did nothing to change this. The Qur'an itself does not deal with the subject of medicine and treatment, but describes God as the cause of healing (Q 26:80), although the Qur'an addressed numerous other areas of human life in detail and proposed regulations. When the Qur'an speaks of physical illness, it speaks only in terms of those who are sick enjoying relief to the point of exemption from religious commandments (Q 2:184; 2:196; 5:6; 9:91; or 48:17).

The Qur'anic discourse on illness, on the other hand, only concerns the soul, the mind, or the heart as well as neurotic illnesses such as sadness and anxiety (Q 2:10; 5:52; 8:49; or 22:46). For the healing of such illnesses, the Qur'an consistently points to spirituality as a means of gaining inner peace (Q 10:12; 13:28; 16:53; and 21:83), thus drawing attention to the connection between spirituality and coping with hardships. This led to a rich discussion about the interrelationship between body and soul (Hajatpour, "Islamische Seelenvorstellungen"; Kamran, "Psyche und Seele"). It is therefore obvious to say that the Qur'an speaks of spiritual care, either directly through spiritual guidance or indirectly by freeing the person concerned from commandments/prohibitions and, if necessary, curbing the mental impairment that can arise from religious obligations.

The prophetic tradition, on the other hand, devotes numerous texts to the subject of medicine. In the major collections of hadiths, such as those of al-Buḫārī, Muslim, at-Tirmiḏī or ibn Māǧa, there are chapters of varying length entitled *kitāb aṭ-ṭibb* (chapters on medicine). The Prophet strengthened the sick by treating the sleep of the sick as worship and their moaning as praise of God. Sayings that promise the sick that their prayers of supplication will be accepted, their sins forgiven, etc., already show their spiritual character. Here, too, a "strict division of health and religion, of body and soul" (Karle, "Chancen und Risken," 58) is hardly to be found. This literature is considered the basis for a medical culture that focuses on the influence of spirituality on the soul and, if necessary, on the healing of the body and on the human being as a holistic being in both health and illness. "Instead, such medical framing should be viewed as key in a conception of the spirit as similar to the body, requiring treatment and care, and consequently, also requiring medicine and physicians to help it" (Ragab, *Piety and Patienthood*, 134).

This practice was enriched with the use of Greek terms and entered Islamic history under the title of prophetic medicine *aṭ-ṭibb an-nabawī* (Ullmann, *Islamic Medicine*, i–iv). Seeking healing through religious rituals such as prayers, supplications, fasting or zikr is a well-established tradition among Muslims (cf.,Tittus-Düzcan, "Spiritualität"). According to Aḥmad ʿĪsā Bek, foundations that promoted the healing of (mentally) ill people through music, sounds, etc. already existed in the 9th–10th centuries (cf. ʿĪsā Bek, *Tarīḫ al-bīmāristānāt fī al-Islām*). The task of those working in such foundations can be described, in the words of the British pastoral care theorist Nolan, as a "hopeful presence" that conveys hope "no longer as hope for recovery, but hope now as hope beyond recovery" (Nolan, *Spiritual Care*, 95, cited in Roser, "Seelsorge," 250). These show that a "culture of care" (Roser, "Seelsorge," 248) was cultivated in Islam from the very beginning, which included caring for the sick and providing social and spiritual services to them and their relatives. The sick were required to work financially for about 15 days upon discharge so that they would be forced to work and face a setback (cf., Abdallah, *Islamische Seelsorgelehre*, 105–108). The Muslim philosopher al-Fārābī (d. 950) described the interrelationship between body and soul as early as the 10th century as follows: "the body is sick when the soul is weakened, and it is impaired when it is impaired: therefore the healing of the body is done through the healing of the soul, by restoring its powers and bringing its substance into right order with the help of sounds that can do this and are suitable for it" (al-Fārābī, "Über den Ursprung," 19).

ISLAMIC SPIRITUAL CARE WITHIN THE CONTEXT OF A CHARGED RELATIONSHIP AMONG THEOLOGY, ETHICS, AND MEDICINE

The Islamic understanding of body and soul as a unity whose two components support and influence each other characterizes Islamic medicine, ethics, and philosophy. Ethics are seen as a kind of "medicine of the soul" (Adamson and Pormann, *Philosophy and Medicine*, 3). A certain connection between morality and medicine as well as a terminological approximation of the good with the healthy runs through this genre of literature (cf., Adamson, *Health*, 104). Muslim physicians contributed to the development of an integrated study of medicine and philosophy, especially of moral philosophy and philosophical psychology. Accordingly, spiritual care in Islam represents a combination of medicine, ethics, and theology and requires an interdisciplinary approach and inter-professional cooperation in order to succeed. Medical practitioners "usually used medicine as a methodological paradigm for ethical studies and, on the other hand, used philosophical theories to explain some of their medical concepts" (Javadi, "Spiritual Medicine," 217).

This genre of literature, which I refer to as counseling literature, shows that in the Islamic traditions, there was a scholarly discourse on "pastoral care" that went beyond concern for the self and one's own soul (in the sense of Foucault, e.g., "Die Ethik der Sorge um sich als Praxis der Freiheit") but went further and developed concepts for dealing with suffering, comforting oneself and others in the event of illness, loss, conflict, prison or homesickness in the diaspora. This literary genre suggests methods for increased resilience and spiritual guidance in times of demanding and taxing situations, a kind of disaster and suffering ethic—for dealing with emotions of discomfort. It is noticeable in this type of literature that "it . . . offers practical tips and everyday solutions with reference to concrete emotional stress situations" (Özkan-Rashed, *Die Psychosomatik*, 137) and has certain structures that can be compared with spiritual care today.

The scientific subject of such literary works is the human being with his or her physical and emotional burden. Abū Zayd al-Balḫī (d. 934), for example, speaks explicitly of internal and external forms of therapy for negative experiences, emotions and feelings. These forms of therapy are intended to protect the patient who is plagued by obsessive conversations. As the title of his work suggests, the text is conceived in two parts and includes medical treatment and prophylaxis for the body on the one hand and external and internal remedies for the soul on the other. The inner remedies include, above all, useful thoughts (spirituality) that help the soul to endure bad circumstances and support the search for meaning. External remedies include listening to healing music and socializing with other people who can help by giving reminders, good advice or spiritual inspiration.

Friends—or today spiritual consultants—should act as mentors when acting and instructing with regard to spiritual health. This support triggers relaxation reactions and restores an individual's confidence in his own abilities. Furthermore, al-Balḫī recommends to the mentally ill person that he should satisfy his needs for nourishment by enjoying food and drink, sexual pleasures, music and beautiful images, as all of these would abhor sorrow (cf., al-Balḫī, *Maṣāliḥ al-abdān wa al-anfus*, 142–45). Loneliness and turning away from pleasure, which many sick people tend to do, would only harm the patient more. Spiritual guidance helps the soul, just as good food makes the body healthy and thus regain its strength. The genre of counseling literature suggests that spiritual care within the Islamic tradition is understood as a lived and intellectually developed spirituality that aims to make people aware of their inner experiences. An approach for today's patient- and family-oriented model as well as physical and spiritual self-care can be further elaborated on. (It seems reasonable to say that such an approach is given for a pre-model for the well-known patient- and family-oriented approach and body and spiritual self-care.)

The Heidelberg-based historian Schipperges describes this intertwining of religion and health in Islam as follows:

> We have . . . to take into account that Islam is the only high religion that already has the word "health" in its title and has thus made this central concept the foundation of its world view and way of life. "s l m" = "salam" means all-round well-being of body, soul and spirit, i.e. healing. The reflexive form of "salam" is "islam," the total devotion to salvation. Anyone who professes this salvation is a "Muslim." (Schipperges, *Gesundheit und Gesellschaft*, 25)

Two sciences came into being as a result: "the science of healing and the science of medicine. The 'ḥākim', the theologically informed jurist, acted as the representative of the science of healing. The representative of medicine was the 'ḥakīm', the philosophically trained physician" (Schipperges, *Gesundheit und Gesellschaft*, 25). In practice, this division still prevails today. We can see that medicine had no inhibition in using different aspects as a model in developing a medical approach that can help—even if that should lead to the philosophizing of medicine (Adamson, *Health*). The recovery of the patient was central. We are all concerned with the patient's well-being, whether we are doctors, pastoral caregivers, or nurses—in other words: "We are all in the same boat."

ISLAMIC SPIRITUAL CARE: CHALLENGES AND POSSIBILITIES OF INTERFAITH CAREGIVING

"As a special relationship, spiritual care is a response to the spiritual need of another involving caring gestures such as a reassuring presence in the time of loss, a gentle touch in a time of pain, a prayer in time of need, a listening ear in time of confusion, the validation of another's emotions or cry of distress, or the celebration of new-found meaning" (Schipani, 113).

This meaning is congruent with the understanding of Islamic pastoral care, which encompasses concern for questions of faith and meaning, existential needs, emotional aspects, cultural aspects, quality of life, social support, relationality, and character development of the person seeking help and has been exemplified and established as an "indispensable and fundamental way of human interaction" in Islam (Ziemer, *Seelsorgelehre*, 14). Through the example of the Prophet in his spiritual and therapeutic care for and support and accompaniment of sick people, this practice became an Islamic commandment. Numerous traditions highlight the sick person's entitlement to visits from friends or fellow believers and, taking things a step further, draw up guidelines for talking to the sick. "When you are with [someone who is] sick, tell him good things (positive things about health), because this helps the sick person, but it does not change his condition (literally fate)."

It can be argued that visits to the sick are placed in the realm of spirituality, as in Islam both health and illness are seen as coming from God. Those who visit the sick and assist them with as much sincerity and presence as possible experience a mutual exchange of divine grace and mercy. The same, in fact, also applies to doctor-patient relationships. These traditions suggest that spiritual care also means perceiving the reality of people's lives, taking an interest in how people live, what they are shaped by, etc. Spirituality, therefore, is not a contradiction to materialism and the soul is not in opposition to the body. The commandment to assist people in times of crisis (Abdallah, "When a Crisis Empties Mosques," 223–39) and anguish also applies to non-Muslims. This means that Islamic spiritual care—in contrast to the traditional understanding of spirituality—must not perceive spirituality as a part of religiosity or ethics and character formation. Ultimately, Islamic spiritual care must be committed to or engage with pastoral professional ethics. An example of this is the code of the American Association of Pastoral Counselors (AAPC). It sets out seven ethical principles for professional practice, including 1. recognizing the commitment to different theologies, traditions, value systems, and faith communities and the recognition of the dignity and worth of each individual; and 6. inter-professional cooperation within an interdisciplinary network (cited in Schneider-Harpprecht, "Die Person des Seelsorgers," 199). This requires a compassionate and responsible attitude of solidarity on the part of chaplains in order to act in accordance with the demands of their profession. The challenge of Islamic spiritual care is how to develop patient- and client-centered concepts for a secular context from the tradition described above so that it contributes to the development of a free, liberating, and individually designed practice of spirituality. To this end, it is essential to build a consensus on a definition of spiritual care that is "compatible with both theological and therapeutic professional groups as well as representatives of different religions and worldviews" (Roser, "Seelsorge," 246).

Islamic pastoral care can be characterized by four aspects: Mercy, protection of life, human dignity, and letting oneself be touched by the suffering of others. It shows parallel tasks and structures with spiritual care. Both put the individual person at their center, work in an interdisciplinary and interreligious manner, are located in secular institutions, and can be marked by "particularly high spirits with regard to the own and the new" (Drechsel, 2014, 62, cited in Reichenbach, "Seelsorge," 258). Spiritual care differs significantly from ISC in that, among other things, the former promotes the target group's ability to reason and make decisions on the basis of transparent knowledge, while the latter seeks to shape faith through the spiritual and ritual practice of religious practice. Spiritual care is advantageous for Islamic pastoral care in a certain sense. It will advance interdisciplinarity and open up the profession to new groups, new practices, and new worldviews.

This is where I see great potential for Islamic pastoral care to connect with spiritual care. Birgit and Andreas Heller speak of five ethical principles with regard to spiritual care: "compassion/empathy, responsibility, non-intentionality, humility, and service" (Heller and Heller, *Spiritualität und Spiritual Care*, 35). These values can be found again in the Prophet Muḥammad's accompaniment of people in stressful situations, as I showed using the example of ʿAmmār *ibn Yāsir* (d. 657) (see Abdallah, "Islamische Seelsorge ohne religiöse Unterweisung," 391–92). Nonetheless, today in particular the perception of diverse spiritual-religious paths must be further sharpened and the offer of discussion in the religious-spiritual landscape must be conceptually opened and further developed. This is where Roser's distinction seems useful to me. He suggests distinguishing between everyday spirituality and faith spirituality. "The conscious distinction enables the differentiated intertwining of a general spiritual care and a special pastoral care of the faith community." (Roser, "Seelsorge," 249) To accomplish this successfully, Islamic pastoral care must initiate a profound discussion about the image of the human person in Islam. Accompanying clients in their religious and spiritual practices must not be deductive or normative, but distributive, i.e. it does not specify what this practice should look like, but rather engages with the individual perspective (Roser, 2019).

In an article from 2016, I set out to show that the image of humanity should be rethought if ISC also aims at benefitting people of other faiths or people who describe themselves as spiritual but not religious. At least five aspects need to be considered: religion, religious diversity, intra-Islamic plurality—via tolerance—by appreciating differences, and social support (Abdallah, "Bei den Menschen sein"). In practice, this means refraining from giving advice and proposing solutions, concentrating on "being" rather than acting, and not equating spiritual care with the pursuit of ethical and religious perfection. Islamic spiritual care thus encompasses—according to Foucault's perspective—those measures "which enable the individual, by his own efforts or with the help of others, to carry out a series of operations on his body or soul, his thinking, his behavior and his mode of existence, with the aim of changing himself in such a way that he attains a certain state of happiness, purity, wisdom, perfection, or immortality" (Foucault, *Technologien des Selbst*, 26).

REFERENCES

Abdallah, M. "Bei den Menschen sein." Islamische Seelsorge und soziale Arbeit. Neudenken des Menschenbildes im Islam." In: Khorchide, M. and Karimi, M., eds., *Jahrbuch für Islamische Theologie und Religionspädagogik: Was ist der Mensch?* 5 (2016) 147–76.

Abdallah, M. "Islamische Seelsorge ohne religiöse Unterweisung! Zur ethischen Dimension Islamischer Seelsorge am Beispiel von Schulseelsorge." In *Wege zum Menschen* 76 (2024) 379–92.

Abdallah, M. *Islamische Seelsorgelehre. Theologische Grundlegung und Perspektiven in einer pluralistischen Gesellschaft* (Theologie des Zusammenlebens—Christliche und muslimische Beiträge = ThdZ 4). Ostfildern: Grünewald, 2022.

Abdallah, M. "When a Crisis Empties Mosques: A Case Study of Muslim Responses to the Pandemic's Challenges in Regards to Spiritual Care and Communal Rituals in Austria and Germany." *International Journal of Practical Theology* 26/2 (2022) 223–39.

Adamson, P. and Pormann, P. E. *Philosophy and Medicine in the Formative Period of Islam*. London: Warburg Institute, 2017.

Adamson, P. "Health in Arabic Ethical Works." In *Health: A History*, edited by P. Adamson, 105–35. New York: Oxford University, 2019.

Ajouaou, M. and Bernts, T. "Imams and Inmates: Is Islamic Prison Chaplaincy in the Netherlands a Case of Religious Adaptation or of Contextualization?" *International Journal of Politics, Culture, and Society* 28 (2015) 51–65. https://doi.org/10.1007/s10767-014-9182-y.

Ahmed, S. and Amer, M., eds. *Counseling Muslims: Handbook of Mental Health and Issues and Interventions*. New York: Routledge, 2013.

al-Balḫī, A. Y. *Maṣāliḥ al-abdān wa al-anfus*, edited by. M. Badrī, M. and M. ʿAšawī, M. Riyāḍ, Saudi Arabia: *Markaz al-Malik Fayṣal li al-buḥūṯ wa ad-dirasāt al-islamīya*, 2010. (Orig. publ. 1424 after hijra.)

al-Fārābī, A. N. "Über den Ursprung der Wissenschaften (*De ortu scientiarum*): Eine mittelalterliche Einleitungsschrift in die philosophischen Wissenschaften." In

Beiträge zur Geschichte der Philosophie des Mittelalters, edited by C. Baeumker, vol. 19, no. 3. Münster: Aschendorff, 1916.
Best, M., Leget, C., Goodhead, A. and Paal, P. "An EAPC White Paper on Multidisciplinary Education for Spiritual Care in Palliative Care." *BMC Palliative Care* 19 (2020) 9. https://doi.org/10.1186/s12904-019-0508-4.
Chilian, L., and Coors, M. "Zur moralischen Dimension von Spiritualität im Gesundheitswesen. Eine ethische Perspektive auf Spiritual-Care-Diskurse." *Zeitschrift für Evangelische Ethik* 67 (2023) 22–33.
Dziri, A. "Muslimische Seelsorge im Aufbruch—Konzepte theologischer Fundierungen." In *Muslimische Seelsorge in Kanton Zürich*, edited by H. Schmid, and A. Lang, 12–15. Freiburg: Schweizerisches Zentrum für Islam und Gesellschaft, SZIG Papers 8. https://folia.unifr.ch/unifr/documents/308891.
Edwards, A., Pang, N., Shiu, V. and Chan, C. "The Understanding of Spirituality and the Potential Role of Spiritual Care in End-of-life and Palliative Care: A Metastudy of Qualitative Research." *Palliative Medicine* 24/8 (2020) 753–70.
Foucault, M. "Die Ethik der Sorge um sich als Praxis der Freiheit." In *Foucault, Ästhetik der Existenz: Schriften zur Lebenskunst, mit einem Nachwort von Martin Saar*, edited by D. Defert, and E. Ewald, E., with F. Lagrange, translated (from French to German) by M. Bischoff, U. Bokelmann, H.-D. Gondek, and H. Kocyba, 253–79. Frankfurt: Suhrkamp/Fischer, 2007.
Foucault, M. *Technologien des Selbst*. Edited by R. Martin, L. H. Martin, W. Paden, K. Rothwell, H. Gutman, and P. H. Hutton, P. H., translated (from French to German) by M. Bischoff. Frankfurt am Main: Fischer, 1993.
Frick, E. "Spiritual Care zwischen Kirche, Theologie und Medizin." *Epistula (Herzogliches Georgianum)* 61 (2012) 20–26.
Gilliat-Ray, S., Ali, M., and Patterson, S. *Understanding Muslim Chaplaincy*. Ashgate AHRC/ESRC Religion and Society Series. Farnham: Ashgate, 2013.
Glicksman, G. G. and Glicksman, A. "Apples and Oranges: A Critique of Current Trends in the Study of Religion, Spirituality, and Health." In *Handbook of Bioethics and Religion*, edited by D. E. Guinn, 333–44. Oxford: Oxford University, 2006. https://doi.org/10.1093/0195178734.003.0016.
Hajatpour, R. "Islamische Seelenvorstellungen und die Herausforderungen der Moderne." In *Grundlagen muslimischer Seelsorge: Die muslimische Seele begreifen und versorgen* edited by T. Badawia, G. Erdem, and M. Abdallah, 73–88. Research. Berlin: Springer, 2020.
Heller, B. and Heller, A. *Spiritualität und Spiritual Care: Orientierungen und Impulse*. Palliative Care. Boston: Hogrefe, 2018.
'Isa Bek, A. *Tarīḫ al-bīmāristānāt fī al-Islām*. Damascus: al-Maṭbaʿah al-Hāshimiyah, 1939. Facsimile https://sites.dlib.nyu.edu/viewer/books/nyu_aco001201/1.
Isgandarova, N. "Islamic Spiritual Care in a Healthcare Setting." In *Spirituality and Health: Multidisciplinary Explorations*, edited by A. Meier, A., T. St.J. O'Connor, and P. L. VanKatwyk, 85–104. Waterloo, ON: Wilfred Laurier University, 2005.
Javadi, M. "Spiritual Medicine in the Muslim World with Special Emphasis on Rāzī's Book." In Barcelona: Edicions de la Universitat Barcelona, 2008.
Kamran, T. "Psyche und Seele—eine mystische Betrachtung." In *Grundlagen muslimischer Seelsorge. Die muslimische Seele begreifen und versorgen*, edited by T. Badawia, G. Erdem, and M. Abdallah, 127–36. Berlin: Springer, 2020.

Karle, I. "Chancen und Risken differenter Systemlogiken im Krankenhaus." *Spiritual Care* 7/1 (2018) 57–6.

Mezger, M. *Religion, Spiritualität, Medizin: Alternative Religiosität und palliative Care in der Schweiz*. Bielefeld: Transcript, 2018.

Naser, S. H., ed. *Islamic Spirituality: Foundations*. World Spirituality 19. London: Routledge, 2008.

Nehring, A. "Spiritualität im religiösen Pluralismus." In *Spiritualität: Theologische und humanwissenschaftliche Perspektiven*, edited by L. Allolio-Näcke and P. Bubmann, 47–61. Stuttgart: Kohlhammer, 2022.

Nolan, S. *Spiritual Care at the End of Life: The Chaplain as a "Hopeful Presence."* London: Jessica Kingsley, 2012.

Özkan-Rashed, Z. *Die Psychosomatik bei Abū Zaid al-Balḫī, Mit einer Reproduktion der zweiten Abhandlung von Abu Zaid al-Balhis Handschrift Masalih al-abdan wa-l-anfus in Faksimile*, 2nd ed. Düren u. Maastricht: Shaker, 2016.

Polat, M. "Spiritualität als pädagogischer Ansatz: Eine islamische religions- und moralpädagogische Betrachtung." *Zeitschrift Österreichisches Religionspädagogisches Forum* 25 (2017) 107–16.

Ragab, A. *Piety and Patienthood in Medieval Islam*. Routledge Studies in Religion. London: Routledge, 2018.

Reichenbach, C. K. "Seelsorge als geistliche Begleitung." In *Seelsorge im Plural*, 2nd ed., edited by U. Pohl-Patalong and A. Lüdtke, 255–65. Berlin: EB-Verlag, 2019.

Roser, T. "Seelsorge als Spiritual Care." In *Seelsorge im Plural*, 2nd ed., edited by U. Pohl-Patalong and A. Lüdtke, 244–254. Berlin: EB-Verlag, 2019.

Schipperges, H. *Gesundheit und Gesellschaft: Ein Historisch-Kritisches Panorama*. Schriften der Mathematisch-naturwissenschaftlichen Klasse 12. Berlin: Springer, 2013.

Schneider-Harpprecht, C. "Die Person des Seelsorgers als Gegenstand der Seelsorge." In *Handbuch der Seelsorge: Grundlagen und Profile*, edited by W. Engemann, 182–205. Leipzig: Evangelische Verlagsanstalt, 2016.

Tittus-Dužcan, R. "Spiritualität in der islamischen Seelsorge." In *Grundlagen muslimischer Seelsorge. Die muslimische Seele begreifen und versorgen*, edited by T. Badawia, G. Erdem, and M. Abdallah, 137–50. Berlin: Springer, 2020.

Ullmann, M. *Islamic Medicine*. Edinburgh: Edinburgh University, 1978.

Ziemer, J. *Seelsorgelehre. Eine Einführung für Studium und Praxis*. Göttingen: Vandenhoeck & Ruprecht, 2008.

11

The Muslim Counseling Helpline (MuTeS)

An Example of Spiritual Care from an Islamic Perspective

Mohammad Imran Sagir and Omar Adham Youssef

The Muslim community in Germany, largely composed of migrant workers who arrived in the 1960s and 1970s, traditionally relied on family, friends, self-help groups, worker unions and mosque leaders for support in religious and existential matters, emphasizing a strong cultural community bond. Contrasting socio-economic backgrounds between European and American Muslims reveal greater integration challenges for European Muslims due to laborer roles and lower incomes, while American Muslims tend to integrate more fully into society. MuTeS, an organization providing spiritual care through a phone helpline, is embedded in an Islamic framework, aiming to address these challenges. This chapter explores MuTeS's approach, staff training, and the complexities of integrating religion and spirituality into phone counseling, concluding with practical examples to illustrate theoretical concepts in practice.

MUTES

The Muslim Telephone Helpline (MuTeS—**Mu**slimische **Te**lefon-**S**eelsorge) was founded in 2009 to offer anonymous telephone counseling to the predominantly Muslim community in Germany. Addressing a wide range of issues such as depression, employment, marital conflicts, and racism, MuTeS operates round-the-clock with a team of 67 volunteers. Since its inception, it has fielded over 72,000 calls. Even amidst the COVID-19 pandemic, during which it saw a 50% surge in call volume, only a small fraction related directly to the virus, which suggests robust familial and societal support in Germany. MuTeS attempts to fill gaps in mental health services, particularly within the Muslim community, providing culturally sensitive assistance grounded in Islamic values. It confronts the stigma surrounding mental health, advocating for seeking help, including therapy, while upholding principles of anonymity, confidentiality, and data protection.

Unlike other counseling services that often have lonely older callers as their demographic, MuTeS primarily assists younger callers who find themselves grappling with their problems alone, offering a safe and respectful environment regardless of religion. It aims to address concerns of confidentiality, language barriers, boundary maintenance, and cultural awareness, emphasizing inclusivity by welcoming both Muslims and non-Muslims to share their struggles without fear of judgment. Through such efforts, MuTeS strives to empower individuals to overcome the stigma of mental health and to encourage to engage the support they need, including therapeutic interventions, from other providers such as therapists or counselors.

THE ISLAMIC FRAMEWORK EMBEDDED AT MUTES

MuTeS, deeply rooted in Islamic principles, integrates religiosity and spirituality into its counseling framework. It emphasizes the significance of intentionality in religious practices, considering them as manifestations of one's spiritual stance. Motivated by Islamic teachings, volunteer counselors emulate Prophet Muhammad's compassion and forge interfaith alliances to care for those in distress. The organization underscores the importance of spiritual support, drawing upon hadiths and Qur'anic verses advocating for visiting the sick and alleviating others' concerns. Spiritual support is crucial not only during phone conversations but also in times of illness, as emphasized by the following hadith Qudsi, a divinely inspired form of prophetic tradition:

> On the Day of Resurrection, Almighty God will say: "O son of Adam, I was sick, and you did not visit Me." He will say: "O Lord, how could I visit You when You are the Lord of the worlds?" God will say: "Did you not know that one of My servants was sick, and you did not visit him? Did you not know that if you had visited him, you would have found Me with him?" (von Denffer et al., *Allahs Gesandter*, 235)

In counseling sessions, religion serves as a source of trust and comfort for Muslim callers, while respecting the preferences of those of different faiths or having no belief. MuTeS employs Islamic principles like patience, steadfastness, and gratitude, and may incorporate prayers or Qur'anic readings based on the caller's religious context and counselor's competence. In Islam, even everyday actions and practices can take on a spiritual significance when done with the intention of pleasing God. This is supported by a famous saying of Prophet Muhammad, "Deeds are according to intentions!" (Schaible, *An-Nawawi*, 8). It highlights that in Islam, the true value of a virtuous act lies in the intention behind it, emphasizing that religiosity is expressed through one's spiritual stance (Sagir, "Das Muslimische SeelsorgeTelefon").

Alongside the Qur'an and the traditions of Prophet Muhammad, MuTeS upholds five Islamic maxims essential for humanitarian services: protection of religion, life, intellect, family, and property. These values manifest in MuTeS's daily practice, including safeguarding reason during psychological distress, preserving family unity in conflicts, intervening in thoughts of suicide or violence, addressing existential needs or addictions to protect property, and guiding individuals towards purposeful living to protect religion (Hamidullah, *Muhammad*). Overall, MuTeS embodies an empathetic and pastoral approach rooted in Islamic teachings, extending support to individuals in need within and beyond the Muslim community.

THE ROLE OF RELIGION AS A MEANS OF PASTORAL CARE

> Have you not considered how Allah presents an example, [making] a good word like a good tree, whose root is firmly fixed and its branches [high] in the sky? It produces its fruit all the time, by permission of its Lord. And Allah presents examples for the people that perhaps they will be reminded. And the example of a bad word is like a bad tree, uprooted from the surface of the earth, not having any stability.
>
> —SURAT 'IBRĀHĪM 14:24–26

Religion holds a pivotal role in MuTeS, providing a sense of security and motivation for predominantly Muslim callers. While MuTeS doesn't position itself as an informational service about Islam, religious elements such as the Islamic greeting may be integrated into counseling sessions as valuable sources of encouragement, if instigated by the caller. The organization only delves into religious matters if initiated by the caller, respecting their approach.

In specific counseling situations, attitudes like patience (*sabr*), steadfastness (*istiqamah*), and gratitude (*shukr*) are integrated, aligning with the caller's preferences. Suggestions such as prayers and Qur'anic readings are offered for calming practices. Depending on the caller's religious context and the counselor's competence, examples from the Qur'an, the life of the Prophet, or the wisdom of Muslim scholars may be introduced to provide strength, consolation, or meaning. These contributions are well-received by callers, irrespective of their faith backgrounds. Interestingly, individuals from different faiths also express appreciation and deep emotion in response to such sentiments. Occasionally, at the end of a conversation, a *dua'* (supplication/prayer) is collectively offered, guided by the explicit wishes of the caller or if it aligns with the conversation's nature.

In addressing moral dilemmas or fears of divine retribution, discussions on repentance, God's mercy, and His constant forgiveness offer solace and reassurance to callers.

MUSLIM COUNSELING HELPLINE

MuTeS, the Muslim Counseling Helpline, offers a non-judgmental and inclusive space for individuals seeking understanding and guidance, regardless of their faith or background. Rooted in Islamic principles, MuTeS operates under key principles such as:

- *Understanding and Compassion*: There is no judgment, only a compassionate understanding of the caller's situation, which may involve various interpretations or views. Caregivers establish boundaries to prevent any misinterpretations.
- *Service to the Community*: MuTeS provides aid to anyone in need, irrespective of their denomination or creed, and topics discussed need not have Islamic relevance.
- *Islamic Framework*: While adhering to national laws and Islamic principles, MuTeS emphasizes understanding the humanity of the person without judgment.

- ***Multilingual Support***: Conversations primarily take place in German, with flexibility to accommodate callers' preference for languages including Turkish, Arabic, Moroccan Arabic, Urdu, and others.
- ***Anonymity and Confidentiality***: Both caller and caregiver enjoy complete anonymity, with no personal data or contact information exchanged or documented. Conversations remain confidential, enhancing caller trust, and are used for training and supervision purposes in anonymized form.
- ***Free of Charge***: MuTeS services are provided without charge to any caller, ensuring accessibility to all.
- ***24/7 Reachability***: MuTeS is accessible around the clock, including holidays and weekends, although occasional limitations may occur due to its volunteer-based nature.

These principles ensure MuTeS provides a safe and supportive environment for those in need, upholding its mission of offering compassionate assistance rooted in Islamic values. The goal is to foster a supportive space where individuals can express their thoughts about their situations. Through conversations guided by counselors, callers can gain insights, understand their emotions better, and share their burdens (Klessmann, *Seelsorge*).

THE IMPLEMENTATION OF A RELATIONSHIP-PROMOTING ATTITUDE

Other than the previous principles presenting the structural framework of MuTeS's concept, these are 9 fundamental guidelines that focus on the interpersonal level between caregiver and caller, which is promoted throughout the screening and training of the caregivers and beyond:

1. ***Acceptance***: Callers are embraced without judgment.
2. ***Caller-Centric Approach***: Conversations prioritize the caller's perspective.
3. ***Emotional Connection***: Caregivers build trust and empathy through emotional rapport.
4. ***Collaboration, not Argumentation***: Possible next steps are discussed together, encouraging the caller to adapt a solution that's suits for them, without trying to persuade them of one's own views.
5. ***Emotional Awareness***: Caregivers maintain sensitivity by reflecting on their own emotions.

6. ***Non-Judgmental Attitude***: Callers are respected without judgment.
7. ***Contextual Understanding***: Caregivers grasp the caller's situation within their context.
8. ***Caller-Centered Focus***: Caregivers adjust their approach to meet caller needs.
9. ***Equality***: Callers are treated as equals, fostering respect and trust.

Volunteer selection focuses on suitability, with comprehensive training covering self-exploration, religious inputs, and practical skills relevant to counseling. Ongoing evaluation and improvement are ensured through a quality circle. Training activities include group discussions and interactions with trainers from diverse religious backgrounds.

MuTeS addresses suffering from an Islamic perspective, emphasizing divine destiny and the belief in manageable burdens. With its commitment to inclusivity, MuTeS offers compassionate support to individuals in need, regardless of their background.

CASE STUDIES

The following examples highlight a range of MuTeS counseling-sessions, often centered on attentive listening without the need for immediate action. These exchanges capture the complexity of human experiences, including emotions like tears, laughter, and regret. However, challenges such as miscommunication and differing expectations can arise, impacting the effectiveness of the conversation. Some callers may also need time before they feel ready to fully discuss their issues, prompting them to reconnect later for further support.

Case A: A Moral Dilemma

During the early hours of the night, a young man in his twenties reached out, conveying a profound sense of unease and an inability to find solace or sleep since returning home an hour or two earlier. During his journey home, he had accidentally collided with a parked car but chose not to report the incident to the police. Now, he sought guidance on how to address this situation in accordance with Islamic principles and feared potential police investigation and penalties. Upon delving deeper into the details of the situation, the focus shifted to exploring ways the caller could alleviate his conscience and act in accordance with his personal Islamic values. It became evident that he recognized the necessity of reporting the incident to the police to avoid repercussions for a hit-and-run. Contemplating whether or not to report it, he grappled with the time discrepancy. In addressing this dilemma, the counseling work centered on fortifying the caller's resolve and encouraging him to follow through with the decision to report the incident. Despite lingering concerns about potential penalties, the caller experienced relief by the end of the call, knowing that he was choosing the right course of action in alignment with his Islamic principles.

Case B: Pregnancy Conflict

In the afternoon, a non-Muslim German woman in her late 30s contacted MuTeS to discuss her pregnancy dilemma. Already a mother of two, she found herself in the second month of pregnancy with a third child, conceived after a separation from her husband in an attempt to reconcile. However, it became apparent that reconciliation was not in their future, prompting her contemplation of abortion. The counselor inquired if she was aware that MuTeS was a Muslim service, not to discourage her but to ensure she had intentionally sought this service and was aware of its nature. The caller clarified that she intentionally chose MuTeS as a Muslim service, anticipating a stricter stance on abortions. The counselor affirmed this expectation, explaining that, in Islamic contexts, abortions are generally allowed only for medical reasons. This transparent approach also conveyed the counselor's uncertainty in handling such a challenging topic with a non-Muslim caller.

The ensuing discussion weighed the pros and cons in context of her personal reality of a potential abortion, independent of the beliefs of the counselor, acknowledging that the ultimate decision rested with the caller, to ultimately empower her to resolve her own conflict. The caller weighed the decision of abortion based on her desire to reconnect with the father and concerns about being a single mother, while also considering the child's right to life. Importantly, she asserted that it had not been morally right, from her standpoint, to conceive the child solely to bind the father to her. Expressing positive feelings toward the child, she hesitated to proceed with abortion to avoid a guilty conscience about the father. The counseling process supported her through this journey, offering understanding and space for introspection. By the conversation's end, she felt more confident in her decision to carry the child, seeking further clarity on its alignment with the child's best interests and her own moral stance.

Case C: Marriage-Seeking Young Man with Commitment Issues

A young man in his mid-20s called in the middle of the night. He came from a Muslim family with roots in the Balkans. He was sitting in his car because he couldn't find peace at home. The restlessness stemmed from the fact that, on the day of his engagement to a woman from the Arab cultural circle, he had declined a possible marriage. He felt guilty because she cried due to this rejection. He knew that this refusal was mainly due to his fear of commitment, which arose from two long, unhappy relationships where he was abandoned. Six months ago, he had started actively practicing his religion. His mother was also a practicing Muslim, and his father, while Muslim, only practiced occasionally. He had a good relationship with both parents. He also brought up his father's opinion that a marriage across cultural boundaries would not work well, even though he wasn't really against it.

The counselor, allowing the caller to express his situation, identified three key themes: guilt toward the former fiancée, commitment issues, and paternal resistance. The caller sought guidance on addressing these challenges. Acknowledging that commitment issues were the primary factor; the counselor affirmed the caller's viewpoint and discussed the father's perspective.

Together, they developed a step-by-step approach. They developed a plan together, with the caller aiming to discuss his commitment issues with his former fiancée. The counselor recognized potential disappointment but supported the decision, agreeing to address the father's concerns later. Counseling prioritized active listening and support, with minimal emphasis on Islamic aspects. The counselor's closing dua' provided comfort, leaving the caller feeling more determined to address his challenges.

CONCLUSION

In conclusion, MuTeS operates within a Muslim framework, incorporating spirituality and religiosity even in cases where religion is not explicitly discussed. Spiritual elements such as Qur'anic verses and supplications are integral to the service, reflecting the team's Islamic understanding that every action has a spiritual dimension. This approach, coupled with an open and non-judgmental stance, allows MuTeS to effectively assist Muslim and non-Muslim seekers, without the intention to proselytize.

MuTeS caregivers undergo comprehensive training, emphasizing the importance of understanding Islamic faith and addressing daily challenges faced by Muslims. The service provides one-on-one counseling via phone, empowering individuals to navigate their life situations using systemic resources. Additionally, MuTeS offers spiritual pastoral care for reflection and guidance, operating anonymously and free of charge. Through its holistic approach and commitment to inclusivity, MuTeS serves as a valuable resource for individuals seeking support, embodying the principles of compassion, understanding, and empowerment within the Muslim community and beyond.

REFERENCES

Hamidullah, M. *Muhammad, Prophet des Islam: Sein Leben, Sein Werk*. Ostfildern: Patmos, 2016.
Klessmann, M. *Seelsorge: Begleitung, Begegnung, Lebensdeutung im Horizont des christlichen Glaubens*. Neukirchen-Vluyn: Neukirchner, 2015.
Sagir, M.I. "Das Muslimische SeelsorgeTelefon: Ein Projekt mit vielen Dimensionen." In *Handbuch Christentum und Islam in Deutschland*, edited by M. Rohe, M. Khorchide and H. Engin, 2426–45. Freiburg im Breisgau: Herder.
Schaible, T., ed. *An-Nawawi, Riyad-us-Salihin*, Vol. 1. Garching, Munich: Dar-us-Salam, 1996.
Surat ʿIbrāhīm. Quaran.com, 2024. https://legacy.quran.com/14/24-30.
von Denffer, A., el-Shabassy, E., el-Shabassy, O., and Waltter, A. *Allahs Gesandter hat gesagt*. Lützelbach: Haus des Islam, 1984.

12

Spiritual Care in Light of COVID-19: A Jewish Perspective

Mychal B. Springer

It's wonderful to be invited to contribute to this anthology of the IASC (International Association for Spiritual Care). To frame where I am coming from, I am a hospital chaplain, a Conservative rabbi and a certified Educator in ACPE: *The Standard for Spiritual Care and Education*. I stopped working in the hospital when my older daughter was born, 20 years ago—I continued to do the work but at the Jewish Theological Seminary, where I created the Center for Pastoral Education. In May 2019, I came back to the hospital setting at New York Presbyterian Hospital in Manhattan. I was so excited to be back in a hospital environment. Of course, I never could have imagined what that year would bring with the COVID-19 pandemic. I have given thanks every day for having the opportunity to be here, to be part of our team, and to have provided care during that challenging time. As an Educator the focus of my position is supervising chaplain residents. But during the height of the pandemic we shifted all chaplains' focus to direct care and, as it happened, I was serving as the interim rabbi at one of the campuses at that period. So every day I visited patients, spoke with family members, and took care of staff, and it's those experiences that I want to draw on.[1] Here at the outset, I want to give thanks to my students, colleagues. and friends, who taught me so much and accompanied me in the whole-being work that being present during COVID-19 required.

In a crisis, we call on what we know; we call on the foundations that we have laid. A disciplined spiritual life requires that we have to be laying those foundations all the time, because we don't know what will happen. What are my foundations?

As we entered into COVID-19, this rabbinic passage was before me all the time. (All the texts are Hebrew and Aramaic texts, but I'll mostly present them here in English, for the diversity of our readers.)

> Therefore but a single person was created in the world, to teach that if anyone has caused a single life to perish from Israel, that one is deemed by Scripture as if they had caused a whole world to perish; and anyone who saves a single soul from Israel, that one is deemed by Scripture as if they had saved a whole world. (Mishnah Sanhedrin 4:5;[2] adapted for gender neutral language)

This text was in front of me because, with the sheer numbers of people who were afflicted with COVID-19 and continue to be afflicted today, the image of a person as a whole world came to me over and over again. We all descend from the same first person, Adam, so all of humanity throughout the world comes from one person. And with each death that I witnessed and each death that I heard about from others who witnessed them, I felt the loss of a whole world. The severity of that loss and the need to continue to cherish each person as a whole world was a guiding principle for me, because it would have been too easy to get lost in the numbers.

Our morgues were filled to overflowing and soon there were refrigerated trucks out in the parking lot with human beings waiting to be picked up, so that they could be buried. Two of my friends and colleagues, Chaplain Linda Golding and Chaplain Jenny Kent, provided great leadership early on paying attention to the morgues—paying attention to the people who were working in the morgues, paying attention to the distress of the people who were worried about their loved ones who could not be in the proper facilities, and paying attention to what was happening to people whose bodies were being stored in the parking lot. So Linda organized a virtual *shemirah*—the guarding of deceased bodies—dividing up the Psalms

---

1. Key identifying information about patients and families has been altered or withheld to protect the identities of patients and their families.

2. Except where otherwise indicated, citations of texts were accessed on Sefaria.org, *Living Library of Torah*, https://www.sefaria.org/texts.

among the whole community of people who would recite Psalms and hold these people in mind. Jenny would walk by the refrigerated trucks every day and she brought me with her one day. I made it my practice to look, pause, and say a prayer for our beloved human beings who were waiting in those trucks. Each person is a whole world.

And the Mishnah continues:

> Again [but a single person was created] to proclaim the greatness of the Holy Blessed One; for humans stamp many coins with one seal and they are all like one another; but the King of kings, the Holy Blessed One, has stamped every human with the seal of the first human, yet not one of them are like another. Therefore everyone must say, "For my sake was the world created." (Mishnah Sanhedrin 4:5; adapted for gender neutral language)

Now, this part of the text continues that theme of the preciousness of each human being. While the first passage designates "Israel," the impact of causing a "soul from Israel" to perish or be saved, this continuation of the Mishnah broadens into a statement celebrating the distinctiveness of every human being. By reaching all the way back to Adam, it powerfully includes all of humanity in its teaching. Each life is precious and unique. And it adds that each person has to say, "For my sake was the world created," which gives each of us a sense of purpose and efficacy, even in the moments when we feel least able to help. "For my sake the world was created," and I have an obligation to act in this world, with the recognition that my actions matter. And in a time of overwhelming loss and need we have to feel capable, even as we feel incapable. The spiritual imperative is to feel that what I can contribute is what I was born to contribute, I was born for this moment, every day going to work, knowing there's so much I can't do. And yet, I was born for today. And the world was created for today. And the world was created for me to do what I can on this day.

Michelle Friedman spoke beautifully in our IASC webinar about *contagion*—the fears of contagion and the inadequacy of the PPE and the difficult decisions that needed to be made, or that we anticipated would need to be made, about scarce resources. The Talmud discusses what it is to visit the sick, and some of the danger we encounter in visiting them. One passage explores a *baraita*. A *baraita* is the oldest layer of the Talmud, composed by rabbis who mostly lived in the first two centuries of the Common Era, known as *tana'aim*. The *baraita* takes a verse, Exodus 18:20, and in a classic *tannaitic* move associates each phrase with an action that we are commanded to perform. The verse says: "And you shall teach them the statutes and the laws, and shall show them *the path* wherein *they shall walk* and the action that they must perform" (Exodus 18:20; emphasis added).

The *baraita* says that the word הדרך "the path," teaches us to perform *gemilut hasadim*, acts of kindness, and the word ילכו, "they shall walk," teaches us about *bikkur holim*, visiting the ill. But the Gemara—compiled around the year 500 CE—takes issue with the parsing of the verse:

> The Gemara analyzes the *baraita*. The Master said: With regard to the phrase "they shall walk," that is referring to visiting the ill. The Gemara asks: That is a detail of acts of kindness; why does the *baraita* list it separately? (Babylonian Talmud Bava Metzia 30b)

The *Gemara's* question concerns a perceived duplication between acts of kindness and visiting the sick. Isn't visiting the sick an example of an act of kindness? Why do we need a whole separate category? According to Talmudic reasoning, there should be no meaningless duplication; every phrase has a unique meaning.
The Gemara answers:

> The reference to visiting the ill is necessary only for the contemporary of the ill person, as the Master said: When one who is a contemporary of an ill person visits him, he takes one-sixtieth of his illness. Since visiting an ill contemporary involves contracting a bit of his illness, a special derivation is necessary to teach that even so, he is required to go and visit him. (Babylonian Talmud Bava Metzia 30b)

The *Gemara* resolves this problem of a seeming duplication by pointing out that they are actually different. Unlike *gemilut hasadim, bikkur cholim* involves a unique risk. When "a contemporary" visits the ill, that visitor takes away one-sixtieth of the ill person's illness. You might think that the contemporary might not be required to visit the ill, that only people who want to take on this risk would do so. The creation of the special category of *bikkur cholim* teaches us that, nevertheless, despite the risk, the contemporary is required to go and visit the ill.

The phrase in Hebrew for "contemporary" is *ben gilo*, someone your same age, someone who is like you (Kestenbaum, "The Gift of Healing Relationship," 6–7). When we visit someone who is like us, there is a special contagion that happens. So, for me, in this epidemic, the moment when I felt that contagion the most was when I got a call from a woman whose husband was dying and she was completely bereft, in a very palpable way, on the phone, telling me, pleading with me, that I had to help save him. The doctors had determined that he was dying and this woman was convinced that if her husband could hear her voice, if he could be surrounded by prayer, if he could see her, if he could receive care, that he would continue to live. She had a very strong spiritual sensibility. And that pleading got me in the *kishkes*—which means your literal and metaphorical guts—and gave me a very acute stomachache. Not while I was caring for her, but later.

I spoke with the doctor about this patient. This doctor had seen many patients in this situation and was certain, based on all of his medical knowledge and experience, that this patient was going to die. And this wife was refusing to let her husband die. And so, I did everything she wanted. I advocated with the staff. She emailed me pictures and prayers that I printed out and we put them in her husband's room and we arranged for her to FaceTime visits with her husband every day. I couldn't go in the room, because of the PPE situation,[3] but these visits impacted her husband's fate, and he lived, and he went home. Her husband's fate had not, in fact, been sealed.

Now, I wish I could say that this happened for everyone. But we know that it didn't. But sometimes it did. And part of providing spiritual care is being willing to risk failing, because sometimes people do live, and I want to be on the side of hope, I want to be on the side of being ridiculous. Because the doctor may say that this man is dying. But we are not in charge of life and death. We are only in charge of the hope that we bring and the fervent nature of the prayers as we facilitate and advocate for the spiritual wellbeing of the patients and the families, who are willing to do everything they can think of to partner with the divine in leading to more life.

The Babylonian Talmud, in Tractate Brakhot, offers essential wisdom about spiritual care in the form of stories:

> Rabbi Ḥiyya bar Abba fell ill. Rabbi Yoḥanan entered to visit him, and said to him: Is your suffering dear to you? Rabbi Ḥiyya said to him: I welcome neither this suffering nor its reward. Rabbi Yoḥanan said to him: Give me your hand. Rabbi Ḥiyya bar Abba gave him his hand, and Rabbi Yoḥanan stood him up and restored him to health. (Babylonian Talmud, Berakhot 5b)

This text captures an essential Jewish stance toward suffering—it does not have to be embraced as meaningful. There is an embedded belief here that suffering leads to reward, but in the depths of his suffering Rabbi Hiyya bar Abba rejects this paradigm. Instead of arguing with him, or rebuking him, Rabbi Yohanan supports him and says: "Give me your hand." It is this act, this "Give me your hand" that is at the heart of Jewish spiritual care. Something happens in the giving of the hand, that enables Rabbi Hiyya bar Abba to stand up and be restored to health.

---

3. "PPE" refers to personal protective equipment and associated health precautions.

We might think that the essence of this healing resides in Rabbi Yohanan, who is a powerful rabbi. So it's important to continue in the text:

> Similarly, Rabbi Yoḥanan fell ill. Rabbi Ḥanina entered to visit him, and said to him: Is your suffering dear to you? Rabbi Yoḥanan said to him: I welcome neither this suffering nor its reward. Rabbi Ḥanina said to him: Give me your hand. He gave him his hand, and Rabbi Ḥanina stood him up and restored him to health. (Babylonian Talmud, Berakhot 5b)

In this continuation of the text, it is now Rabbi Yohanan who falls ill. Since we know that he has the power to help another stand up and be healed, we might think that he can do the same for himself, but in this passage Rabbi Yohanan is in need of the care of Rabbi Hanina, who asks the same question and says the same phrase: "Give me your hand." The Talmud asks this very question: "*Why* did Rabbi Yoḥanan wait for Rabbi Ḥanina to restore him to health? *Let Rabbi Yoḥanan stand himself up.* The Gemara answers, *they say: A prisoner cannot free himself from prison*" (Babylonian Talmud, Berakhot 5b).

The *Gemara* understands that what we can do for another we cannot do for ourselves. Even a great healer needs another person to extend the hand. There is something in the relationship between the person who is ill and the one who comes to visit, that enables healing to happen. And the *Gemara* draws an analogy to a prisoner. There is something about illness that constrains us and diminishes our power. But the extended hand of the other gives us access to healing and resilience that we do not possess on our own.

While I delivered the talk that this piece is based on in July, 2020, I am writing this adaptation in October, 2023, just three weeks after the terrorist group Hamas massacred over 1,200 Israelis—whole families, old people, babies—including citizens of 30 other countries, and dragged approximately 250 people into captivity. As we read the words of the Gemara: "They say: A prisoner cannot free himself from prison" I cannot help but think of the hostages who, please God, are still alive, praying that they will be redeemed from captivity. And they cannot free themselves. This reality brings home the truth that the world of the one who is suffering and the world of the ones who are in a position to extend a hand are inextricably connected. Even when we are not physically proximate, and even when the reality of war makes it challenging to secure their freedom, we must keep the captives in our prayers and not abandon them. According to Moses Maimonides, "There is no greater mitzvah than the redemption of captives" (Maimonides, "Mishneh Torah, *Sefer Zeraim*, Gifts to the Poor 8:10," 1341). There is much more to say about being spiritual-care focused in the midst of mortal conflict, but I will leave that for another paper. For now, let me simply state that Judaism deeply values all human life, as I have articulated above.

Returning to our passage in the Talmud, the relational act at the heart of the healing in the stories of Rabbi Yohanan, "Give me your hand" echoes the book of Job, where friends come to comfort Job:

> When Job's three friends heard about all these calamities that had befallen him, each came from his home—Eliphaz the Temanite, Bildad the Shuhite, and Zophar the Naamathite. They met together to go and console and comfort him. When they saw him from a distance, they could not recognize him, and they broke into loud weeping; each one tore his robe and threw dust into the air onto his head. They sat with him on the ground seven days and seven nights. None spoke a word to him for they saw how very great was his suffering. (Job 2:11–13)

In this first moment of encountering Job, his friends fall silent in recognition of his distress. This is arguably the most spiritually attuned moment in their attempts to comfort Job. Presence—joining someone in their inconsolableness—is a greater source of comfort than words. And eventually Job begins to speak, articulating his lament. Almost as if he cannot help himself, Eliphaz the Temanite begins to speak at length. Eventually he says:

> See how happy is the man whom God reproves;
>   do not reject the discipline of the Almighty.
> He injures, but He binds up;
>   He wounds, but His hands heal.
> (Job 6:17–18; New JPS, 1985, p. 1346)

In these words, we hear an echo of the question that the rabbis ask: "Is your suffering dear to you?" and the response: "I welcome neither this suffering nor its reward." While Eliphaz emphasizes the happiness of someone who embraces their suffering as just, as something that will bring a person closer to God, Job is of the school of the rabbis, rejecting the suffering and maintaining that it is not just. Instead of trying to get Job to repent, Job's friends would be wiser to stand with him in his protest, to embrace his lament. This is what Rabbi Yohanan and Rabbi Haninah model when they give room for the one who is sick to disavow the value of their suffering and extend a hand to lift him up.

This image of extending a hand lends itself to being understood, metaphorically, as other acts of spiritual sustenance. An essential piece is offering prayer, as we read in the following text, from Rabbi Moses Maimonides' *Mishneh Torah*:

> When one comes to visit a sick person, one should not sit on a bed, nor on a chair, nor on a bench, nor on a high place, nor above the invalid's head. Instead, one should wrap oneself in a tallit, sit below the sick one's head, *entreat God for mercy on the sick one's behalf* and depart. (Moses Maimonides, *Mishneh Torah, Sefer Shoftim,* Mourning 14:6; emphasis added and adapted for gender neutral language)

When I began my journey as a chaplain I was afraid that people might want me to pray for them. What scared me is that I did not believe that prayer is effective. This belief—or non-belief—troubled me greatly. How could I offer prayer if I did not believe God would respond to those prayers? This bind led me to feel like a fraud. I have endless gratitude for my first ACPE Educator, Sr. Theresa Brophy, may her memory be for a blessing, who held me in these fears and both gave me the space to give voice to the experiences that shaped my non-belief and encouraged me to accompany the patients, seeing where our pastoral encounters would lead. I was blessed to care for a patient who wrestled with prayer as I did, Miriam. This woman in her 40s had terminal cancer. She told me that she wanted to pray but did not know how, and asked me if I would help her. I told her that I did not know how, either. While I knew many prayers in our prayer book, I did not know how to open my heart to the kind of prayer that she needed. But together we stumbled into prayers—and sometimes prayers for prayers. In the process, I discovered that if I allowed myself to offer the prayers, and worried less about how God would or would not receive the prayers, then the prayers themselves became efficacious. Miriam and I both experienced God with us as we found our way in prayer, and that was a source of great relief, especially as she moved towards dying, much too young.

Though I had journeyed with prayer over many years since my first experiments praying with Miriam, what was new for me in COVID-19 was that so much of the praying that I did was public, because I wasn't usually going in the rooms. I would stand outside the door of the hospital room and enter into prayer. And the staff would all watch me, because we were all on top of each other, and they would hear my prayer and they would witness my prayer, and mostly they wouldn't say very much. Sometimes they would engage me in conversation about it. One day I was outside the room of a woman who was dying. As I was praying for her, a doctor came over to me and she said, "What are you doing?" I introduced myself and she introduced herself. I then told her I was praying for the patient. As she looked at me, I could tell that these prayers meant something to her. She said to me, "Let's call the family together." And I felt that I had a partner in a whole new way.

We joined together and we called the family. They were amazed that we had initiated a call simply because a rabbi and a doctor had been outside the room of their dying mother. And we knew that our proximity gave us power.[4] By calling them we shared that proximity with them, and we enabled them to participate in the end of her life in a different way. When they were able to be outside her room for a brief visit, that was a tremendous gift to them. But knowing that those of us who were in the hospital were serving as a conduit, living in between the world of the hospital and the world beyond, in between this world and the next world, brought them tremendous comfort. Spiritual care providers serve a mysterious mediating role between the human and the divine. We hover on the threshold, between worlds. The Jewish relationship to the threshold is shaped by the *mezuzah*. The word *mezuzah* literally means doorpost, and it is commonly known as the small object that holds passages from the Bible, including those that instruct us to place God's words on our doorposts: "Inscribe them on the doorposts of your house and on your gates" (Deuteronomy 6:9, New JPS, 1985). The outside of the parchment on which the Biblical verses are written contains the name for God, *Shaddai*, which is also read as an acronym for *Shomer D'latot Yisrael*, Who Guards the Doors of Israel. There is an awareness that crossing the threshold has potential danger and we are in particular need of protection from the Divine. Inside the parchment is the *Shema*, the proclamation of God's oneness that has sustained the Jewish people, that we have lived by and died reciting. "Hear, O Israel! Adonai is our God, Adonai is One" (Deuteronomy 6:4). As spiritual caregivers we help people access spiritual sustenance, the protection that comes from being bound up with the Divine, even as we face the unknown, even as we transition into the next world, even as we face existential threats, we are not alone. שמע ישראל "Hear, O Israel! Adonai is our God, Adonai is One."

REFERENCES

Kestenbaum, I. "The Gift of Healing Relationship: A Theology of Jewish Pastoral Care." In *Jewish Pastoral Care: A Practical Handbook from Traditional and Contemporary Sources*, 1st ed., edited by D. Friedman, 3–15. Woodstock: Jewish Lights, 2001.
Maimonides "Mishneh Torah" In New JPS, *Tanakh: A New Translation of the Holy Scriptures According to the Traditional Hebrew Text*. Philadelphia: New JPS, 1985.
Sefaria.org. *A Living Library of Torah*. https://www.sefaria.org/texts.
Stevenson, B. *Just Mercy: A Story of Justice and Redemption*. New York: Delacorte, 2018.
Tanakh: A New Translation of the Holy Scriptures According to the Traditional Hebrew text. Philadelphia: Jewish Publication Society, 1985.

4. In my understanding of the power of proximity, I have drawn on "An Evening with Bryan Stevenson," author of *Just Mercy*, sponsored by the Jewish Community Center Manhattan on Oct. 10, 2018.

13

What Is Spiritual Care in Light of Crisis? from the Perspective of Orthodox Judaism

Michelle Friedman

I am honored to be included in this discussion of Jewish perspectives on spiritual care, in light of the stresses of the COVID-19 pandemic and the war between Israel and Hamas. I begin with a few words of personal introduction to give readers a sense of where I'm coming from. I am a psychiatrist and psychoanalyst in New York City. I maintain a private practice and also teach in two capacities, as an Associate Professor of Clinical Psychiatry at the Icahn School of Medicine at Mt. Sinai Hospital and at Yeshivat Chovevei Torah (YCT) Rabbinical School. Regarding the latter, for the past twenty years, I have been developing, directing, and teaching the pastoral counseling program at YCT, an Orthodox rabbinical seminary. There I have the privilege of teaching students committed to vocations in Jewish communal service as pulpit rabbis, chaplains, educators and other forms of leadership. Clergy out in the field reached out to me as well and I have facilitated pastoral counseling seminars in North America and Israel. My work amplified with the pandemic and has continued to escalate with the stresses of the October 7, 2023, Hamas attack on Israel and the ensuing war in Gaza.

The COVID-19 pandemic pushed issues of pastoral counseling to the limit. Ordinary citizens, government workers and health care professionals face conditions and crises not encountered in our lifetimes. Clergy of all faiths are called upon more than ever to comfort, support, and guide all strata of society. Looking across global faith traditions as well as the Jewish denominational spectrum, I feel that we have more in common than we have differences. As I am tasked with discussing specific issues and responses pertaining to Orthodox Judaism, I will first sketch an overview of Judaism and then touch on four areas in the context of the Orthodox community; medical, economic, the social and political moment, and pervasive isolation.

Judaism rests on two basic tenets, ethical monotheism and humankind's relationship with God as expressed through *mitzvoth*, specific actions rooted in daily activity. These *mitzvoth* derive from the Torah, the five books of the Bible (Old Testament), and encompass all areas of life ranging from marking time (Sabbath and holiday observance), diet, sexual life, prayer, charity, and medical care, to name some of the major areas. The differences between the denominations (Orthodox, Conservative, Reform, Reconstructionist, Renewal) can most simply be understood as the degree to which adherents see the Torah, or the written law, as the divine word of God and therefore binding, and to what degree they adhere to the traditional forms of the oral law, the *Halakha* (the exposition of Biblical law) as evolved through centuries of rabbinic interpretation. The degree to which Jews turn to rabbinic law for authority and guidance is highly correlated with the degree to which they embrace or eschew modernity and contemporary culture. I will note that certain commonly known traits, such as clothing and marital practices portrayed in movies about Hassidm, are rooted more in sociocultural history than a religious text.

COVID-19 imposed enormous challenges on the medical world. Health care professionals faced unprecedented situations of personal risk, triage decision-making, and emotional strain caring for large numbers of very sick and dying people who suffer in profound isolation. While we know that the virus is respiratory borne and therefore highly contagious, basic science has yet to clarify issues of vulnerability, treatment and immune status. Further complicating the picture was inadequate systemic preparation such as the lack of sufficient PPE (personal protective equipment). The anxiety of personal exposure as well as possibly transmitting COVID-19 to family at home added to the daunting challenges of providing medical care to identified patients. Participating in emergency cardiopulmonary resuscitation became a threat to all present as COVID particles would be aerosolized during the proceedings. Medical care itself was limited. Hospital workers felt demoralized by the deluge of extremely sick people for whom treatment was often supportive at best. This was especially pronounced during surges when, in addition to feeling that the virus was a largely unknown and scary entity, medical personnel also anticipated shortages of basic life-saving resources and equipment such as ventilators. As time went on, the confusion and chaos regarding mask wearing, testing, and efforts to find a vaccine added to the sense of a broken system.

Orthodox Judaism reveres the preservation of life. Observant healthcare providers turn to sacred text and rabbinic commentary for support on decisions such as personal exposure and triage of scarce resources. We at YCT conducted a Zoom conference in March on rationing care. Dr. Kenneth Prager, a pulmonologist and ethicist at Columbia/Presbyterian Medical Center in NY and Rabbi Dr. Jason Weiner, chaplain at Cedars Sinai Medical Center in LA discussed issues such a ventilator assignment in a time of potential scarcity and patient triage.

The isolation of the sick and dying imposes huge strains on medical staff. Trying to render treatment and comfort for severely ill and dying patients while garbed in layers of protective gear and managing anxiety about one's own health set up a situation in which caregivers spent little time at patients' bedsides. This further dispirited those on the medical front line as it flies in the face of years of training. Family members were also restricted from the bedsides of loved ones for fear of spreading the virus. These limitations also applied to chaplains who tried to offer supportive spiritual care to patients and families via phones and other remote devices.

The economic downturn accompanying the pandemic impacted all communities. For Orthodox Jews, religious life entails certain additional expenses. Families are often large, kosher food costs more, and religious schools require tuition. Many families already on the financial margins faced poverty and those who never needed assistance before and who may even have been pillars of charity themselves were hard hit. Schools and communal institutions were forced to furlough workers. All this adds to the burden of providing for basic needs and to the burden of humiliation, shame, and depression that accompanies severe financial crisis.

The Black Lives Matter movement further cast a spotlight on issues of social and political morality in this fraught time. Climate concerns and the partisan polarization with the 2020 presidential election added to the sense of urgency. While this was a difficult time, it was also an opportune time for value clarification for all communities, especially those with a strong faith base.

Orthodox Jewish life deeply lodges in communal structure. A basic quorum of ten men is required for the recitation of important prayers.

Limitations on the use of electricity on Sabbath and holidays made zoom services unusable during the pandemic. Observant Jews gather for lifecycle occasions such as circumcisions, bar and bat mitzvah celebrations, weddings, funerals and mourning rituals. Restrictions on gatherings impacted all of these basic hallmarks of daily Jewish community life. The general isolation imposed by the pandemic was especially hard on people living alone—elders and singles. Jewish spiritual leaders, educators and community leaders were using technology as much as possible to maintain human connection, provide religious support, guidance and celebration.

The attack of October 7, 2023, on Israeli civilians by Hamas terrorists represents the largest pogrom against Jews since the Holocaust. Unlike earlier waves of murder, rape and kidnapping in Jewish history that went unchecked, this assault was met by Israeli military action. Tragically, that war continues to rage at the time of this writing and has resulted in the suffering and deaths of thousands of Palestinian civilians.

Orthodox Jewish spiritual care faces huge challenges in the wake of October 7th. The enemy in the COVID-19 pandemic was a biological virus that attacked all human beings. While political and religious strife ensued with matters such as mandatory masking and vaccines, these paled in comparison to the issues and controversies raised after October 7th. In addition to the shock and horror of the attacks themselves, failure on the part of intelligence and military agencies to protect the people led to a deep crisis of faith in long vaunted Israeli strength. Uncertainty about actions taken in reprisal continue to roil Israeli citizens as well as Jews in diaspora communities.

On an immediate, most basic level, Israel could not cope with the huge death toll of October 7th. Jewish tradition teaches that burial happen as soon as possible, preferably within a day. The capacity of basic mortuary and funeral systems was overwhelmed by the devastation of the crime scenes at the site of the Nova Music Festival in the Negev and the ravaged kibbutzim. Uncertainty about who was abducted and difficulty in identifying burnt human remains further complicated the situation. Compounding the pain of not knowing who was dead and who was kidnapped were questions of theodicy—how could devastation of such magnitude befall young people celebrating life at a music festival? How could Holocaust survivors and members of some of the most liberal, peace-loving communities in Israel be slaughtered so viciously?

Psychological and spiritual care was and continues to be desperately needed. Zaka Search and Rescue, a religious volunteer group committed to dignified burial of human remains, came south to collect and properly care for body parts. Trauma experts and clergy continue to offer support to survivors, families of the murdered and kidnapped as well as to persons displaced from communities under threatened attack.

The ongoing war in Gaza has triggered an ongoing wave of protest inside Israel and throughout the world. The conflation of anti-Zionist, anti-Semitic and binary rhetoric employing the tropes of colonialism/anti-colonialism, oppressed/oppressor has engulfed college campuses and governments. Jews around the globe, who themselves hold divergent opinions about the war, experience unprecedented isolation and incidents of frank antisemitism.

Jewish history has vast experience with suffering and crisis. We draw on the power of our sacred texts and the received wisdom of long spiritual tradition to sustain belief that this painful time will pass into one of peace and appreciation of the joy of life.

14

Understanding Spiritual Care: A Christian View[1]

Daniel S. Schipani

The content of this chapter stems from years of clinical work, teaching and supervision, extensive research, and collegial consultation and collaboration. Such practical and theoretical work has been carried out with a Christian perspective that informs both a vision of reality and normative criteria regarding human life in community. That *location* therefore conditions the response to the question, "what is spiritual care?" offered in this chapter. That response will be presented *in italics* the following sections of this essay right after the heading that succinctly characterizes spiritual care generally across traditions and disciplines.

---

1. Some of the themes in this chapter—and many more concepts that are too extensive to be included here—are elaborated with case examples in Schipani, *Spiritual Care*.

SPIRITUAL DIMENSION: MANY (RELIGIOUS AND NONRELIGIOUS) "FAITHS," ONE HUMAN SPIRIT

> *Human life has a spiritual dimension[2] (also called the "human spirit") that is bio-psychologically grounded and socio-culturally fashioned. It manifests itself as a longing for wisdom with a search for meaning and truth, connectedness and communion, purpose and vocation. On the one hand, the spiritual dimension confronts spiritual (also called "existential") threats such as meaninglessness and emptiness, condemnation and alienation, and despair and sense of lostness. On the other hand, spiritual growth and revitalization (also called "inner healing") defines a flourishing life with enhanced creativity and character hallmarks such as love, peace, joy, generosity, courage, and more.*

Simply stated, we are humans because we are spiritual beings. The spirit is an essential dimension of being human; hence the Jewish and Christian claim about our being created in God's image according to the words of Genesis 1:26–27. So, *spirituality* can be understood as the ways in which our spirit manifests itself through searching for, experiencing ("inner" sensations), and expressing ("outer" manifestations) *meaning* (truth, wisdom, faith); *communion* with others, nature, the Divine, and oneself; and *purpose* (life orientation, vocation). The claim that these dimensions of spirituality—meaning, communion, and purpose—name fundamental experiences and expressions of our human spirit is based on consistent and converging confirmation stemming from various sources. Among these are evidence-based clinical work and supervision, study and comparative analysis of sacred texts across traditions, contributions from cultural anthropology, intercultural and interfaith case studies, and literature in the fields of pastoral and spiritual care, and spiritual direction in particular.

The construct of *spirit* is inseparable from that of *psyche*; so, the spiritual dimensions related to "longing" or "searching for" are viewed in continuity with ongoing psychic process and content. In other words, the *psychological* and the *spiritual* dimensions are integrated and inseparable—yet they are also distinct and distinguishable. Psychotherapist Russell Siler Jones says it well: The body-rootedness of 'spirituality' and 'religion' reminds us that spirit is inseparable from body. But spirit is also inseparable from 'psyche' and from the relational and social fabric of our lives . . . A spiritual experience is also a physical experience, a psychological experience, and a social

---

2. "Spiritual dimension" (and "spirituality," for that matter) is not meant a synonym for "religious dimension" (or "religiosity"). The category of spiritual dimension may include religion however viewed, experienced and practiced, but not necessarily so.

experience" (Jones, *Spirit in Session*, 37). The spiritual dimension is integrated and interwoven with all the other dimensions of human experience (mind, body, relationships, and more). It is present, affecting care receivers' health and wellbeing for better or worse. Implicit spiritual experiences occur at the fuzzy intersection of the psychological and the spiritual; and those explicit and implicit spiritual experiences are always a resource to draw upon in helping people stabilize, change, and heal (Jones, *Spirit in Session*, 9, 37–40).

In the case of Christian theology, this model can be related to Trinitarian anthropological conceptions developed through the history of Christian thought, from Augustine to Catherine LaCugna. Further, from a theological perspective a direct connection between these facets of the spiritual self and the gifts of faith, love, and hope can be visualized (see Figure 1 below). Possibly, caregivers from other traditions, including humanism, can also broadly consider the categories of (religious and nonreligious) faith, love, and hope, as potentially helpful to name main sets of existential experiences and spirituality as such. That consideration can in turn illumine the tasks of spiritual assessment, setting goals, and evaluation of caregiving processes.

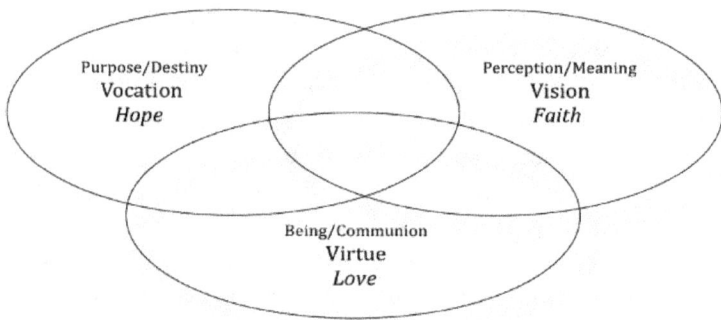

Figure 1. **Threefold Expression of the Wholesome Spiritual Self (within Family, Social, Global, and Cosmic Contexts)**

The heuristic potential of this model of the human spirit and spirituality has also been tested in research on the structure and dynamics of religious fundamentalism from a spiritual health science perspective. The toxicity of fundamentalism can thus be assessed across cultures and traditions in terms of religious trauma and the threefold collapse that characterizes all fundamentalisms as closed systems: collapse of meaning into dogmatism, a caricature of faith (epistemological failure); collapse of communion into sectarianism, a caricature of love (ethical failure); and collapse of purpose into proselytism/realized utopia, a caricature of hope (political failure) (Schipani, "Fundamentalism," 178–207).

The heuristic potential of the model can be realized also regarding the whole range of spiritual-moral struggles (Pargament and Exline, *Working with Spiritual Struggles*), including the category specifically identified as "moral injury" (Brock and Lettini, *Soul Repair*; Graham, *Moral Injury*; Kelle, *Moral Injury*). Testimonies of veterans from the Vietnam and Middle East wars point to the collapse of military indoctrination analogous to the fundamentalist system alluded to in the previous paragraph: ideology of nationalism/patriotism and "noble cause" (vision/meaning); clear cut division us/good-them/bad (virtue/communion); and "noble mission" that justifies sacrifice and destruction of enemies (vocation/purpose). Further, diverse expressions of psychological and spiritual distress include dealing with existential anxieties associated with meaninglessness, guilt-condemnation, despair and annihilation (Ramsay and Doehring, *Military Moral Injury*).

COMMON GROUND: WISDOM AS NORM, PROCESS, AND GOAL IN SPIRITUAL CARE

> *Diverse spiritual and religious traditions have explicitly addressed the spiritual dimension and its existential quests throughout millennia, as documented in sacred texts and other artifacts. They can be called wisdom traditions because they offer ways to growth in wisdom (or "spiritual-moral intelligence"[3]) and human wholeness. Philosophical and theological traditions started much later to also explicitly address the spiritual dimension. Further, the systematic scientific study of, and engagement with, the spiritual dimension in clinical psychology is relatively recent.*

Religious wisdom traditions are usually associated with the life of faith communities. They are both creators and custodians of those traditions while also being shaped, sustained, and transformed by them. Caregiving activities practiced within ("intra-faith") and in representation of religious communities ("interfaith") always connect directly with those wisdom traditions and their visions of reality and of human wholeness. Further, in addition to the more obvious question of caregiving goals that define resolution or the

---

3. The term, "moral-spiritual intelligence" is connected to the main understanding of *wisdom* as a holistic way of knowing that includes discernment, making good choices, and living well in community. Form a psychological point of view, there is abundant support for such understanding (Sternberg and Glück, eds., *Cambridge Handbook of Wisdom* and *The Psychology of Wisdom*.) It is also the case with main tenets of Positive Psychology (e.g., Keys and Haidt, *Flourishing*; Peterson and Seligman, *Character Strengths and Virtues*).

completion of a caregiving process, wisdom traditions share in common their applications in hermeneutic (interpretive) process—often practiced as a way of discernment and making wise choices. Comparative studies illstrate the commonality alluded to in the previous remarks (Schipani, *Multifaith Views*).

Recent writings explicitly representing Christian (Malony and Augsburger, *Christian Counseling*; see also chapters by Mombo and Son, this volume), Jewish (Friedman and Yehuda, *Art of Jewish Counseling*; see also chapters by Springer, and Friedman, this volume), Islamic (Hussein, *Islamic Counselling*; Bajwa *Mantle of Mercy*; see also Abdallah, this volume), Hindu (Chander and Mosher, *Hindu Approaches*), and Buddhist wisdom traditions (Sanford, *Kalyāṇamitra*; see also Luraschi, this volume) further help us to perceive not only the uniqueness and potential complementarity among those traditions but also considerable common ground in terms of normativity criteria, process, and goal.

Wisdom in the Jewish and Christian Biblical Traditions

Two main reasons undergird the proposal to reclaim wisdom as the heart of pastoral and spiritual care and counseling (Schipani, *Way of Wisdom*, 37–63). First, wisdom, a significant part of the biblical tradition and of the Judeo-Christian theological heritage, represents a unique way of doing practical theology. Second, biblically grounded wisdom language and orientation are especially suitable when redefining care and counseling as a psycho-spiritual practice. The following paragraphs explicate that rationale.

Taken as a whole, the biblical wisdom tradition presents a distinctive way of doing theology, for it deals with the fundamental questions of human existence and destiny in the light of divine action and will while focusing on everyday, mundane experience. Walter Brueggemann summarizes six aspects of scholarly consensus regarding biblical wisdom. Biblical wisdom is: (a) a theology reflecting on creation; (b) with lived experience as its data, generally not overridden by imposed interpretive categories or constructs; (c) in which experience is viewed as having reliability, regularity, and coherence, (d) including an unaccommodating ethical dimension; (e) a natural theology that discloses to serious discernment something of the hidden character and underpinnings of all of reality, i.e., what is given as true arises in lived experience rightly (or wisely) discerned; (f) a natural theology that reveals and discloses the God who creates, orders, and sustains reality—the generous, demanding guarantor of a viable life-order that can be trusted and counted on, but not lightly violated (Brueggemann, *Theology of the Old*

Testament, 680–81). This tradition offers guidance for wise living through both pedagogy and counsel. It defines wise people as those who daily seek the way of wisdom and walk in that way.

Jesus, Wisdom of God

For Christian caregivers and practical theologians any understanding of a biblically and theologically grounded view of wisdom includes a focus on the life and minstry of Jesus. The Gospels portray him as a teacher of wisdom and a sage guided by the vision of the reign of God. Scholars suggest that he would have been seen as a Jewish prophetic sage whose message and style reflected the confluence of Hebrew sapiential, prophetic, apocalyptic, and legal forms and ideas.

Jesus can be considered as the clue, both hermeneutically and existentially, to grasping the connection between the two foundational biblical motifs of God's reign (envisioned as normative culture and "beloved community") and wisdom in the light of God (discernment of how to live well within and for "Beloved community." Jesus communicated God's alternative wisdom, with an ethic and a politics of compassion particularly reflective of divine grace. His ministry thus became subversive as well as transformative and recreative because he confronted the established conventional wisdoms of his time; he challenged values, attitudes, practices, and understandings of goodness and wellness, and he transformed them (Borg, *Heart of Christianity*, 80–100; Levine, *Short Stories*). Jesus' style of ministry was consistent with the larger wisdom tradition and, specifically, with a biblically grounded wisdom in the light of God. Jesus' way of wisdom entails a counter-order—an alternative, subversive wisdom "from below"—against the status quo or the values of the powerful and the privileged in the context of neoliberal capitalism (Weiss, "Christian Care and Counseling," 144–61).

Biblically grounded and theologically viewed notions of wisdom blend moral and spiritual dimensions by presenting wisdom and becoming wise as living in accordance with the knowledge and the love of God. Further, God's wisdom is acknowledged as the ultimate ground and goal of our human endeavors to sponsor wholeness and fullness of life. Therefore, wisdom is claimed to be the heart of spiritual care that awakens, nurtures, and develops people's moral and spiritual intelligence. Caregiving is a unique setting which offers the possibility of becoming wiser, an extraordinary setting where formation and transformation are expected to happen ultimately as a divine gift.

Christian practical theologians have recently offered views on, and applications of, existential and practical wisdom consistent with the notions articulated in the previous paragraphs[4] (Bass and Dykstra, *For Life Abundant*; Bass et. al., *Christian Practical Wisdom*). For their part, researchers on the philosophy and psychology of wisdom coincide on highlighting the spiritual-moral dimension of wisdom (Hall, *Wisdom*; Boelhower, *Choose Wisely*).

DISCERNMENT AS PRACTICAL WISDOM

Discernment defines wisdom as a practice and discipline. Becoming wiser always involves the disposition and the capacity to discern not only the better means to reach our life goals, but especially which goals are truly worth valuing and seeking. Discerning is an indispensable process when one is confronted with existential challenges (for example, needing to make key vocational decisions) and struggles (for instance, facing the death of a loved one). Discernment, including deliberation and judgment, is thus a key to both process and content in spiritual care counseling, and it must be seen and guided as inseparable from the outcome(s) being sought (for example, making and implementing an important vocational decision, grieving in a wholesome way, healing). Put in the simplest terms, we behave wisely whenever we are able to discern what is the right thing to do, and act in such a way as to bring this about. In spiritual care, goals (caregiving objectives, expected outcomes, or *what for*) must be considered together with discernment as key to the questions of process (caregiving process, strategy, or *how*) and content (agreed-on caregiving focus, or *what*). The main role of spiritual caregivers is to guide the process, because guidance and wisdom go hand in hand.[5] The following section includes de description of such fundamental process in spiritual care practice.

COMMON GROUND: CAREGIVING ENCOUNTERS AND PATTERNS OF CREATIVE IMAGINATION

> *Throughout the ages and across cultures, diverse forms of caregiving practice have been available in order to focus on, engage, guide,*

---

4. It should be noted that our understanding of wisdom (*sophia*)—which includes apprehension and appreciation as well as critical reflection and an orientation to practice based on life experience—incorporates the Aristotelian notion of practical reason and knowledge with moral import and ends (*phrónēsis*).

5. There is indeed an interesting connection between *wisdom* and *guidance* in light of etymological considerations. The word *guide* comes from an ancient Romanic word *widare*, which means *to know*. The words *wise, wisdom, wit,* and *guide* all share the same origin.

> support, reorient and/or heal the human spirit thus understood. Fundamentally, as a compassionate response to human suffering (broadly speaking),[6] spiritual care is a special way (process) of companioning; and all forms of spiritual care have always consisted in connecting wisdom traditions with care receivers' spiritual resources, longings and struggles in socio-cultural and contextually pertinent ways. Such can be, therefore, a broad response to the question, "what is spiritual care?" Multiple forms of dialogical-narrative and hermeneutical process (i.e. discernment as practical wisdom) are normally involved in such ways of companioning.

Most kinds of caregiving situations such as counseling, psychotherapy, chaplaincy, and other helping professions, involve patterned partnerships. They are human encounters in which time and effort are invested in accompaniment as manifold expressions of *therapeutic love*. On the one hand, it is possible to trace developments in the specific ways that caregiving relationships have been structured and performed through the centuries and across cultures. On the other hand, it is also possible to identify persistent continuity in the fundamental pattern(s) of caregiving practice. The work of Catholic practical theologian Maria Harris unveils a remarkable analogy to the fundamental form (*Gestalt*) of caregiving relationships, as depicted in Figure 2 below (Harris, *Teaching*, 23–40):

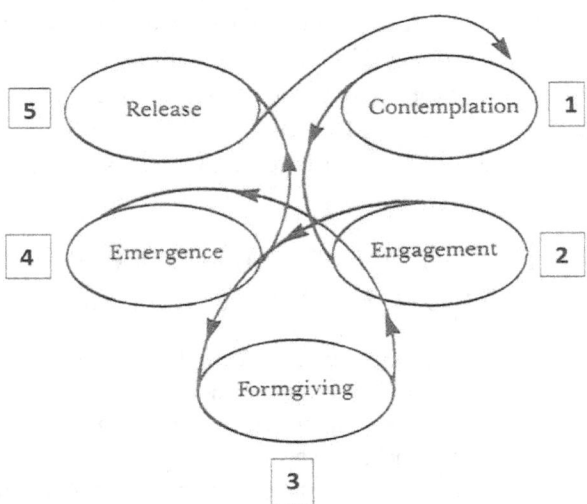

Figure 2. A Five-step Paradigm in Pastoral and Spiritual Care

---

6. In this context and broadly speaking, *suffering* can be understood as "dis-ease, that is, "disturbance of ease" in situations ranging from mild disorientation to severe trauma.

The graphic represents a process that starts with **contemplation** as an attitude of respect, appreciation, receptivity, and reverence. Such welcoming, gracious openness is often reciprocated by carereceivers. Caregivers also contemplate the actual caregiving event and themselves and the Source of grace, wisdom, and power with which/Whom they work. Thus understood, contemplation remains as an indispensable attitude of presence (or, "being present") throughout the caregiving process.

Engagement defines the interaction and interchange involved in getting acquainted, clarifying expectations, and establishing goals and boundaries in the caregiving relationship. The rapport that is generated facilitates the therapeutic conversation focused on the care receivers´ agenda, their needs and potential to move towards reoriention. **Formgiving** in turn names the dialectical, co-creating activity of searching for clarity and for the path to some form of resolution in the face of specific life´s challenges and struggles while activating internal and external resources for such purpose. This moment is oriented to making wise decisions for the way forward in light of shared criteria of human wholeness and flourishing life in community.

As a result of the dialogical and hermeneutical work of formgiving, **emergence** in due time happens as care receivers find themselves in a new and better place in their life journey. This moment usually includes appropriate verification that, indeed, some form of resolution has taken place, or is taking place. (Obviously, necessary emergence thus viewed cannot be guaranteed, and should not be rushed by caregivers. Neither should the caregiving process be prolonged beyond the sought for resolution or reorientation). Opportune **release** is, therefore, a necessary final moment in the caregiving relationship. In all kinds of fruitful caregiving processes and in all settings, release is the step that marks the culmination of such partnership.

ON THE CONTRIBUTION OF PASTORAL AND SPIRITUAL CAREGIVERS

A holistic approach in caregiving practice and theory is the unique contribution of spiritual caregivers involved in all of the health care disciplines. They are expected to consistently demonstrate holistic spiritual caregiving competence. Competence can be described and assessed with a profile of interrelated sets of distinct competencies in the domains of knowledge and ways of knowing, personal character, and multiple caregiving skills. Competencies in turn correlate with standards, that is, expectations of caregiving excellence on the part of institutions and programs and, especially, care receivers themselves.

A unique contribution of pastoral and spiritual caregivers in any health care team is that they can view and work with the care receivers holistically while primarily engaging them psychologically and spiritually. Further, spiritual caregivers must be able to navigate cultural and spiritual-religious difference amidst growing global pluralization and increasing number of multifaith contexts. To do so, spiritual caregivers develop core competencies. Their main task is to connect people in crisis to their spiritual resources and community. That task requires professional and ministerial wisdom with a profile of competency (Schipani, "Competencies," 167–77; Cadge and Rambo, *Chaplaincy*, 61–189, 269–71). A necessary competence for Christian spiritual caregivers relates to self-reflexivity regarding their religious location, especially in terms of distinct theological claims and spirituality (Greider, "Do Justice," 90–92; "Religious Location," 31–37).

A FOUR-DIMENSIONAL FRAMEWORK FOR SPIRITUAL CARE

Spiritual care that is intentionally and consistently offered and reflected upon as a spiritual health discipline also calls for what can be called a four-dimensional view of reality, as depicted in Figure 3 below.

The relatively recent and ongoing "recovery" of spirituality in health care and, especially, counseling and psychotherapy includes emphasis on spiritual assessment (Richards and Bergin, *Spiritual Strategy*, 219–49), engaging clients' spirituality (e.g., beliefs, sources of meaning and hope, etc.) during therapy (Alten and Leach, *Spirituality and the Therapeutic Process*), and integration of spirituality into the therapeutic process including issues and practices such as meditation, prayer, sacred readings (Plante, *Spiritual Practices*). From a Christian theological perspective, however, a psychological framework and approach is always necessary but it is not sufficient. From that viewpoint, together with an explicit recognition of the reality of the spiritual dimension of human life there is also the reality of evil and, especially, a dimension of boundless Grace and divine participation in the caregiving process as well (Appleby and Ohlschlager, *Transformative Encounters*; Loder, *Transforming Moment*; Holeman, *Theology*; Norberg, *Consenting to Grace*; Tan, *Counseling and Psychotherapy*).

A four-dimensional framework for spiritual care

CONCLUSION

In this essay, I have articulated a comprehensive response to the question, "what is spiritual care?" from a Christian perspective. It seeks to represent a tradition that is itself diverse.[7] It is offered with the recognition that any Christian perspective cannot sufficiently address all the main issues involved in the field of spiritual care across disciplines. Along the way, I have also highlighted significant commonality among the multiple religious and theological traditions (Schipani, Introduction, *Multifaith Views*, 1–14; "Exploration," 36–50). That intention reflects a commitment for collaboration and mutual enrichment for the sake of excellent spiritual care consistent with the mission of the International Association for Spiritual Care.

---

7. A variety of Christian frameworks includes Evangelical, Reformed, Wesleyan, Pentecostal, Anabaptist-Mennonite, and many other contributions including many "mainline Protestant," Catholic and Orthodox churches. The author of this chapter, however, has chosen not to make distinctions among those streams of Christian thought in spiritual care due to a lack of space.

REFERENCES

Alten, J. D., and Leach, M. M., eds. *Spirituality and the Therapeutic Process: A Comprehensive Resource from Intake to Termination.* Washington DC.: American Psychological Association, 2009.

Appleby, David W. and Ohlschlager, G., eds. *Transformative Encounters: The Intervention of God in Christian Counseling and Pastoral Care.* Downers Grove, IL: InterVarsity, 2013.

Bajwa, Muhammad A., Omer, A., Kholaki, S., and Starr, J. *Mantle of Mercy: Islamic Chaplaincy in North America.* West Conshohocken, PA: Templeton, 2022.

Bass, D. C., Cahalan, K. A., Miller-McLemore, B. J., Nieman, J. R., and Scharen, C. B., eds. *Christian Practical Wisdom: What It Is, Why It Matters.* Grand Rapids: Eerdmans, 2016.

Bass, D. C., and Dykstra, C., eds. *For Life Abundant: Practical Theology, Theological Education, and Christian Ministry.* Grand Rapids: Eerdmans, 2008.

Boelhower, G. J. *Choose Wisely: Practical Insights from Spiritual Traditions.* New York: Paulist, 2013.

Borg, M. *The Heart of Christianity: Rediscovering a Life of Faith.* San Francisco: HarperSanFrancisco, 2003.

Brock R. N., and Lettini, G. *Soul Repair: Recovering from Moral Injury after War.* Boston: Beacon, 2012.

Brueggemann, W. *Theology of the Old Testament: Testimony, Dispute, Advocacy.* Minneapolis: Fortress,1997.

Cadge, W. and Rambo, S., eds. *Chaplaincy and Spiritual Care in the Twenty-first Century: An Introduction.* Chapel Hill: University of North Carolina Press, 2022.

Chander, V. and Mosher, L., eds. *Hindu Approaches to Spiritual Care.* London: Kingsley, 2020.

Friedman M. and Yehuda, R. *The Art of Jewish counseling: A Guide for All Traditions.* London: Routledge, 2017.

Graham. L. K. *Moral Injury: Restoring Wounded Souls.* Nashville: Abingdon, 2017.

Greider, K. J. "Do Justice, Love Kindness, Walk Humbly: A Christian Perspective on Spiritual Care" In *Multifaith Views in Spiritual Care*, edited by D. Schipani, 85–108. Kitchener, ON: Pandora, 2013.

———. "Religious Location and Counseling: Engaging Diversity and Difference in Views of Religion." In *Navigating Religious Difference in Spiritual Care and Counseling*, edited by J. Snodgrass, 11–44. Claremont, CA: Claremont University Press, 2019.

Hall, S. S. *Wisdom: From Philosophy to Neuroscience.* New York: Knopf, 2010.

Harris, M. *Teaching and the Religious Imagination: An Essay on the Theology of Teaching.* San Francisco: HarperSanFrancisco, 1991.

Holeman, V.T. *Theology for Better Counseling: Trinitarian Reflections for Healing and Formation.* Downers Grove: InterVarsity, 2012.

Hussein, R. G. *Islamic Counselling: An Introduction to Theory and Practice.* London: Routledge, 2016.

Jones, R. S. *Spirit in Session: Working with your Client's Spirituality (and Your Own).* West Conshohocken, PA: Templeton, 2019.

Kelle, B., ed. *Moral Injury: A Guide for Understanding and Engagement.* Lanham, MD: Lexington, 2020.

Keys, C. L. and Haidt, J. *Flourishing: Positive Psychology and the Life Well-lived*. Washington, DC: American Psychological Association, 2003.

Levine, A.-J. *Short Stories Jesus Told: The Enigmatic Parables of a Controversial Rabbi*. New York: HarperOne, 2015.

Loder, J. E. *The Transforming Moment: Understanding Convictional Experiences*. Colorado Springs: Helmers & Howard, 1989.

Malony H. N. and Augsburger, D. W. *Christian Counseling: An Introduction*. Nashville: Abingdon, 2007.

Norberg, T. *Consenting to Grace: An Introduction to Gestalt Pastoral Care*. Staten Island: Penn House, 2006.

Pargament, K. I., and Exline, J. J. *Working with Spiritual Struggles in Psychotherapy: From Research to Practice*. New York: Guilford, 2022.

Peterson, C. and Seligman, M. E. P. *Character Strengths and Virtues: A Handbook and Classification*. New York: Oxford University Press, 2004.

Plante, T. G. *Spiritual Practices in Psychotherapy*. Washington, DC: American Psychological Association, 2009.

Ramsay, N. J. and Doehring, C., eds. *Military Moral Injury and Spiritual Care*. St. Louis: Chalice, 2019.

Richards P. S. and Bergin, A. E. *A Spiritual Strategy for Counseling and Psychotherapy*, 2nd ed. Washington, DC: American Psychological Association, 2005.

Sanford, M. *Kalyāṇamitra: A Model for Buddhist Spiritual Care*. Manotick, ON: Sumeru, 2021.

Schipani, D. S. "Competencies for Wise Interfaith Spiritual Care." In *Multifaith Views in Spiritual Care*, edited by D. Schipani, 167–77. Kitchener: Pandora, 2013.

———. "An Exploration of Common Ground in Pastoral and Spiritual Care: Religious Community, Human Spirit, Wisdom, and Creative Imagination." In *Care, Healing, and Human Well-being within Interreligious Discourses*, edited by K. H. Weiss, D. L. Federschmidt, D. Luow, D. and L. S. Bredvik, 36–50. Stellenbosch: African Sun Media, 2021.

———. "Fundamentalism as Toxic Spirituality: Exploring the Psycho-spiritual Structure and Dynamics of Violent Extremism." In *Teaching in a World of Violent Extremism*, edited by E. S. Fernandez, 178–207. Eugene, OR: Pickwick Publications, 2021.

———. *Spiritual Care in Our Multifaith World: A Primer on Practice and Theory*. Eugene, OR: Wipf & Stock, 2024.

———. *The Way of Wisdom in Pastoral Counseling*. Elkhart, IN: Institute of Mennonite Studies, 2003.

———, ed. *Multifaith Views in Spiritual Care*. Kitchener, ON: Pandora, 2013.

Sternberg, R. J. and Glück, J., eds. *The Cambridge Handbook of Wisdom*. Cambridge, UK: Cambridge University Press, 2019.

———, eds. *The Psychology of Wisdom: An Introduction*. Cambridge: Cambridge University Press, 2022.

Tan, S-Y. *Counseling and Psychotherapy: A Christian Perspective*. 2nd ed. Grand Rapids: Baker Academic, 2022.

Weiss, H. "Christian Care and Counselling in the Context of Neoliberal Capitalism and Vulnerability." In *Care, Healing, and Human Well-being within Interreligious Discourses*, edited by K. H. Weiss, D. L. Federschmidt, D. Luow, D. and L. S. Bredvik, 144–61. Stellenbosch: African Sun Media, 2021.

15

Spiritual Care from an African Christian Perspective

in Light of COVID-19

Esther Mombo

What is spiritual care in the light of COVID-19 from an African Christian perspective? I will locate my response in a personal story and in the Book of Lamentations. In the context of COVID-19, we read many statements about God. For example, "The churches are locked down, but God is not." "God is in control." "All things work together for good." "Trust in God and Him alone." And many more.

A few months before the pandemic, I lost my mother. She had been sick with dementia for a number of years, but it was not dementia that killed her. She fell and broke her hip bone and did not survive the operation meant to heal her. The morning she died, all her children surrounded her, and spoke to her, each one of us giving her a form of affirmation and telling her how we love her. I was the last one to speak, and I said to her, "Mum, we love you, and you have had a long journey," and "Rest." After speaking, before I finished, she breathed her last. We all looked at each other with shock but with a sigh of relief that she had rested from her pain. When the news went out, we were surrounded by family and friends during the days of planning for her funeral. Asked by a friend how I coped, I said I coped because I had time to lament. I had time to grieve and mourn her.

A colleague lost her mother during COVID-19. The funeral was done very fast and only a few people attended. With others sharing my load, I had felt that I was allowed to lament, and thus I was feeling better. But she was still angry, feeling that her mother did not even have a proper funeral because of the hurriedness in which it was done, since it was in the period of the pandemic.

COVID-19 impacted all strata of society. The experience was expressed in different ways—in funerals, in economics, in politics, everywhere people discuss or reflect upon COVID-19. While it was a difficult time, one of the greatest difficulties was the reality of death, which was everywhere. It was the anxiety that everybody was dealing with. It was a time of death, as it were. What does it mean to die alone, without family or friends surrounding you? We know that the quality of life, health, and well-being is just as important as the end of life. During such a time, spiritual care is vital. In the case of having a holistic life, one needs to be cared for spiritually. So the relationship between the spiritual and the non-spiritual has a strong impact on people's ways of dealing with attitudes or emotions. There was a lot of anxiety—anxiety about the disease itself, but also anxiety in terms of the way we deal with those rites that are very important for us. Those rites form part and parcel of our healthy living. So spiritual care, which has to deal with the provision of compassion and empathy during such a difficult time is very important.

I wish to discuss aspects of spiritual care in the context of COVID-19 from an African context and from my own country (Kenya) because Africa is large. I speak from a Christian tradition. Africa houses all the Christian traditions that are in the world. Africa is one whose Christianity is vibrant, whose Christianity is full of life in terms of the way people pray, in terms of the way people read God's word, and in terms of the way people worship. Prayer is important, such that in my own country Kenya, sometimes public events are started by prayer. Any community gathering will have that aspect of prayer, whether you are beginning a journey, or you are finishing a journey, there is prayer. Bible reading and preaching are also very significant in times of worship. Praise and worship are also important segments of worship life.

With COVID-19, the churches were closed. Measures to mitigate the pandemic included physical distancing and a reduction of public gatherings. As a result, common worship, prayer, preaching, and sacraments could not take place in gatherings. So the rites of baptism, confirmation, weddings, and most importantly, funerals could not be carried out. In a context where funerals are very important, they are big, and people travel from far and wide to give their relatives a good send-off. In the villages, church gatherings are centers for social events, for garnering news, for teaching, and even for getting supplies. In my country, as soon as the first case was noted, as soon as the Ministry of Health said that we had a first case of COVID-19, churches were closed down. People could not go out to worship. And this brought a shock to everybody because churches were centers of spiritual life. So the questions around spiritual care were daunting: "What will happen if we do not go to worship?"

The leadership of the church was going through a sense of guilt: "It's like we have abandoned our congregants, we haven't buried their dead, we haven't baptized their children, we have not been able to accompany them during the times of grief." The sense of loss was a strong aspect in the community. Questions arose such as how, and why, and for how long were we going to struggle with COVID-19? We could not gather, we could not mourn our dead as families. And we are in a society that is now haunted by the many issues over and above the medical health perspectives of COVID-19. In the society, there was an increase in isolation, sadness, loneliness, depression, and helplessness. We saw a rise in cases of gender-based violence. And we saw pastors feeling increasingly that they were not able to accompany their congregants.

In this regard, therefore, I look to lament and hope as a form of spiritual care. This is drawn from the Christian tradition—because God is not ignorant of the sufferings of the people of God's creation. God has not forgotten us or rejected us. How do we survive a pandemic—or any catastrophe? How do we offer spiritual care in such a context? I say that it is through lament and hope. Among Christians, one heard more voices of lament and hope during the pandemic. Lament and hope are deeply rooted in the Christian tradition and drawn from the Bible, which is the center of Christian teaching. A practice of lament is a biblical practice. When we look at the Psalms, in part or in full, they offer a cry of lament to God. And in the Bible, especially the Old Testament, when their crops failed or they were defeated in a war, they would gather together to grieve. That is why there are so many laments in the Bible, including more than a third of the 150 psalms. There is, of course, even the whole book in the Old Testament called Lamentations.

To lament is to offer our honest, uncensored pain, heartache and pain to God. It is to take our deepest concerns and grief to God, knowing that God will never reject us for our prayers: no prayer is too honest. To lament is always an act of drawing near to God, with all our raw questions and unpolished prayers. Lament is a place where Christians bring our emotions to God, even if it does not seem 'pretty' or polite. God does not always provide the answers we want in the case of lament, but as we lament, we share in God's own lamenting over the brokenness of creation. We draw near to the safety of God's love and receive God's compassionate embrace when we encounter afresh God's restorative heart for the whole world.

Theologian Emmanuel Katongole in his book *Born from Lament* makes a strong case for the notion that lament is more than a feeling. It is a practice that uses and transforms suffering into hope. Hope, he writes, is not a consolation, but an anguished discipline of turning to and around God. So spiritual care in COVID-19 was spiritual care in isolation. COVID-19 has brought to light many challenges—physically, mentally, socially, and spiritually. When churches were closed, people often felt or were feeling more distanced from God. When we look at Lamentations, we discover that there is a strong aspect of isolation even among the people of Lamentations' time. In this book, we read:

> How lonely sits the city
>   that once was full of people! . . .
> The roads to Zion mourn,
>   for no one comes to the festivals;
> all her gates are desolate;
>   her priests groan . . .
> (Lamentations 1:1, 4a)

Similarly, our worship spaces were deserted. So how could we offer spiritual care, when gatherings for worship are not there? We discovered that spiritual care is not necessarily dependent on a pastor, priest or other official person. Some aspects of care are about attending to our own well-being and connecting with God, in small things and big things. So the physical distancing that happened as one of the ways to mitigate the spread of COVID-19 offered opportunities for renewal, resuscitation, growth, and spiritual development. Praying the psalms, for instance, offered a language to talk honestly and candidly with God, as well as meditation and reading and reflecting on God's word.

For some in our context, it also meant connecting with friends, colleagues, and family through an e-church online. Spiritual care then caused us to reframe our understanding of community, and to seek for alternatives for staying connected and maintaining community during that time.

Spiritual care, at the same time, means taking care of the physical needs of others. COVID-19 exposed disparities that still exist within our African countries and across our continent. It has been said by many that even without COVID-19, hunger would have killed us. Hunger here is a representation of the challenges that many in the church and the wider society are facing. We are faced with many, many challenges. How do we offer spiritual care?

In the Book of Lamentations we also read:

> My eyes are spent with weeping;
>   my stomach churns;
> my bile is poured out on the ground
>   because of the destruction of my people,
> because infants and babes faint
>   in the streets of the city.
> ¹² They cry to their mothers,
>   "Where is bread and wine?"
> as they faint like the wounded
>   in the streets of the city,
> as their life is poured out
>   on their mothers' bosoms.
> (Lamentations 2:11–12)

> The tongue of the infant sticks
>   to the roof of its mouth for thirst;
> the children beg for food,
>   but there is nothing for them.
> (Lamentations 4:4)

COVID-19 challenged us how to offer spiritual care to the total person, not just to the soul. Spiritual care is the base on which we build the wholeness of life. In spiritual care we affirm that life is a gift from God—that we have the privilege to share, protect, celebrate, weep, and for all in the community. This care is inclusive of physical, mental, and spiritual needs. It is for the whole person. Spiritual care means both providing for material needs, and producing theologies that are affirming, rather than theologies that are distractive. It is moving away from interpretations of COVID-19 as a curse or COVID-19 as a sign of the end times. Spiritual care is to listen to the lament and the difficult questions of those who are struggling: "Why God? How long, God?" In the Book of Lamentations, we find that the last questions of the book are:

> Why have you forgotten us completely?
>   Why have you forsaken us these many days?
> Restore us to yourself, O Lord, that we may be restored;
>   renew our days as of old—
> unless you have utterly rejected us
>   and are angry with us beyond measure.
> (Lamentations 5:20–22)

Such pain or calamity in the text of the Bible is sometimes interpreted as punishment from God. The people's lamentations show awareness of that as they speak about that in their suffering. There have been interpretations, even in our modern times, of the COVID pandemic as a punishment for sin. COVID-19 did expose structural sins in our society, and it is those who are poor, for instance, who bear the brunt of these sins. These sins include human greed, inequity, depletion, exploitation, confusion, rage, hate, and lack. These were reflected in our communities during COVID-19 in different ways, including fear, anxiety, and suspicion of the other. For us still, a common thing that we have seen across nations is an increase in domestic violence, as people were forced to share a private space for a longer period of time than usual. COVID-19 eliminated the public space.

In this context, the "why" question is very strong and important. When suffering people are are asking "Why," they may not need our answers as Christians, because sometimes our answers may not be adequate. Sometimes we have used the language of patience, the language of perseverance, but that answer is inadequate to them. They may not be seeking an answer or an explanation for their pain, but a more just solution.

It is a mistake to think that we always need to supply an answer as part of our spiritual care. Often, we will not know the answer, and the best we can do is to keep quiet, to listen, and to interrogate ourselves whether we are part of the problem, and then become part of the answer. Spiritual care means here listening and being available to listen. In Lamentations, as they conclude, we do not hear God speak. God is silent. And maybe there is power in silence. Lamentations forces us to embrace the uncertainty of this silence. "How long?" Or "God, why?" That is why when we think of this book especially we realize that God is there, even though God is silent. So lamentation creates a space for our uncertainties, nothing even uncertainty is outside of God.

Finally, spiritual care is lament and hope. I conclude with the cry of Jesus, "My God, my God, why have you forsaken me?" (Mark 15:34; Matt 27:46) in which he quotes Psalm 22—a radical expression of loneliness and hopelessness. COVID-19 has brought to light a sense of loneliness and hopelessness.

Our hope of ensuring that we listen to the people's lament, the cry of Jesus, and the cries of many today, is a reminder that the issues in our society expect us to bring hope. It is our world that is hopeless, especially during and after the COVID-19 pandemic, especially due to everything that it has exposed. But for us, as Christians, by using the Christian text, we bring hope to this hopelessness. It is our defiance against those things that bring darkness. In my story above, I said that I felt I grieved better because

I was allowed to lament. I think for us as Christians, giving room for lament during COVID-19 provided us that space for lament, and lament is defiance! Lament is a way of hope, a way of bringing us back to God. So COVID-19 was a moment of crisis that confronted us and pushed us to rethink our ways of spiritual care. May the God of hope fill us with all joy and peace, as we trust in Him, so that we may overflow with hope by the power of the Holy Spirit.

REFERENCE

Katongole, E. *Born from Lament: The Theology of Politics and Hope in Africa*. Grand Rapids: Eerdmans, 2017.

16

What Is Spiritual Care from a Christian Perspective?

Pastoral Care for Rage and Joy

Angella Son

Spiritual care from a Christian perspective involves a wide variety of care, such as strengthening people's faith in God, fortifying people's relationships with God and one another, restoring people from relational conflicts, healing from grief from the loss of loved ones or things, releasing from psychological and spiritual burdens, liberating from suffering caused by abuses and injustices, and so forth. Spiritual care from a Christian perspective takes a non-monolithic approach and attends to multiple aspects, including people's relationships to both God and others, people's health in both psychological and spiritual aspects, and well-being for both individuals and society. The aim of spiritual care is more than repair work to bring health to individuals. It also focuses on individual growth beyond healing and societal well-being. Spiritual care from a Christian perspective thus involves healing work of both psychological and spiritual aspects but also the empowering work of people so that they can mobilize their efforts in contributing to others' lives and society and bring healing in others and well-being in society. Spiritual care thus is holistic and cares for individual heart, mind, soul, and societal wellness.

In this discussion, instead of focusing on specific types of spiritual care, I will center my discussion on a major phenomenon of our society today: rage. I will discuss two types of rage, *angry rage* and *wounded rage*. I will then suggest spirituality of joy as a basis of spiritual care in the rage-filled society we live in. In so doing, my attention to spiritual care will address a wider concern with a specific focus on rage instead of spreading attention to a wide variety of care issues, i.e., focusing on the spiritual care of those who experience various vulnerabilities and losses.

Rage is rampant today in the United States. It manifests in an array of various intensities—everything from mild or moderate forms such as emotional upset, screaming, and abstaining from speaking to one another to the more extreme forms evident in physical and emotional abuse and the shooting massacres that have become an epidemic today. Regrettably, we are not skillful in dealing with our rage. What is more troublesome about rage is that, while it is more common and frequent than people think, rage in private interactions is often tolerated or even considered to be an inconvenient but normal part of life. Extreme rage expressed in severe abuse situations is often tolerated because of power differentials that create a loss of control and agency in the victims. Mass shootings shock people, but more attention is directed to the horrific nature of shootings than the rage behind such extreme violence. Rage is identified but often not registered in people's minds. Or, in some situations, it is not even identified. According to *USA Today*, on November 7, 2018, a 28-year-old white male, Ian David Long, walked into Borderline Bar and Grill, a western dance bar, in Thousand Oaks, California, and shot at the patrons for nearly three minutes resulting in many injuries and 11 fatalities, including the death of Ian David Long himself (May and Miller, "What We Know"). Long's horrendous shooting spree might have been prevented if his rage had been identified and addressed at the time of his domestic dispute when Ventura County Sheriff Geoff Dean and his department were dispatched to his home in April.

It is imperative to provide effective care for rage in our personal and societal lives for the well-being of people and society. I propose that spiritual care of rage from a Christian perspective is paradoxically informed by a spirituality of joy. In what follows, first, I classify rage into two categories: (1) *angry rage*—a posture of offense manifesting in a loss of control because of one's unreasonable and disproportionate and thus unfulfilled expectations and (2) *wounded rage*—a posture of resignation manifesting in a loss of control because of one's loss of self-agency inflicted by others. Second, I propose that spirituality of joy grounds in the grace of God and enfolds two aspects—connectedness and undeserving. Third, I offer a theology of excess as a starting point for the spirituality of joy. I then discuss the spirituality of joy and its application to spiritual care.

ANGRY RAGE

Heinz Kohut's understanding of narcissistic rage is very illumining in our understanding of *angry rage*. According to Kohut, narcissistic rage ensues when we experience a loss of control of ourselves and our surroundings including others, which we experience as a part of ourselves. This lack of control, according to Kohut, is akin to the lack of control that an adult may feel when he loses control over different parts of his body, such as the ability to move his arms, bend his knees, open and close his mouth, etc. (Kohut, *Analysis of the Self*, 27). We then experience others or surroundings as a problematic part of us, or "a flaw in a narcissistically perceived reality" when we lose control of them. Our rage then aims to attack others or surroundings in an effort to recover our sense of control.

As an example, I have suggested that Moses killed an Egyptian taskmaster out of narcissistic rage (Son, "Making a Great Man"). Moses' murder of an Egyptian taskmaster was an out-of-proportion response in which he resorted to extreme measures. Moses seems unable to differentiate himself from both the Egyptian carrying out the beating and the abused Israelite. When he finds the Egyptian beating up the Israelite, he experiences the Israelite as a part of himself and thus experiences the beating firsthand as if it were being done to him. On the other hand, he likewise experiences the Egyptian as a part of himself and expects him to behave as he wishes. When the Egyptian does not act in the way he expects and beats up the Israelite, he experiences himself as beating the Israelite and the Egyptian as a malfunction of a part of himself. As a result, he experiences narcissistic injury on dual counts, one by being beaten up and the other by having lost control over his own self in the beating of an Israelite, one of his kinfolks. Moses's narcissistic rage seeks to completely eradicate that bad and useless part of himself. Thus is the delivery of the murder.

I call the narcissistic rage described by Kohut the angry rage. Angry rage usually happens to those whose self lacks a firm boundary, and thus tends to experience others and situations as part of the self. Those who tend to experience angry rage are overwhelmed by a lack of control of one's self which extends to things, others, and situations. Angry rage is conceived by an inability to access realistic expectations of one's self, resulting in a need to seek control of self, others, and one's surroundings, including God. As a result, one is bound to fail because of unrealistic expectations of one's ability or situation. When others, who are experienced as part of the self, do not think and act the way the self desires, one experiences the loss of self-control over these others who are then considered to be the bad part of the self that should be demolished.

WOUNDED RAGE

Kohut's notion of narcissistic rage is illuminating, especially in understanding it within the frame of angry rage. It is, however, limited in explaining rage of all kinds. I would thus augment Kohut's notion of narcissistic rage and add one more category of rage—*wounded rage*. Wounded rage is often the ignored and forcibly unrecognized side of rage experienced by victims of oppression. This rage is not caused by a loss of control because of one's unrealistic assessment of one's own ability and situations that are eventually undelivered, but rather a loss of control inflicted by others who deny the self's needs, rights, aspirations, etc. The response of wounded rage is also different from that of angry rage in that, unlike the *posture of offense*, it takes the *posture of resignation* and is often expressed in powerlessness because their options and power are deprived by others or situations. It is thus silent and this lack of expression of rage is imposed on the powerless by those with power. Societal epistemology defined by those with power will oppress the powerless to ignore any harm or hurt done to them and disregard their rage as an erroneous response. This process of oppression is not a conscious experience, but it is so ingrained in a natural flow of lifestyle and structure that oppression often escapes any notice from either the oppressor or the oppressed.

A paradigmatic case of *wounded rage* comes from the global scene. *Comfort girls-women*[1] are girls and women from various Asian-Pacific countries who were forced into sexual slavery often by deceit and coercion during the latter part of World War II by the Japanese military. The Japanese military misused its authority and used young girls as mere instruments to function as sexual machines that granted soldiers sexual relief and their age could be as young as 11 and usually not older than 18.[2] Through repeated

---

1. I created the term *comfort girls-women* to replace the widely used term "comfort women," often placed inside quotations. This term has three significant aspects: (1) the italics signify that the word *comfort* has a different meaning—sexual slavery—than its usual meaning in the term "comfort women" of entertaining and providing pleasure to men; (2) the addition of the word *girl* underscores the young age of the victims who were put into sexual slavery; and (3) the word *woman* reflects the long period—about three-quarters of a century—they endured without a satisfactory resolution of their situation.

2. For a discussion about why Korean girls were the main target for recruitment as *comfort girls-women*, see Son, "Inadequate Innocence."

exploitation and violation to the extreme with brutal injury, objectification, and degradation, their sense of self was eroded until it gradually became empty and self-agency was almost bankrupt. Even though they were wrongly victimized, they saw themselves as impure, immoral, and irredeemable. Their sense of shame and unworthiness as moral beings pushed them into experiencing alienation even back in their homes or country and kept them in isolation and silence. This sense of shame and bankrupt self-agency kept many Korean *comfort girls-women* from revealing their unjust treatment by the Japanese military as well as from requesting financial, housing, and medical subsidies from the Korean government when the issue became public. Their rage thus was kept in silence for half a century until one of the *comfort girls-women*, Kim Haksun, broke the silence in 1991.

Spiritual care thus must address rage to assist people to be less affected by loss of control or deprivation of their agency in their lives and prevent various rage manifestations that can deteriorate individual and societal health and well-being. I propose that spirituality of joy can play a crucial role in assuaging rage and shoring up the level of resilience in people that spiritual care from a Christian perspective appropriates spirituality of joy as its foundation.

SPIRITUAL CARE IN A FRAMEWORK OF SPIRITUALITY OF JOY

I offer a spirituality of joy as a basis for spiritual care of rage as well as other care issues from a Christian perspective. Spirituality of joy is grounded in the grace of God and emphasizes two aspects—connectedness and undeserving. God desires connectedness with us even though we are undeserving of restoration of our relationship to God and relates to us in God's grace. God reaches out to us, who are undeserving of God's grace, to restore God's relationship with us and allow us to reach the fullness of life. Our society regrettably directs its priority on what is the opposite of the grace of God. In our society, we are obsessed with accuracy and exactness. We are in full gear to train ourselves to competently plan and execute things in our lives with accuracy and exactness. This heightened fixation on accuracy and exactness in our lives makes us more susceptible to experiencing a loss of control in our lives and as a result angry rage. Furthermore, our preoccupation with accuracy and exactness prevents us from recognizing the joys in our lives imputed by God. When we are engrossed with our achievement with accuracy and exactness, joys in life are restricted because we only focus on our efforts and the result of our work. In so doing, we miss God's interventions in our lives and fail to see the work of the grace of God in our lives.

Jesus' parable of workers in the vineyard from Matthew 20:1–16 depicts how the grace of God operates and the human approach to accuracy or exactness based on fairness. The landowner in the parable hires workers at five different times–early in the morning, about nine o'clock, about noon, about three o'clock, and about five o'clock. When it was time to be paid, all the workers received the usual daily wage. The grace of God does not calculate what the reward is by precisely computing the amount of effort. Instead, the grace of God claims excess as normalcy within the context of needs. The workers who were hired early in the morning operate in the framework of accuracy and exactness and think that they should be paid more than those who were hired later. They complained "against the landowner, saying, 'These last worked only one hour, and you have made them equal to us who have borne the burden of the day and the scorching heat.'" (Matthew 20:11–12) Because the workers' perspectives are in the frame of accuracy and exactness, they experienced rage at the unfairness of the landowner and demanded more pay with their complaints. The landowner's response shows how the workers hired early in the morning received a fair wage and thus they were not wronged. But the real point is how excess was provided to other workers who were hired later out of the generosity of the landowner. The focus is not a universal notion of fairness but a contextually sensitive response. All the workers need the usual amount of wage for their livelihood and some workers may have circumstantial situations that hinder them from being hired early in the morning.

In the operation of the grace of God, excess and generosity are not exceptions but normalcy. In the working of the grace of God, contextual needs take priority over fairness. Spiritual care thus directs its effort into transforming people's obsession with accuracy and exactness based on fairness into that of excess and generosity. When excess and generosity are considered normal practices while considering contextual needs, more joys are created in life. Spiritual care from a Christian perspective thus aims to facilitate an environment reflecting the grace of God and emphasizes how undeserving we may be, we are fully accepted as we are and we can free ourselves from fixating on accuracy and exactness in our lives. Spiritual care from a Christian perspective underscores the essential aspect of connectedness among us, others, and God. Spiritual care from a Christian perspective encourages us to experience the joys God has spread in our lives while fully accepting good and bad things in life. Spiritual care from a Christian perspective supports people in their effort to be free from any violation of their dignity and oppression that prevents them from living the fullness of life that God grants to them.

Based on the discussion above, spirituality of joy starts with what I call a *theology of excess*. I draw this theology of excess from Leviticus 19:9–10 and 23:22 and Deuteronomy 24:19–22, which demonstrate this frame of excess and generosity in response to contextual needs. Leviticus 19:9–10 says: "'When you reap the harvest of your land, do not reap to the very edges of your field or gather the gleanings of your harvest. Do not go over your vineyard a second time or pick up the grapes that have fallen. Leave them for the poor and the foreigner. I am the LORD your God."

According to these verses, we should not glean to the last grain or strip the last olive by counting all that we deserve from our efforts. We should not always try to be exact in keeping track of what we own such as a sheaf left in the field. We should not determine all that we reap with our efforts is our own, but a portion should be set apart as excess that belongs to others in need. These verses normalize a lifestyle for people to set apart a portion of what they produce or own as excess for those who are in need. The theology of excess refuses people to hoard excess for themselves but promotes setting apart the excess already built into what people have. A theology of excess advocates a lifestyle that presumes an essential presence of extra space in all aspects of our lives. Instead of having accurate and exact patterns in our lives, we treat extra space as a natural part of our lives and allow breathing room in our lives.

Spirituality of joy categorizes people into two categories and they are what I call *joyrefusers* and *joyfinders* (Son, *Spirituality of Joy*). Joyrefusers are those who are under the control of an accurate and exact lifestyle, whereas joyfinders are those who live based on the theology of excess or having extra space as a natural part of their lives. Spiritual care within the frame of a spirituality of joy is the work of joyfinders to help joyrefusers heal from their wound and to find a lifestyle informed by the grace of God and the theology of excess. Spirituality of joy encourages people to find joy or in-spite-of joys in their lives and the lives of others around them and encourages them to focus on connecting with joys sprinkled by God all around us. To assist people in freeing themselves from angry and wounded rage and practicing the spirituality of joy, I suggest that spiritual care emphasizes four things: Receive, Flow, Discover, and Collaborate.

1. Receive: For those with angry rage, mobilize them not to blame anyone or any group, but to receive any difficulties or suffering in life as a guest who has come to live with us for some time. For those with wounded rage, mobilize them not to blame themselves, but receive any oppression as an unwanted guest who needs to leave—the sooner the better.

2. Flow: For both angry and wounded rage, encourage them to (1) stop trying too hard to make it on their own; (2) lower or even suspend their expectations, especially trying to live in a mode of accuracy and exactness; (3) wait for things to be worked on that are naturally revealed by the situation; (4) catch helping hands extended to them; and (5) search actively for the grace of God.

3. Discover: For both angry and wounded rage, reinforce them to give time to themselves in (1) finding and defining themselves that can provide joy and fulfillment in their lives, (2) finding creativity in them that can fuel their passion and vision and (3) finding any hobby or interests that might naturally develop in the situation.

4. Collaborate: For both angry and wounded, support them to find ways to connect and collaborate with one another in their way to healing and flourishing. As they find themselves stronger, motivate them to reach out to those at higher risk of angry and wounded rage.

Spiritual care based on a spirituality of joy is like giving life to the dry bones in Ezekiel 37:1–10. Just as the dry bones were given the shape of a body by being pulled together, covered by sinews, flesh, and skin, spiritual care is pulling together the scattered and useless pieces of people's wounded rage and angry rage and covering them with affirmation and understanding. Just as the shaped bodies of the dry bones were finally given the breath of life, spiritual care then breathes joy into their life. Spiritual care thus creates life in people by spreading the joy that springs from the grace of God through Jesus Christ and is expressed by the work of the Holy Spirit.

REFERENCES

Kohut, H. *The Analysis of the Self: A Systematic Approach to the Psychoanalytic Treatment of Narcissistic Personality Disorders*. Madison: International Universities, 1971.

May, A., and Miller, R.W. "What We Know about the Mass Shooting at a Thousand Oaks, California, Dance Bar." *USA Today*, November 8, 2018. https://www.usatoday.com/story/news/nation-now/2018/11/08/mass-shooting-southern-california-dance-bar-what-happened/1927903002/.

Son, A. "Inadequate Innocence of Korean *Comfort Girls-women*: Obliterated Dignity and Shamed Self." *Pastoral Psychology* 67.2 (2017) 175–94.

———. "Making a Great Man, Moses: Sustenance and Augmentation of the Self through God as Selfobject." *Pastoral Psychology* 64.5 (2015) 751–68.

———. *Spirituality of Joy: Moving Beyond Dread and Duties*. Seoul: Jeyoung Communications, 2013.

17

Beyond the "Art of Doing Nothing"

Reflections on Indigenizing Clinical Pastoral Education to the Buddhadharma

Upayadhi S. Luraschi

Long before I started any kind of formal Clinical Pastoral Education, I remember showing up on my first day at a hospice residence of the Visiting Nurse Services of New York as a volunteer "spiritual caregiver." I was enthusiastically welcomed by the Resident Manager and before I could mumble much of a self-introduction, she exclaimed: "I *love* Buddhists! You people know how to do nothing! We need that." She was not wrong. Years of long hours sitting steady in meditation halls, shrine rooms, and zendos, even as the mind jumps off the wall and itches beg to be scratched, do train one in forbearance, receptivity, and the ability to be with what arises. . .and does not arise. The manager longed for caregivers who could be with, and be curious about, so-called nonresponsive hospice residents, without getting caught up in feelings of inadequacy or ineffectiveness. New York is a notoriously frenetic place, steeped in a culture of hyper-productivity. I love its energy. That hustle has a long and storied history that cuts across social strata. It's about survival, ingenuity, and grit. Yet, to sit and just be, to offer a "ministry of presence" as Christians call it, to become transparent without dissociating, to taste the timelessness between two ticks of the clock on the wall--this is an act of resistance of the highest order, an affront to the (capitalist) compulsion to prove one's worth by doing, by producing. Including, of course, producing a commodifiable and Instagrammable self, even a good little Buddhist self.

Though administrators certainly clocked me as a Buddhist, this only rarely came up with hospice residents, and later with the hospital patients I served. As chaplains know, it's not about us. Like most non-Christians who may not visibly present as such, assumptions are quickly made. I mostly let those be and allow myself to be projected upon as needed, unless a situation calls for some kind of minimal self-disclosure for the sake of integrity, care, or self-care (such as a rare theological question about my own beliefs, or the need to set boundaries when requested to perform liturgy). My job did not involve walking around with a neon sign flashing above my head:"Buddhist spiritual care provider"! Instead, the invitation was to *be* the practice, to live rooted in the tradition, and to respond appropriately and spontaneously from that wisdom and compassion––which is not mine, not yours, and logo-free. Buddhists certainly have no monopoly over practices such as meditation, even Buddhist meditation, for that matter. While those many years of burning off karma on the meditation cushion may have been critical to my ability to cross the threshold of a hospice or hospital room and not shy away from the rage of a patient, the despair of a family member, or the beyond-burnout of a nurse, actual professional training in contemplative pastoral care with an experienced supervisor and a peer group is invaluable. But what does that look like for Buddhists in a US context?

The Buddhist world is vast and variegated. "Buddhist spiritual care" is as confounding a generic formulation as "Christian spiritual care." Ritual needs and theological conversations related to existential distress in the face of death, change, illness, loss, incarceration, war, climate despair, calamity, or injustice play out differently among Lutherans, Presbyterians, Evangelicals, Methodists, Baptists, Christian Orthodox, Pentecostals, Catholics and so on. And so it is also among Buddhists, perhaps even more so, yet our diversity easily collapses under the pressure of a dominant frame and low religious fluency. Furthermore, most care offered by Buddhist chaplains in American settings does not actually involve caring for self-identified Buddhists, who remain less than 1% of the US population (Smith, "America's Changing Landscape"). Once in a blue moon, my heart skips a beat in the excitement of being called to visit an actual Buddhist patient. Then comes the reality check. A visit with a Buddhist most often means stepping into a huge linguistic and cultural gulf between the patient's expectations and needs, and my own capacities and idiosyncratic formation as a Buddhist of a particular Indo-British lineage, presenting as a white-bodied middle-class Franco-American female. I am not a Cambodian monk in *kāṣāya-civara* (saffron robes), a Tibetan Yogi in red and white *ngakpa* robes, or a Korean Won minister sporting a brown *pômnak* with its recognizable golden circle. I have thus sought to educate myself in the Buddhist traditions demographically most likely to be encountered where I live. These are most often Buddhist communities that originated in Japan such as the Soka Gakkai International (SGI) and the Jodo Shinshu tradition, which themselves could not be more different. I have tried to learn some basic chants and to familiarize myself with core ideas, texts, and important festivals. I remember trying to chant the vow of *Nam-myoho-renge-kyo* at the request of an ailing SGI patient, and seeing him grimace as I got the pace and the tune invariably wrong. I learned to quickly admit defeat and to keep a rolodex of contacts among local *sanghas,* so as to bring in more appropriate interlocutors than myself to the situation. Coordinating Buddhist care as a Buddhist requires an unbiased and non-sectarian education in our own intra-religious complexity, a deliberate effort to cultivate cultural humility, and a willingness to navigate linguistic divides. This kind of education is not so easy to find, though a new generation of educators, scholars, and thought leaders have made a difference with greatly helpful publications in recent years (see, e.g., McMahan, *Buddhism*; Mitchell, *Buddhism in America*; Han, *Be the Refuge*; Gleig and Mitchell, *Oxford Handbook of American Buddhism*).

Students of history and religious studies know that the construction of a singular "Buddhism" is a modern development of the colonial era, one that Buddhists themselves wrestle with. Sometimes it can be harder to contend with our own intra-religious diversity than to engage in an overtly interfaith context. Buddhists don't always have what Christians call a "theology of religious diversity"—*of Buddhism itself.* While concepts such as *upāya* (skillful means) or the "84,000 doors to the Dharma" can make much room for the intra-religious other, the diversity of cosmologies, lineage commitments, cultural histories, practice styles, and languages (both literal and symbolic) go easily undetected in the West under the weight of a religious version of the Model Minority Myth (*"Buddhists are so nice: don't they all just get along?"*). As Buddhists of various stripes slowly but surely make their way through the American chaplaincy system, as did Jews and Muslims before them, we are simultaneously accommodating a dominant frame for the sake of access, accepting a certain burden of representation despite its absurdity, and gently re-negotiating that frame, bringing distinctive contributions to the field, such as "the art of doing nothing" (more accurately called bearing witness and turning towards suffering). Buddhists have of course been engaging in pastoral work for a long time, going back to when they first set foot in Hawaii and then on the US continent by way of Angel Island in the 1800s (Hsu, "We've Been Here All Along"; Williams, *American Sutra*).

This has included developing pastoral training and theorizing pedagogy. Yet it mostly happened outside of the American mainstream systems that recognize and codify such spiritual labor, and that bear down on the norms of employability in secular institutions.

Things started to change in the early 2000s, perhaps in part as a result of the HIV/AIDS epidemic and the rise to some prominence of Buddhist hospices, such the Zen Hospice Project in San Francisco. By 2006 an initial white paper was published by the Association of Professional Chaplains (APC) titled "Equivalency Issues for Buddhist Candidates for Board Certification," mapping out possible pathways for aspects of Buddhist training to count towards the certification of Buddhist chaplains (Vardell, "Equivalency Issues"). In 2020 a significant update to the state of the affairs was published by the Chaplaincy Innovation Lab, "The Path to Buddhist Chaplaincy: Academic Education, Religious Endorsement, Professional Board Certification" (Gauthier et al., "The Path to Buddhist Chaplaincy"; see also Gauthier, "Buddhist Chaplaincy"). A small but growing number of intrepid Buddhist chaplains began to obtain APC Board Certification and, most importantly, Educator status with the Association for Clinical Pastoral Education (ACPE). A tiny number of Buddhist projects and organizations became accredited to deliver Clinical Pastoral Education, with more on the way. Importantly, several accredited Buddhist graduate degrees oriented towards actual ministry began popping up around the country (the Chaplaincy Innovation Lab maintains up-to-date listings). Some arose from pre-existing Buddhist educational organizations that arduously obtained higher-education affiliations and/or accreditations. Others are the result of extensions into Buddhist chaplaincy by historically Christian and now ecumenical seminaries and universities (for a breakdown, see Zhen, "Buddhist Chaplaincy"). Within Anglo-European Higher Education, this is a departure from the more typical Buddhist Studies degrees which emerged out of Area Studies, and before that, Oriental Studies. Congruent with the colonial project and later with Cold War politics, programs in Buddhist Studies were institutionally fueled by the drive to produce knowledge as a form of control. Degrees were *about* Buddhists but not *for* Buddhists. By the start of the 21st century, various permutations of working groups led the Buddhist chaplaincy charge, with increasing care for intra-Buddhist diversity, and accelerated by the global pandemic (Kandil, "Pandemic's Suffering"). Upwards of fifteen institutions are now part of the Buddhist Ministry Working Group, initiated at a conference held at the Harvard Divinity School in 2014.

It is noticeable that many (though not all) of the first programs to obtain Higher Education accreditations or CPE training site status (and sometimes both) came out of predominantly white convert Buddhist organizations. It is also widely acknowledged that there is a dearth of research dedicated to Buddhist pastoral care happening within the *sangha* (congregational) settings of the Asian diaspora. Still, these initial pathways into mainstream institutional credibility created the potential for more recognition and employability. It also made long-standing inequities uncomfortably visible, and new set of challenges were then foregrounded, such as disparate access to credentialed professional training and the legacies of economic and racialized stratification within American Buddhism. Our institutional *dukkha* (unsatisfactory-ness, suffering) cannot be reduced to issues of Christian dominance; it also bound up with the karmic momentum of white supremacy.

While American Buddhist chaplains continue to wrestle with these issues, they have also increasingly looked abroad for inspiration and collaboration. Promising international exchanges have intensified, particularly with chaplains in Japan, where Buddhist spiritual care, in the aftermath of the traumatic events of the 2011 Tōhoku earthquake and tsunami (and subsequent nuclear disaster), has arguably undergone both a renaissance and non-sectarian professionalization (Watts, *This Precious Life*). Conversely, the growth of Buddhist chaplaincy in the US has piqued the interest of scholars and practitioners invested in the re-imagination and/or the expansion of Buddhist care into sectors of Japanese society from which, for historical reasons, it had been shut out, or neutered of its political edge (Watts and Jin, "Development"; Watts, "Is Buddhist Chaplaincy"). Other Asian thought leaders are analyzing developments in American chaplaincy as they think through their own issues of secularism, sectarianism, and monastic/lay divides, with the hope, for example, of actualizing the vision of the great 20th century Chinese Buddhist modernist Taixu (Zhen, V. G. "Taixu,'" and "Buddhist Chaplaincy"). Important developments are unfolding in Buddhist counseling and care all over Asia, albeit steeped in an incomparably longer Buddhist history.

Though the situation is far from perfect in the US, Buddhists now have a seat at the table in the growing field of chaplaincy, as a result of the painstaking work of Buddhists and non-Buddhist allies. Despite these heroic efforts, statistically, Buddhists who train to become chaplains rarely experience having other Buddhists in their peer groups or working with a Buddhist ACPE Educator—a still too rare unicorn sighting! Even in Buddhist-friendly contexts, efforts to educate Educators and peers about basic tenets of the tradition can result in a superficial engagement with the "theological reflection" component of CPE, leading to missed opportunities for challenge and spiritual maturation. This heightens the importance of access to long-term robust spiritual formation and supervision within

Dharma community settings—something unaffiliated Buddhists or the Buddhist-curious often struggle with.

There is perhaps something of a historical precedent to this moment: the World Parliament of Religions of 1893, held in Chicago. At this landmark event, modern ideas of what a "religion" is (and is not) became reified within a fraught colonial context of European universalism being preserved under the guises of religious pluralism (Masuzawa, *Invention*). Before this moment, to be "religious" meant to be Christian; the rest of us were heathens. Disciples of the Buddha would have spoken of the *Buddhadharma* (teachings of the Buddha) or the *Buddhasasana* (the philosophy and practice of the Buddha), but not of a Buddhist "religion" in the Western sense of the concept. Some prominent Buddhist reformers and change-makers from Sri Lanka and Japan were selectively invited to speak at the proceedings in Chicago, leaving a lasting mark on what the rest of the world would understand Buddhism to be, the particularities of their agendas mostly invisible to the Anglo-European audience. For example, the idea that meditation was somehow the marker of Buddhism, even though statistically most Buddhists do not meditate, was solidified at this point. A new kind of race and religion war was in fact playing out, with Buddhists (and Buddhophiles like the Theosophists) resisting the missionizing force of Christianity by asserting Buddhism's superior compatibility with science and the values of the European Enlightenment. To claim that Buddhism was a "philosophy, not a religion" and that meditation was but a "science of the mind" were ingenious moves to triumphantly showcase the tradition's compatibility with secularism and modernity. Generations later, this discourse, historically constructed yet presented as perennial, has helped to normalize the contemporary presence of mindfulness meditation in healthcare settings. It was also meant to pacify those who deemed Buddhism demonic. Those fears have not left us, however. Some Christian influencers consider Meditating Barbie to be satanic and have demanded Mattel to produce a Bible Study Barbie. They have a point: they have not succumbed to the discourse of innocent meditative secularity, nor to the viability of decoupling contemplative practices from their soteriological context.

Will something of this dance play out again, as our post-modern understandings of chaplaincy and pastoral care continue to reconfigure themselves? This time, which schools of Buddhism will be at the table of the APC and the ACPE, as norms and regulating standards are re-articulated to make room for Buddhists? How does this support and challenge the development and maturation of Buddhist spiritual formation in the US? How will this impact, and be influenced by, the increasing number of SBNRs ("spiritual but not religious") and "NONEs" (no religious affiliation), many of whom declare themselves to be "Buddhish" (Smith, "America's Changing Landscape"; Oakes, "Meet the 'Buddhish' Nones")?

A significant challenge for eclectic religious minorities trying to puncture pre-existing dominant systems is definitional—internally and externally. On the one hand, there is understandable pressure driven inwards to find a set of "somethings" (qualities, practices, concepts, etc.) that capture a unifying "essence" of Buddhism and distinctively Buddhist spiritual care. Yet finding that red thread has been elusive for both practitioners and scholars of Buddhism alike. Debates about authenticity and authentication of teachings among Buddhists have been unfolding since the time of the First Council in the 5th Century BCE. This backdrop gets exacerbated by the modern quest for a *kerygma* ("core message" of Christianity) or a kind of irreducible essence, which is a likely Christian carry-over from the early Orientalists. At best, a fluid assembly of "family traits" in the Wittgensteinian sense might be reluctantly agreed upon, for the benefit of readability to the outsider (Silk, "What, if Anything"). These are the kinds of arduous negotiations behind the scenes in the production of school textbooks on religion. They also play out in delicate matters of APC Board Certification: in a profession dominated by Christians yet making a sincere effort to open up, who decides what is a *bona-fide* Buddhist community, when religious endorsements by previously unknown *sanghas* and teachers are presented by applicant chaplains? Furthermore, while some Buddhist communities do not offer chaplain endorsements, do those that do have a shared understanding of what is being endorsed? (For a comprehensive account of these issues see Gauthier, "Buddhist Chaplaincy"). Notwithstanding the challenges of "pinning down" what Buddhism is, the definitional pressures internally bearing down on Buddhists are driven by understandable pragmatic and ethical concerns.

On the other hand, externally, Buddhists are asked to define themselves and their approaches on the basis of *equivalency*. This is of course of great benefit to the mission of getting Buddhist pastoral care training recognized outside of denominational settings. Years of very robust discussions were needed to ascertain how exactly Buddhist spiritual formation prepares individuals to care skillfully for religiously diverse populations. According to Pamela Ayo Yetunde, an experienced Buddhist-Christian pastoral care counselor and writer, the equivalency process "was not a capitulation to Christian supremacy, but a demonstration, if you will, of how Buddhism works." It required "a Herculean effort in Buddhist-Christian dialogue" (Yetunde, personal communication). I have personally witnessed the undeniable developmental gains in the equivalency process: Buddhists have had to let go of speaking in insider shorthand and have needed to articulate themselves "theologically" and to make their "theologies of pastoral care" far more explicit to a non-Buddhist audience. I am grateful for the ways in which I was challenged and at times confronted by Christians and Jews in the seminaries where I trained (Union Theological Seminary and the Jewish Theological Seminary, both in New York). I am more self-aware and grounded in my own Buddhist tradition as a result. Still, this also means leaving that which is paradigmatic unquestioned (equivalent to *what*?), and asking those at the periphery to respond to a predetermined norm. Even if, at best, Christians and Buddhists were presumed to be equal partners in the conversation, the conversation itself structures the outcome: Buddhist-Muslim, Buddhist-Sikh or Buddhist-Hindu dialogues would have likely generated different maps of pastoral care skills.

What happens when equivalency is not the starting point? This is the probing question asked by Monica Sanford, a trailblazing scholar in the field of Buddhist pastoral care, and the Assistant Dean for Multireligious Ministry at Harvard Divinity School. Sanford's primary concern is the need for Buddhists to have models of spiritual care that are from *within* their tradition. "I contend that, as Buddhists, we must proactively discover, develop, and explicate our own norms for spiritual care, rather than simply continue reacting to Christian standards" (Sanford, "Practice of Dharma Reflection," 48). She notes the value of working with Christian archetypes (the shepherd, the wounded healer) and Jewish ones (*tikkun 'olam*), but claims that they "fail to connect to the Dharma that motivates and guides our work" (Sanford, *Kalyāṇamitra*). This is a departure from writings that have made an effort to understand or illustrate such models from Abrahamic traditions through the lens of the Dharma. For example, a notable thesis submitted by Adele Smith-Penniman in 2006 titled "Buddhist Resources in Pastoral Care" did a robust job of aggregating Buddhist and secular mindfulness approaches (which have their root in Buddhism) in service of chaplaincy (Smith-Penniman, "Buddhist Resources"). She did not, however, challenge the overall Protestant paradigm, which is perhaps unsurprising given her Unitarian affiliation. Sanford's move is also a departure from the relatively abundant contemporary body of works in the Anglosphere composed by Buddhist chaplains and counselors, which I tentatively typologize as follows:

1. Buddhist approaches to *skills* for chaplaincy: listening, meditation, etc. (see, e.g., Halifax, Back, Bauer-Wu and Rushton, "Compassionate Silence".
2. Buddhist approaches to *psychology and counseling*, including Buddhist psychologies and the Western psychological sciences (see, e.g., Jennings, *Mixing Minds*; Lee, *Guide*)

3. Buddhist approaches to *life transitions and crises*: end-of-life care, illness, disaster, incarceration etc. (examples include Halifax, *Being with Dying*; Ostaseski, *The Five Invitations*; Michon, "Refuge")

4. Buddhist chaplaincy as a *profession* in particular environments: healthcare, education, military, criminal justice, etc. (see, e.g., Fisher, "Benefit Beings!")

5. Buddhist reflections on care grounded in Buddhist teachings and practices, or what the ACPE calls "*theological reflection*" (see, e.g., Giles, "Beyond the Color Line")

6. Buddhist contributions to providing *contemplative care to non-Buddhists* (see, e.g., Fisher, *Three Yanas*) and *within Buddhist communities* (Michon and Fisher, *Thousand Hands*)

7. Buddhist *testimonial* essays, case studies, and autobiographical narratives written by chaplains (see, e.g., Giles, "Beyond the Color Line"; Han, *one long listening*; and Yetunde et al., "Right Here")

8. Works that (re)frame and develop a theory of *chaplaincy as Engaged Buddhism* in the modern sense, often including a social analysis of systemic suffering (see, e.g., Watts "Is Buddhist Chaplaincy"; Yetunde and Owens, "What Does Being Black and Buddhist Tell Us").

All of these works are valuable contributions, and publications of this nature have only continued to grow in recent years. Yet Sanford is most interested in supporting the *formation* of chaplains when we are freed up from retrofitting Buddhism into non-Buddhist frameworks. Based on her empirical research among Buddhist chaplains, she convincingly argues that *kalyāṇamitratā*, a Buddhist concept translated as spiritual friendship, noble friendship, or beautiful friendship, could be an efficacious paradigm for the formation of Buddhist chaplains, and one which is indigenous to the tradition (Sanford, "Kalyāṇamitrā"; *Kalyāṇamitrā*). Sanford makes the point that *kalyānamitrata* appears in the Pali Canon, the Perfection of Wisdom literature, works of Shantideva, the *lojong* and mind training texts, as well as other key source texts—in fact, it's hard to find a lineage that does not emphasize it in some way. She also grounds her pedagogical model in what are known as the Three Levels of Knowing, or Three Levels of Wisdom (*Prajñā*), a set of teachings identifiable in a great number of Buddhist traditions. These are the wisdom derived from *listening*, the wisdom derived from *contemplating*, and the wisdom derived by *practicing*. These terms are her translation choices for *śrutamayīprajñā*, *cintāmayīprajñā*, and *bhāvanāmayīprajñā* (other versions used include cognizing/hearing, contemplating/reflecting/

meditating, and embodying/exemplifying). Combining these frameworks, she theorizes a "Three Prajñās Framework for Spiritual Care" with successive stages: Self, Student, Chaplain and *kalyāṇamitra*. From this she builds out a comprehensive pedagogical matrix that stands as a robust alternative to the action-reflection-action model advocated by the ACPE, without being incompatible either.

Sanford's lifting up of *kalyāṇamitratā* as a paradigm for chaplaincy certainly validated my own experience. In many Buddhist contexts, spiritual friendship is a practice of the highest order. At its best, when it is truly *kalyāṇa*, this kind of friendship cannot be confused with mere camaraderie, enmeshment, or even empathy (which is finite and prone to fatigue). It is a mutually transformative and restorative experience for both chaplain and care-seeker. In my own community, we are frequently reminded of the exhortation of the Tibetan Buddhist master Gampopa (d. 1153) in *The Jewel Ornament of Liberation* to regard the ordinary friend as the most precious of teachers. Gampopa lists four types of teachers according to their level of realization, and counter-intuitively claims the ordinary human as the most cherished: without a relatable spiritual friend, the gates to the Dharma remain closed (Gampopa, *Jewel Ornament*). Scanning contemporary literature, I also notice a number of personal accounts of Buddhist chaplains that seem to substantiate Sanford's theorization. Chenxing Han's autobiographical work in *one long listening: a memoir of grief, friendship, and spiritual care* could be read as an exquisite example of chaplaincy as *kalyāṇamitratā* (Han, *one long listening*). Yet, I am also left wondering if Sanford's model could be interpreted (and too easily misapplied) as mostly developmental, placing a strong emphasis on stages of progression, and privileging a transcendent orientation to practice and pastoral formation. Though she claims the model is both "recursive and cumulative," I am less sure that her proposed matrix has the dimensionality of a Buddhist *mandala*, in the sense of explicitly integrating regressive cycles and shadows of the psycho-spiritual life.

When Thomas Kilts wrote his journal article "A Vajrayana Buddhist Perspective on Ministry Training" in 2008, he was an ACPE supervisor and the Director of Spiritual Care at the John Muir Medical Center in Concord, California (Kilts, "Vajrayana Buddhist Perspective"). At the time, Kilts reinterpreted the ACPE framework for the training of chaplains (with the three-fold categories of pastoral formation, identity, and functioning) into the traditional Mandala of the Five Buddhas, in his capacity as a Vajrayāna practitioner. The Mandala represents the distinctive qualities of five types of wisdom, each embodied by a particular Buddha figure. Each of the five Buddha figures transforms a singular type of poison (conceit, hate, craving, envy, and ignorance) into an aspect of the awakened mind-heart. A characteristic aspect of the Vajrayāna is to see obstacles as blessings on the path: the seed of wisdom is (only) found within the defilement. This is why the language is usually one of transmutation and transformation, as opposed to cessation or relinquishment, more commonly found in Early Buddhism. The Five Buddha Mandala utilizes obscurations for the purpose of awakening (or in the case of Kilts' adaptation, pastoral effectiveness). It's worth noting that there are many Vajrayāna Buddhisms: Kilts aptly named his article "A Vajrayana Buddhist Perspective." There are vast resources for pastoral care within Vajrayāna Buddhisms that have yet to be articulated to a more pan-Buddhist audience and beyond. This includes a particular relationship to Tibetan medicine, its cosmologies and understandings of the body and mind that are quite different from what is ordinarily found in American healthcare settings (von Bujdoss, "Caregiving").

In her literature review, Sanford appreciated Kilts' work but deemed it to be excessively sectarian: though interesting, she saw it as too specific to the Vajrayāna schools. She has a point, yet perhaps this specificity is its very strength. I do note that at least two institutions not rooted in Vajrayāna Buddhism and offering training in Buddhist ministry have included Kilts works in their syllabi (University of the West and The Upaya Institute). Furthermore, mandalas are pervasive in Buddhism, and can be traced back to some of the earliest symbolic language of the Buddha himself, such as the use of the *dharmachakra* (the wheel turning Dharma) in his very first sermon. Buddhist mandalas frequently serve as maps that are cosmological and psycho-spiritual. Since the days of Lama Govinda and C. G. Jung, Europeans have taken a great interest in Buddhist mandalas and powerfully related them to Western psychology (Govinda, *Foundations*; Jung, "Concerning Mandala Symbolism"). While Sanford's pedagogical model of *kalyāṇamitratā* and the Three Ways of Knowing is compelling, Kilts also captures something particularly important for chaplaincy. His is a mandala model for growth and maturation *through* and *with* difficulty, as well as a critical stop gap to spiritual bypassing. In this sense, our "training" is never complete, so long as habitual tendencies and obscurations remain. As Kilts states: "In my tradition, integration is seen as being even more imperative than 'knowledge.' Integration is the most effective path toward realization of the divine or the truest nature of what is" (Kilts, "A Vajrayana Buddhist Perspective"). In my reading, Kilts offers us a paradigm that is *both* progressive and regressive, and that centers the need for embodiment. In my own work, I have found this model to be highly effective: it allows for continual chaos and reordering. It pulls me out of habitual toxic shame for messing up: being undone is part of the process, and reframing my defilements as seeds of wisdom invites a deeper inquiry, without letting me off the hook.

Still, it might come across as an overly conceptual framework, especially for Buddhists unfamiliar with the Five Buddha Mandala.

Another approach to Buddhist chaplaincy sidesteps the need to broker doctrinal or cosmological alignment altogether. This is found in the work of Jenny Quek, who made a notable contribution to Buddhist chaplaincy formation, this time grounded in the modern Theravada tradition. It was not included in Sanford's literature review, likely due to the challenges of sourcing it. Her book, originally a doctoral dissertation, was self-published in Singapore in 2007 and titled: *The Buddha's Technique and Practice of Counselling as Depicted in the Pali Canon* (Quek, "Buddha's Technique"). Although her concern is pastoral counseling (which has some overlap with chaplaincy yet is its own distinct field more akin to psychotherapy), Quek's methodology is noteworthy for what Sanford is getting at. In essence, she draws out the pedagogical and caregiving methods from the Buddha's life as templates for interpretation and exemplification in the pastoral encounter. Although she is certainly not the first nor the last Buddhist to reference stories from the Buddha's life in her theorization of spiritual care, her systematic approach is noteworthy. This is congruent with a Theravada sensibility, as these schools of Buddhism pay particular attention to a historical Buddha and see themselves as charged with the safeguarding of the Early Buddhist canon through memorization, recitation, and exemplification. The historical Buddha's teachings are nearly always delivered in a narrative context, as the result of some kind of (arguably pastoral) encounter. Although presumably not highly realized Buddhas just yet, chaplains can nevertheless seek inspiration and guidance from the famously varied ways in which the historical Buddha met the suffering of those he engaged with.

What Quek is pointing to is not simply an inventory of the Buddha's exemplary interventions, but a foundational paradigm to Buddhist ethics: *upāya*, typically translated as skillful means. In short, *upāya* signifies that a practitioner might deploy means that appear unconventional or even antinomian to the unawakened mind, for the sake of their soteriological and healing efficacy. A concept that went on to become critical to the Mahāyana schools, *upāya* can be understood as the creative and skillful ability to respond appropriately to the very particular ways any given being suffers, as the fruition of unfathomable causes and conditions coming together over many lives. Contemplating the Buddha-as-Chaplain, drawing upon his life as it is recounted in scripture, arguably creates a genre of "buddhological reflection" that stands on its own footing (and does not simply mimic Christian methods). It is also deeply pertinent to the Four Noble Truths, which follow a methodology of ancient Indian medical diagnostic practice (the ailment, the cause of the ailment, the possibility of the end of the cause, and the pathway to that end). A powerful example of this narrative approach can be found in the work of Pamela Ayo Yetunde, who drew on the story of the Buddha's encounter with Angulimāla, a notorious serial killer, in her reckoning as a Black woman with a white male patient who confessed homicidal thoughts towards her (Yetunde, "I Know"). She drew upon this episode of the Buddha's life both in caring for her patient and for herself in this charged and tenuous situation.

We all have stories of crises and of transformative responses to spiritual distress in our lineages. In the heat of the moment, stories can be easier to recall than a conceptual diagram or even a teaching. It's not hard to imagine expanding Quek's Theravada-inspired method to the broader Buddhist tradition, considering the Bodhisattva-as-Chaplain, the Yogini-as-Chaplain, the Mahāsiddha-as-Chaplain and so forth. A story that is seminal to my own tradition and that I return to over and over is that of the Bodhisattva Avalokiteśvara (or Quan Yin in the female form) becoming overwhelmed with hearing the unending cries of the world as they attempt to alleviate the suffering of countless beings. Avalokiteśvara explodes into millions of pieces, literally. The great red Buddha Amitabha then appears and lovingly puts Avalokiteśvara back together—yet this time with a thousand arms, and numerous heads. Each hand holds a different implement to address the specificity of the suffering of each being. As Avalokiteśvara resumes their endless work, they hold Amitabha (the ACPE Educator?) above their head.

From a pedagogical standpoint, if the chaplain's Buddhist practice is still largely unintegrated, a story will often be a greater resource than the recall of a fleeting meditative insight. Stories operate as their own kind of *sādhanā*, or visualization practice wherein we eventually become that which we cultivate imagining. A strength of this method is that it is multilayered and generative: stories are living things, they are always rewriting themselves in the process of being shared anew. A narrative method also has a capaciousness that exceeds a Buddhist context, and perhaps offers a bridge between chaplaincy and narrative medicine. After all, are not the verbatims we write in Clinical Pastoral Education the retelling of a story—our own and our care-seeker's?

Sanford has offered a powerful model for the formation of Buddhist chaplains, well rooted in tradition. She has made several theoretical moves that unquestionably advance the state of the field. I also appreciate the pragmatic argument for a Buddhist pedagogy that can act as some kind of common denominator amidst our eclectic and messy reality. There is, after all, great wisdom in Gayatri Spivak's expression of "strategic essentialism," even for an anti-essentialist tradition such as Buddhism. By her own admission, Sanford's intellectual orientation is toward systems thinking and synthesis.

Her conclusions also derive naturally from her qualitative research method ("grounded theory") and her decision to examine a pan-Buddhist sampling of chaplains. At present, she teaches in an institution serving a pan-Buddhist and Buddhist-curious student body. Yet, I remain perplexed by the quest for a unifying frame, as it could risk diluting the power of the very diversity of Buddhist approaches to care. Specific schools have distinct teachings and practices to bring to bear, as we have barely touched upon with Kilts and Quek. Many other examples come to mind, such as The Three Tenants of the Zen Buddhist Peacemakers (not knowing, bearing witness, taking action), the end-of-life practices of *phowa* in Tibetan Tantric Buddhism, the *mizuko kuyō* or memorial services for "water children" (lost to miscarriage, stillbirth, or abortion) of a number of Japanese Buddhist communities, or the social application of the Four Noble Truths led by the Village Awakening Councils of the Sarvodaya movement in Sri Lanka, to name but a few. Some approaches have a political edge, others are more humanitarian in nature. Some are individuated and psychological, others are more collective. Some are concerned with confronting root causes, others work more downstream to tend to trauma's rippling karmic effects. Some are highly devotional and liturgical, and others champion a kind of liberatory analytical rationalism. Some are self-empowering (as in the Vipassana schools), while others are decidedly other-power-oriented (as in the Pure Land schools). Some are non-sectarian, others occur mostly within denominational contexts. Some are egalitarian, others are rarified and limited to the initiated.

A truly salient challenge for Buddhists might be less to find a universal pan-Buddhist framework for spiritual care, and more to learn deeply from the strengths of each other's traditions, including transnationally, in ways that are historically and culturally informed. This might lead us to mutually negotiate the thorny ethics of deploying and adapting each other's powerful practices and ideas without formal transmission, and to what extent. It might also serve as an antidote to culturally habituated "bright-siding" and the propagation of a rootless feel-good vanilla mindful mush attributed to Buddhists and championed by the wellness industry, for better and for worse (on the theological origins of American toxic positivity see *Dhammacakkappavattana Sutta*; Bowler, *Everything Happens for a Reason*; and on the shadow sides of wellness see Kelly, *American Detox*).

As we can see, Buddhist chaplains have much to offer beyond an uncommon ability to "do nothing," as my cherished former hospice Residence Manager exclaimed all those years ago. I would also like to think that we have come a long way since the Parliament of World Religions in 1893, at the very least in the sense that a greater diversity of Buddhists are dialoguing and collaborating, nationally and internationally, to define and advance on a global stage what is understood to be the field of "Buddhist contemplative care" in a burning world. (For a helpful account of the strategic shift from "spiritual" to "contemplative" among some American Buddhists, see Watts and Jin, "Development of Buddhist Chaplaincy.") Yet, a certain legacy of strategic ambiguity forged in 1893 endures. Back then, several Buddhist thought leaders, namely Anagārika Dharmapāla and D.T. Suzuki, simultaneously accommodated and resisted dominant frames of respectability (McMahan, "Making of Buddhist Modernism"). In so doing, they played an important part in expanding and changing what was understood to be "religion." Will the very idea of pastoral care, in a similar way, be drawn out from its original Christian frame? Will it simply be expanded to make elbow room for "religious others," or will it be reimagined—and if so, how can chaplain training evolve and even transform? What will be the Buddhist contribution to that process? And what is at stake for Buddhists themselves?

Differently than in 1893, Buddhism is now a more visible part of American religious life. Issues of respectability and legibility have shifted. For some American Buddhists, professional chaplaincy is a way to combine their practice and livelihood, Right Livelihood being a crucial component of the Eightfold Path. Furthermore, a life devoted to Buddhist practice and materially supported by a congregation is inaccessible to most lay Buddhists, and even to many ordained and/or transmitted Buddhist teachers. The economic system of *dāna* (generosity) which sustains large parts of the transmission of the tradition in Asia is simply alien, if not antinomic, to American capitalism. At stake in the interreligious professionalization of chaplaincy training is perhaps the ability to be a Buddhist at all, or at least certain kind of Buddhist. Many Buddhist chaplains see their work as the natural outpouring of "a Dharma life," and one that offers some modicum of sustainability. It also means being potentially gainfully employed and not having to endure the samsaric hustle of freelance mindfulness gigs, nor does it require them to mute their Buddhist identity (as might be the case for a secular mindfulness jobs). Even if it involves trade-offs, chaplaincy is a way for certain Buddhists to negotiate being *in* the world, yet not entirely *of* the world, as the expression goes. Others understand chaplaincy as a potent vehicle for societal change, placing themselves in the very hell realms where injustices are most compounded, animated by the vision of challenging and interrupting systemic forms of violence. In so doing, American Buddhists are not simply adding a social analysis of suffering to pastoral work. Rather, it is their very starting point; and they come to the table with robust theories and practices of transformation, offering a distinctive voice to justice-informed chaplaincy.

The field of modern pastoral care training in the West was founded by a clergyman, Anton Boisen, at the fascinating juncture of the fields of mental health and practical theology. In the context of his own intense personal suffering and multiple institutional failures to adequately meet that suffering, two disciplines came to be in conversation and challenged one another. Something quite new arose out of that encounter. This history gives me hope for the future of Clinical Pastoral Education, and its capacity to reconfigure itself through both *inter* and *intra*-religious conversation and cooperation. The vitality of Buddhist chaplaincy training could very well depend on the co-arising of least two streams: efforts to re-engineer academic and clinical programs in historically Christian institutions, and efforts to recognize and support small-scale training pathways indigenous to Buddhist communities offering spiritual formation (which itself is in a state of flux and re-configuration at the Buddhadharma takes root in these lands). In the former, pan-Buddhist frameworks (pedagogical, ethical, professional) are likely to continue to be crafted and will render Buddhist-informed care accessible to both Buddhists and ever-growing "Buddhish" cohorts, as well as legible to non-Buddhist institutional authorities. The latter, on the other hand, might be more freed up to steer to a different kind of depth and experiment in important ways within specific lineages, perhaps in coalition with one other, and sheltered from the pressure to center the demands of a dominant or singular frame, even a pan-Buddhist one.

Mutually generative Buddhist-Christian dialogue will undoubtedly remain a key component of the future of Buddhist pastoral care, if anything because Buddhist chaplains are, in the US, working in landscape and culture so deeply architected by Christian paradigms. Robust exchange, collegiality, and solidarity with other religious minorities within the fields of pastoral care will also continue to be critical to the interreligious formation of chaplains. *And*, accredited grassroots Buddhist programs, unapologetically rooted in the Buddhadharma, can offer a creative laboratory and a provisional reprieve from the inevitable power imbalances that arise from Buddhists being less than 1% of the population. There has been much discussion about Buddhist chaplaincy "finding its voice." The conversation among Buddhists about chaplaincy and the formation of Buddhist chaplains is far from settled, but its gifts lie perhaps in its inherent, and indeed indigenous, polyphony.[1]

---

1. Acknowledgments: The author is greatly indebted to Chenxing Han, Monica Sanford, Justin von Bujdoss, and Pamela Ayo Yetunde for suggestions and comments that have significantly helped to improve this article.

REFERENCES

Bowler, K. *Everything Happens for a Reason: And Other Lies I've loved.* New York: Random House, 2018.

Dhammacakkappavattana SuBta. Pali Canon, SN 56.11.

Fisher, D. C. "Benefit Beings!: The Buddhist Guide to Professional Chaplaincy." Doctoral project, Rosemead, CA: University of the West, 2013. ProQuest #1415892772.

———. "Three Yanas for Wise Caring: A Buddhist Perspective on Spiritual Care." In *Multifaith Views in Spiritual Care*, edited by D. Schipani, 45–64. Kitchener, ON: Pandora, 2013.

Gather, J. T. "Buddhist Chaplaincy." In *The Oxford Handbook of Buddhist Practice*, edited by K. Trainor K. and P. Arai, 564–580. Oxford: Oxford University Press, 2022.

Gauthier J. T., Kinst D., Miller L., and Yuen E. "The Path to Buddhist Chaplaincy: Academic Education, Religious Endorsement, Professional Board Certification." Chaplaincy Innovation Lab. 2020. https://chaplaincyinnovation.org/resources/faith-tradition/buddhist-chaplaincy. Also published in *Refuge in the Storm*, edited by J. Michon, 223–32—see below.

Gampopa, *The Jewel Ornament of Liberation: The Wish-fulfilling Gem of the Noble Teachings*, edited by A. K. Trinlay Chödron, translated by K. K. Gyaltsen Rinpoche. Ithaca, NY: Snow Lion, 1998. (Orig. text before 1153 C.E.)

Giles, C. A. "Beyond the Color Line: Cultivating Fearlessness in Contemplative Care." In *The Arts of Contemplative Care: Pioneering Voices in Buddhist Chaplaincy and Pastoral Work*, edited by C. A. Giles and W. Miller, 41–54. Boston: Wisdom, 2012.

Gleig, A., and Mitchell, S. A., eds. *The Oxford Handbook of American Buddhism.* Oxford: Oxford University Press, 2024.

Govinda, A. L. *Foundations of Tibetan Mysticism: According to the Esoteric Teachings of the Great Mantra "Oṁ Maṇi Padme Hūṁ."* New York: Dutton, 1960.

Halifax, J. *Being with Dying: Cultivating Compassion and Fearlessness in the Presence of Death*, 2nd ed. Boulder: Shambhala, 2024.

Halifax, J., Back, A. L., Bauer-Wu, S. M., and Rushton, C. H. (2009). "Compassionate Silence in the Patient-clinician Encounter: A Contemplative Approach." *Journal of Palliative Medicine* 12/12 (2009) 1113–17.

Han, C. *Be the Refuge: Raising the Voices of Asian American Buddhists.* Berkeley: North Atlantic, 2021.

———. *One Long Listening: A Memoir of Grief, Friendship, and Spiritual Care.* Berkeley: North Atlantic.

Hsu, F. "We've Been Here All Along." *Buddhadharma: The Practitioner's Quarterly* (Winter, 2016) 24–31. https://www.lionsroar.com/weve-been-here-all-along/.

Jennings, P. *Mixing Minds: The Power of Relationship in Psychoanalysis and Buddhism.* Boston: Wisdom, 2010.

Jung, C. G. "Concerning Mandala Symbolism." In *Collected Works of C.G. Jung*, translated by R. C. F. Hull, Vol. 9, Part I, 355–384. Bollingen Series 20. Princeton: Princeton University Press, 1972. (Orig. publ. 1950.)

Kandil, C.Y. "Pandemic's Suffering Opens Way for Buddhist Chaplains." *Religion News Service.* December 2, 2020. https://religionnews.com/2020/12/02/pandemics-suffering-opens-way-for-buddhist-chaplains/.

Kelly, K. *American Detox: The Myth of Wellness and How We Can Truly Heal.* Berkeley: North Atlantic, 2022.
Kilts, T. "A Vajrayana Buddhist Perspective on Ministry Training." *Journal of Pastoral Care and Counseling* 62/3 (2008) 273–82.
Lee, K. C. *The Guide to Buddhist Counseling.* London: Routledge, 2023.
Masuzawa, T. *The Invention of World Religions, or, How European Universalism Was Preserved in the Language of Pluralism.* Chicago: University of Chicago Press, 2005.
McMahan, D. L. *The Making of Buddhist Modernism.* Oxford: Oxford University Press, 2008.
———, ed. *Buddhism in the Modern World.* Religions in the Modern World. London: Routledge, 2012.
Michon, N. J., and Fisher, D. C., eds. *A Thousand Hands: A Guidebook to Caring for Your Buddhist Community.* Nepean, ON: Sumeru, 2016.
———, ed. *Refuge in the Storm: Buddhist Voices in Crisis Care.* Berkeley: North Atlantic, 2023.
Mitchell, S. A. *Buddhism in America: Global Religion, Local Contexts.* London: Bloomsbury Academic, 2016.
Oakes, K. "Meet the 'Buddhish' Nones." *Tricycle: The Buddhist Review* (Spring, 2017). https://tricycle.org/magazine/meet-buddhish-nones/. Portions of this essay adapted from Oakes, *The Nones Are Alright: A New Generation of Seekers, Believers, and Those in Between.* Maryknoll: Orbis, 2015.
Ostaseski, F. *The Five Invitations: Discovering What Death Can Teach Us about Living Fully.* New York: Flatiron, 2017.
Quek, J. H. H. "The Buddha's Technique and Practice of Counselling as Depicted in the Pali Canon." PhD diss., University of Kelaniya, Sri Lanka, 2007. (URI University of Rhode Island Research Digital Commons). http://repository.kln.ac.lk/handle/123456789/672.
Sanford, M. *Kalyāṇamitra: A Model for Buddhist Spiritual Care.* Vol. 1. Ottawa, ON: Sumeru, 2021.
———. "Kalyāṇamitra or Spiritual Friendship as a Paradigm for Buddhist Chaplains." Conference remarks, Annual Meeting, American Academy of Religion, November, 2019. https://www.academia.edu/41203278/Kaly%C4%81%E1%B9%87amitra_or_Spiritual_Friendship_as_a_Paradigm_for_Buddhist_Chaplains?rhid=294585 48240andswp=rr-rw-wc-44573829.
———. "The Practice of Dharma Reflection among Buddhist Chaplains: A Qualitative Study of 'Theological' Activity among Nontheocentric Spiritual Caregivers" PhD diss., Claremont School of Theology, 2018.
Silk, J. A. "What, If Anything, Is Mahāyāna Buddhism?: Problems of Definitions and Classifications." *Numen* 49/4 (2002) 355–405.
Smith, G. (2015). "America's Changing Religious Landscape." Washington, DC: Pew Research Center. https://www.pewresearch.org/religion/2015/05/12/americas-changing-religious-landscape/.
Smith-Penniman, A. "Buddhist Resources in Pastoral Care." DMin thesis, Andover Newton Theological School, 2006. Proquest #3270209.
Vardell, D. (2006) "Equivalency Issues for Buddhist Candidates for Board Certification Through the Board of Chaplaincy Certification, Inc." Board of Chaplaincy

Certification, Inc., 2006. https://www.apchaplains.org/bcci-site/wp content/uploads/sites/2/2023/07/buddhist_white_paper-002.pdf.

von Bujdoss, J. "Caregiving in the Face of Death: The Dissolution of Elements." *Sowa Rigpa Journal* (Summer, 2024) 74–89.

Watts, J. S., ed. "Is Buddhist Chaplaincy a Form of Socially Engaged Buddhism? Reflections on a Japan-U.S. Dialogue." International Network of Engaged Buddhists (INEB) blog post, June 13, 2024. https://jneb.net/is-buddhist-chaplaincy-a-form-of-socially-engaged-buddhism/.

———, ed. *This Precious Life: Buddhist Tsunami Relief and Anti-nuclear Activism in Post 3/11 Japan*. Yokohama: International Buddhist Exchange Center, 2012.

Watts, J. S., and Jin, H. *The Development of Buddhist Chaplaincy in the United States and Its Meaning for Japan*. Rinbutsuken Institute for Engaged Buddhism (臨床仏教研究所), International Network of Engaged Buddhists (INEB), 2022. https://inebnetwork.org/the-development-of-buddhist-chaplaincy-in-the-united-states-its-meaning-for-japan/.

Williams, D. R. *American Sutra: A Story of Faith and Freedom in the Second World War*. Cambridge, MA: Belknap, 2019.

Yetunde, P. A. "I Know I've Been Changed: Black Womanist Buddhist and Christian Spiritual Formation and Spiritual Care for a Homicidal White Male Buddhist." In *Navigating Religious Difference in Spiritual Care and Counseling*, edited by M. Mazvita, C. Doehring, and R. Robins R., 235–50. Claremont: Claremont University Press, 2019.

———. "Is Buddhist Chaplaincy a Form of Socially Engaged Buddhism? Reflections on a Japan-U.S. Dialogue." International Network of Engaged Buddhists (INEB) blog post, June 13, 2024. https://jneb.net/is-buddhist-chaplaincy-a-form-of-socially-engaged-buddhism/.

Yetunde, P. A., Han, C., Wade, B., Shapiro, Y., and Gomez, C. G. "Right Here with You: Buddhist Chaplains' Inspiring Stories of Spiritual Care." *Lion's Roar* (August, 2023). https://www.lionsroar.com/buddhist-chaplain-stories/.

Yetunde, P. A., and Owens L. R. *What Does Being Black and Buddhist Tell Us about Chaplaincy?* Webinar, Chaplaincy Innovation Lab, February 11, 2021. https://chaplaincyinnovation.org/2021/02/what-does-being-black-and-buddhist-tell-us-about-chaplaincy-recording.

Zhen, V. G. 太虚"佛教宗教师"理念——略论僧信建制与当代北美佛教宗教师专业 "Taixu' Concept of "Buddhist Minister": Its Development of Buddhist Monastic and Lay Ministerial System to the Contemporary Formation and Profession of Buddhist Chaplaincy in the US." Peking University: *Journal of Buddhist Studies* (2020). (北大佛学).

———. "Buddhist Chaplaincy in the United States: Theory-praxis Relationship in Formation and Profession." *Journal of International Buddhist Studies* 13/1 (2022) 44–59.

Epilogue

Spirituality: Oh, What Is This We Call Spirituality?[1]

Ivone Gebara

In general, when we hear someone talk about spirituality, a positive feeling comes over us, assuming that they are describing something good and fair. The kind of emotional positivity that this word often provokes shows us that we feel and understand it as something entirely good—something that transcends the limits of our corporeality, which is marked by needs, afflictions, disputes, and every kind of limit. In this perception, often without realizing it, we develop a certain *dualism* in relation to spirituality: we view our bodies—our material reality—as existing in opposition to something that we imagine as always good and unlimited—that which we call *spirit*. From this perspective, we can imagine worlds different from ours and even worlds full of joy and happiness after our death. We make the fruits of our imagination, which are still an intangible reality in our daily living—a kind of *directive hope* that we project outside of ourselves and seek as a prize or benefit to be lived some future day, or even after we have departed from "this vale of tears," as is often said. We develop a set of beliefs or hopes from our experiences that, although they can help at times, they can also alienate us from the concrete life in which we live and even prevent us from taking certain urgent steps necessary to keep our lives from being taken from us.

Therefore, I would like to analyze both the typical good feeling but also the dis-ease that a deeper reflection on what we call "spirituality" can cause in us.

The first thing that we are invited to observe and perceive carefully is that what we call spirituality happens *within* us, within our body, our living space, our current time, and therefore within the limits of the situations in

1. Translated from the Portuguese by Pamela Cooper-White.

which we live. No one sees or encounters something called "spirituality" on the street. There is no single thing that stands out to us that we call "spirituality." We do not find it outside the limits of our own bodies, even if we consider it to be something superior. So we can conclude that what is called "spirituality" is something that happens in our own bodies, in our behaviors, in our emotions. Spirituality is a dimension of ourselves just like hope, love, despair and hate. For this reason, the consequences of our spirituality are expressed in our bodies, in our daily attitudes, and in our ethical and political choices.

It is also important to realize that no one owns collective spirituality, although some people do have gifts to help others on their journey. We often think that priests, theologians, and biblical scholars are those who have the greatest knowledge of this something called "spirituality," and they share their knowledge with us in celebrations, in preaching, in teachings, and in the counseling they give in churches. In Portuguese, of course I use masculine words for them, because it is men we find in these roles in our Catholic society. Given this reality, it is a mistake to believe that spirituality is the property of a group of privileged people who magnanimously offer us something for our consumption. Likewise, along these lines we often think that spirituality is something that men have more of than women, since in the (Brazilian) society we live in, they appear more often as preachers of the Bible, and as teachers and leaders of spirituality.

This is a very limited conception of spirituality in our times, because it privileges one gender more than the other. Moreover, it specifically privileges men as the greater interpreters of the Bible, as the true experts to discern "God's will" and as the official hierarchical and even sacramental representatives of Jesus. In this way, a gender hierarchy is maintained within our spirituality as it is lived in a plural community.

When talking about the Bible, many people believe that in it we find the purest source of our spirituality—that there is the Word of God, that there are the sources of good and justice, that there are the narratives of the life of Jesus considered our greatest Master. Even without having read most of the biblical texts, deep down, those of us who are Christians consider that our spirituality originates above all from the strength of these writings and especially the writings about Jesus of Nazareth, all of which are considered revelations from God. We can't even imagine how many people who claim to be Christians are illiterate or have never read any book of the Bible. And we don't often appreciate their influence on our lives and the directions they helped us take. We often forget to look, to observe, to feel, to know the people who make up our world, our current history. As Christians, we tend to think with the criteria of a religious elite and end up favoring the maintenance of male hierarchies, those hierarchies of power and knowledge that surround us. The same phenomenon occurs in other religions in that they privilege their oral and written traditions as immutable sources of wisdom without realizing that each generation and each person transforms them in the image of their own needs and contexts.

With both the Bible and the Qur'an, one can justify waging war against many peoples. With the Torah also, the earliest Jewish law, the maintenance of oppression and extermination of a people can be defended. Although sacred texts also contain exhortations to peace, there can be many conflicting interpretations. For this reason, it is good to always remember that religions are born from *us*, and as human writings (even if divinely inspired), they are not entirely "good," or exempt from destruction and many forms of exclusion. They are part of the mix that we are, as people who can have a kind and magnanimous heart, but who can also be petty, violent and focused only on their own interests.

Faced with a social situation full of injustices commanded and legitimized by the Roman Empire, the Jesus Movement denounced the taxes that burdened the poor, provided care for the sick, shared bread with the hungry, visited prisoners, cared for widows, and prevented the stoning of women. Jesus educated through examples and not just pretty words. It thus became a way of acting, an ethic that disturbed the established political situation. From another tradition, we could think of the Buddha who perceived abandonment, pain, suffering as constitutive of life and taught ways to live them and create solidarity in the world. We could also think of some indigenous traditions that do not destroy nature because they consider themselves to be part of the same family as forests, animals, rivers, seas and winds.

I am trying to show that there is a positive and plural dimension in what we call "spirituality"—a dimension that helps in building good relationships between us, although it can also have negative aspects of destruction when we forget our ideals of mutual help and alleviating human pain. Spirituality approaches ethics as a proposal for life in common, for common care that arises from the suffering and limitations of our corporeal condition, and addressing these.

At this point we have reached, I can say that spirituality is what always arises from us humans when we consider ourselves in relation to others in a dimension of personal and collective responsibility. Spirituality then leads us to realize that our life depends on each other, just as it depends on the forces of nature, that is, on the trees, the rivers, the sun, the many stars, the moon and our entire solar system—which is just one of the thousands that exist. It depends on who lived before us and who lives in different situations from us. All of this leads us from our individual perspectives to realize the connection we have with a Greater Whole, and how much our life depends on this Greater Life that always surpasses us.

We get used to calling this Greater Life "God," and unfortunately, we reduce this Greater One to a male image of a powerful bearded old man separated from our human actions. We invent a lot of behaviors in his name and expect him to do *our* will as if it were his. We build and destroy in his name. We judge in his name and reduce him to the image of our own often petty and self-serving judgments.

Today we are living in a privileged moment in History. We are beginning to realize the limits of our speech, the limits of our beliefs, the absurdities we impose on each other. And this can be seen from the confusion that exists among us. Most of us no longer understand ourselves solely or primarily based on our religions, and most of us are no longer able to impose our gods and saints (although some religious leaders still try to do this), because they have been reduced to our own greed and belligerence. These human-conceived gods and saints reveal the worship of money, and show no respect for the dignity of plural lives.

The confusion and violence in our present show that the spirituality of conquest and domination, of imperialism and colonialism that are still present, no longer serve us. Women's movements are showing that it is no longer possible to maintain male deities that exclude women and consider them inferior. Ecological movements are showing that the planet needs to be taken care of and that we must no longer open the womb of the earth and remove minerals and oil to enrich the few. We can no longer burn forests because our breath will cease with their ashes. Indigenous people, Black people, and many despised and uprooted peoples have raised their voices to fight against the white hegemony that some religions have wanted—and still want—to establish in complicity with the dominating empires of this world.

A new spirituality intimately linked and blended to our fragile materiality, to our bodies, is slowly sprouting everywhere in the world. The abandonment of gods of power is happening, and their sacred temples and palaces are being replaced by healthy and flowery dwellings for the poor. We are realizing that we will live with dignity if everyone lives with dignity. It is this gentle and constant breeze that has been crossing the world despite the noise of cannons, despite the mass destruction of people and cities, despite the pollution that infests our lives. There is a breeze in the air, there is also a soft singing capable of awakening human tenderness and that can be heard in the early hours of the morning. There is an immense desire to join hands to plant beans and corn, to knead bread, bake it, and distribute it to satisfy different hungers.

Today we are called to breathe this breeze, to seek it every day of our lives so that we "may have Life and have it abundantly" (John 10:10). Spirituality is the breeze that makes us believe in a possible earthly kinship, in an endless social utopia that always needs to be tried again. Our religious traditions—including our ever-expanding practices of spiritual care—can help us to the extent that we do not make them static truths, dogmas that subject our reason and our hearts to past times, and ideas that no longer express the richness of what is happening in our lives today.